Safety-critical Systems

Safety-critical Systems

Current issues, techniques and standards

Edited by

Felix Redmill and Tom Anderson

CHAPMAN & HALL
London · Glasgow · New York · Tokyo · Melbourne · Madras

Published by Chapman & Hall, 2–6 Boundary Row, London SE1 8HN

Chapman & Hall, 2–6 Boundary Row, London SE1 8HN, UK

Blackie Academic & Professional, Wester Cleddens Road, Bishopbriggs, Glasgow G64 2NZ, UK

Chapman & Hall Inc., 29 West 35th Street, New York, NY 10001, USA

Chapman & Hall Japan, Thomson Publishing Japan, Hirakawacho Nemoto Building, 6F, 1-7-11 Hirakawa-cho, Chiyoda-ku, Tokyo 102, Japan

Chapman & Hall Australia, Thomas Nelson Australia, 102 Dodds Street, South Melbourne, Victoria 3205, Australia

Chapman & Hall India, R. Seshadri, 32 Second Main Road, CIT East, Madras 600 035, India

First edition 1993

© 1993 Felix Redmill and Tom Anderson

Printed in Great Britain by Hartnolls Ltd, Bodmin, Cornwall

ISBN 0 412 54820 8

A catalogue record for this book is available from the British Library

Library of Congress Cataloging-in-Publication data available

∞ Printed on permanent acid-free paper, manufactured in accordance with the proposed ANSI/NISO Z 39.48-199X and ANSI Z 39.48-1984

Contents

PART FIVE: CURRENT DEVELOPMENT OF STANDARDS

List of Contributors
with page references

Barry Barber   238
NHS Management Executive
Information Management Centre
15 Frederick Road
Edgbaston
Birmingham B15 1JD

Ron Bell   273
Health and Safety Executive
Magdalen House
Stanley Precinct
Bootle L20 3QZ

Jeremy Clare   117
Consultant - Human Factors
Cambridge Consultants Ltd
Science Park
Milton Road
Cambridge CB4 4DW

Brian Davies   193
Imperial College
Robotics Centre
London SW7 2BX

Colum Devine   255
Centre for Software Reliability
The City University
Northampton Square
London EC1V 0HB

John Dobson   123
Computing Laboratory
University of Newcastle upon Tyne NE1 7RU

Nigel Dodd   228
Neural Solutions
15 Celandine Bank
Woodmancote
Cheltenham GL52 4HZ

Mike Falla   181
MFR Software Services Ltd
35 Benbrook Way
Gawsworth
Macclesfield
Cheshire SK11 9RT

Norman Fenton   255
Centre for Software Reliability
The City University
Northampton Square
London EC1V 0HB

Anthony Finkelstein   90
Department of Computing
Imperial College
180 Queens Gate
London SW7 2BZ

John Fox   202
Imperial Cancer Research Fund
Lincoln's Inn Fields
London
WC2A 3PX

Kevin Geary   312
Ministry of Defence
Foxhill
Bath BA1 5AB

Denis Jackson   139
Data Sciences (UK) Limited
Meudon Avenue
Farnborough
Hampshire GU14 7NB

Peter Jesty   297
University of Leeds
Safety Critical Computing Group
School of Computer Studies
Leeds LS2 9JT

Jeff Kramer   90
Department of Computing
Imperial College
180 Queens Gate
London SW7 2BZ

John A McDermid   16
Professor of Software Engineering
Department of Computer Science
University of York
York YO1 5DD

Andrew McGettrick   160
Computer Science Department
University of Strathclyde
Livingston Tower
26 Richmond Street
Glasgow G1 1XH

Benjamin Macias   67
University of Cambridge Computer Laboratory
New Museums Site
Pembroke Street
Cambridge CB2 3QG

Bob Malcolm   43
Malcolm Associates Ltd
Savoy Hill House
Savoy Hill
London WC2R 0BR

Bashar Nuseibeh   90
Department of Computing
Imperial College
180 Queens Gate
London SW7 2BZ

Stella Page   255
Centre for Software Reliability
The City University
Northampton Square
London EC1V 0HB

Steven Pulman   67
SRI International
23 Miller's Yard
Mill Lane
Cambridge CB2 1RQ

Bill Quirk   102
Erstwhile of
ERA Technology
Harwell OX11 0RA

Felix Redmill   3
Redmill Consultancy
22 Onslow Gardens
London N10 3JU

Dietmar Reinert   273
Berussgenossenschaftliches Institut
   fur Arbeitssicherheit
Fachbereich 5
Postfach 20 43
D 5205 St Augustine
Germany

Ed Robson   167
The Teaching Company Scheme
Hillside House
79 London Street
Faringdon
Oxon SN7 8AA

Ros Strens   123
Computing Laboratory
University of Newcastle upon Tyne NE1 7RU

David Thewlis   153
GEC-Marconi Limited
The Grove
Warren Lane
Stanmore
Middlesex HA7 4LY

Jim Thomas   173
SD Scicon UK Ltd
101-103 Fleet Road
Fleet
Hampshire GU13 8NZ

Preface

When the Safety-Critical Systems Club came into being in May 1991, it provided a focus for those in a field which was new and growing fast - that of computer systems in safety-critical applications. In this field, the literature is not yet extensive, and training is not standardised; traditional safety engineers and other professionals are frequently not software engineers, and software engineers working in the field are seldom acquainted with safety technology. As a result, new entrants, practicing engineers, and managers are all in search of reliable sources of knowledge. They want introductory information, state-of-the-art reports, advice on emergent technologies, and reports on lessons learned; and they want the opportunity for discussion with others in the safety profession, in their own or in a parallel sector.

With its newsletter, its annual symposium, and several seminars per year, the Safety-Critical Systems Club goes a long way to meeting such needs of safety professionals. Between July 1991 and May 1992, the club hosted five seminars, all well attended. Whereas the speakers were not required to provide written papers with their presentations, they were invited to write chapters - based on their presentations, but expanded to benefit from knowledge and experience which could not have been covered in the time allowed at the seminars. The results are the twenty-two chapters of this book.

While it would be impossible to cover every aspect of safety-critical systems and safety engineering in a single volume, this book tackles a wide range of issues and communicates the knowledge and experience of numerous eminent practitioners in the field. In particular, three of the currently most crucial topics are dealt with at length: Fundamental and Current Issues, in Part One, Education and Training, in Part Three, and Standards, in Part Five. In addition, what is perhaps the single most important aspect of system development, Requirements Capture and Specification, is covered in Part Two; and reports of experience in the Medical Sector - which contain widely-applicable technologies and lessons for all sectors - are published in Part Four. It is hoped that the book will be of interest and use to all in the safety-critical systems domain - engineers, managers, and novices.

Whereas the Club provided the focus for its compilation, this book could not have been published without the good will and effort of the authors. We would like to thank them for their marvellous cooperation and their strong support of the Club.

Felix Redmill and Tom Anderson
December 1992.

The Safety-Critical Systems Club

The Safety-Critical Systems Club exists for the benefit of industrialists and researchers involved with computer systems in safety-critical applications. Sponsored by the Department of Trade and Industry and the Science and Engineering Research Council, its purpose is to increase awareness and facilitate communication in the safety-critical systems domain.

The British Computer Society and the Institution of Electrical Engineers are active participants in the management of the Club, the Centre for Software Reliability at the University of Newcastle upon Tyne is responsible for organisation, and Felix Redmill, an independent consultant, is the Club's Co-ordinator.

The Club's goals are to achieve, in the supply of safety-critical computer systems:

- Better informed application of safety engineering practices;
- Improved choice and application of computer-system technology;
- More appropriate research and better informed evaluation of research.

In pursuit of these goals, the Club seeks to involve both engineers and managers from all sectors of the safety-critical community and, thus, to facilitate the transfer of information, technology, and current and emerging practices and standards.

The club publishes a newsletter three times per year, has initiated an annual three-day symposium, and organises and co-sponsors regular events on safety-critical topics. In these ways it facilitates: the communication of experience among industrial users of technology, the exchange of state-of-the-art knowledge among researchers, the transfer of technology from researchers to users, and feedback from users to researchers. It facilitates the union of industry and academia for collaborative projects, and it provides the means for the publicity of those projects and for the reporting of their results.

To join or to enquire about the Club, please contact:
Mrs J Atkinson
Centre for Software Reliability
The University
20 Windsor Terrace
Newcastle upon Tyne, NE1 7RU
Tel: 091 212 4040; Fax: 091 222 7995.

PART ONE
CURRENT ISSUES

1

Software in safety-critical applications - a review of current issues

Felix Redmill

1.1 INTRODUCTION

Accidents will happen, so it is said; and they do. When an accident involves a new technology, doubts are quite properly raised about the fitness of the technology for the application in question. Is the technology sufficiently mature for safety-critical applications? Is it adequately understood, and are we sure that we can control it? Are its engineers appropriately trained, or even, do we yet understand how to train them? Are there standards in place for development, for quality, for acceptable risk? All these questions, and more, are being raised about the use of software technology in safety-critical applications.

Nor is it the case that these questions are only being raised by the press. The software and safety professionals too are conscious of their responsibilities: they themselves are raising the questions and trying to answer them. They recognize the huge proliferation of computers as control systems and, more specifically, in safety-critical applications. They are committed to achieving safety and they recognize the need to work for it in a technology as young as theirs.

The first electronic computer was built during the last war and commercial use of computers only commenced in the 1950s. In the brief period since then, software-based systems have come to pervade almost every aspect of human life. They are small, cheap, fast in operation, and flexible in that their functionality can be corrected, extended, or otherwise modified easily and rapidly. In these attributes they have no rival, so it is natural that they have taken over almost every function previously performed by the more bulky, more expensive, considerably slower, and far less flexible electromechanical equipment; and that their application has been extended to functions not previously automated.

Nor is it surprising that they are employed in safety-critical applications, for here too economics and supplier competition dictate that size, cost, speed of operation, and flexibility are crucial. And computer systems can, and usually do, enhance safety, particularly when they replace human beings, for the latter are notoriously unreliable. But they also raise the questions asked above, for software technology is a new technology.

In the end, the safety issue can only be resolved in relative terms. Given the human condition, no guarantee can be given that any system is completely safe, whether it is software-based, electromechanical, or of any other technology; and this is particularly so where human beings form part of the system. If a guarantee of complete safety cannot be given, then there must be confidence in there being a level of safety commensurate with the circumstances in which the system is to be used - and this means that the circumstances and associated risks must be analysed and understood. The quality of the engineering of the software is of the highest importance: good software engineering principles and practices, sound project management, and top-down total quality management are recognized as necessary elements of the foundation for the development of safety-critical software. They are necessary, but not sufficient. There are other issues relevant to a 'safety' infrastructure, such as awareness and the acceptance of responsibility, standards, and education and training. It is these issues which are the subject of this introductory chapter, for they are, or should be, of importance to every safety professional.

1.2 AWARENESS

1.2.1 The Issues

The spread of computers into and through the safety-critical domain has been so rapid that it has in many instances outpaced the changes necessary in industry for supporting it. Are companies aware of the latest relevant technologies (for example, safety analysis techniques, software engineering practices and tools, and quality systems)? Are the best development, management and quality practices being employed in all cases? Are education and training adequate and appropriately focused? Are engineers aware of their responsibilities? Are safety professionals sufficiently knowledgeable, experienced, and aware of the limitations of their knowledge and the technology which they use? These and other searching questions are not only being asked, but also researched; and there have been a number of initiatives aimed at raising awareness and competence.

1.2.2 HSE Initiatives

In 1981, the Health and Safety Executive (HSE) published a booklet, *Microprocessors in Industry*, giving its view of the attitude to safety which needed to be developed in order to meet the challenge of the use of computers in control applications. In 1984, the HSE followed this with a lengthy draft document [HSE 84] inviting discussion on the safe use of PESs. Extensive consultation resulted from this and led to the publication in 1987 of more definitive documents [HSE 87]. These have been influential throughout the safety-critical industry.

1.2.3 SafeIT

In 1988, the Government's Inter-Departmental Committee on Software Engineering (ICSE) created a Safety-Related Software Working Group to co-ordinate the Government's approach in this field. Members were drawn from a broad spectrum of Departments and Agencies, with the Secretariat being held jointly by the HSE and the Department of Trade and Industry (DTI). Out of this Working Group came the 'SafeIT' initiative which, in its tangible form, consists of two documents [ICSE 90]. It is worth repeating the SafeIT objectives, for they can be seen to address the questions posed in the introduction to this chapter.

(i)   To facilitate the development of technically sound, feasible, generic international standards together with consistent sector- or application-specific standards which are likely to achieve wide acceptance.
(ii)   To encourage the use of PES technology in safety-related applications and promote the adoption of advanced techniques and best IT practices in relation to PES.
(iii)   To ensure that the application of PES in safety-related applications enhances safety.
(iv)   To find better technical solutions to assure PES integrity.
(v)   To promote, within the UK and internationally, open markets for safety-related PES.

1.2.4 IEE and BCS Report

In 1989, a study, sponsored and partly funded by the DTI and carried out by a joint project team of the Institution of Electrical Engineers (IEE) and the British Computer Society (BCS), produced its report [IEE 89] on 'the problems arising from the specification, design and assessment of software for use in safety-related systems'. This thorough study reviewed the position as it was then and made a number of recommendations which have been influential in determining the subsequent directions of technical research, standards development, practice, and studies into education and training.

One of its observations was that 'a major factor affecting safety is a lack of awareness on the part of individuals and organisations of how and to what extent their work is safety-related', and its related recommendations have been at least partially responsible for the formation of the Safety-Critical Systems Club discussed below.

1.2.5 Research Programme

In 1988, the Joint Framework for Information Technology (JFIT) was set up by the DTI and the Science and Engineering Research Council (SERC) to bring together appropriate activities in information technology research, technology transfer, and education and training.

In 1990, JFIT initiated a safety-critical systems collaborative research programme, and in September of that year a call for proposals was sent out, with a deadline of January 1991. Eighteen projects were accepted, each with collaborating partners from both industry and academia. Projects were chosen not only to cover a broad spectrum of technologies and phases of the life cycle, but also a wide range of industrial sectors. With cross-sector collaboration not only within projects, but also between them, new ideas and technologies for safety engineering in computer systems would receive rapid circulation.

One of the principles of the programme is that technologies developed should receive early trials in industry and, if successful, be made available speedily for more general use. The projects are as yet in their infancy but, when they begin to mature, a good communication infrastructure will be essential. The Safety-Critical Systems Club is expected to contribute significantly towards this.

1.2.6 The Safety-Critical Systems Club

In May 1991, the Safety-Critical Systems Club was launched to 'facilitate the transfer of information, technology, and current and emerging practices and standards'. The Department of Trade and Industry (DTI) and the Science and Engineering Research Council (SERC), who sponsor the Club, have contracted responsibility for it to the IEE and BCS jointly, and these, in turn, have sub-contracted the day-to-day organization to the Centre for Software Reliability at the University of Newcastle upon Tyne.

The Club exists to increase awareness and facilitate communication in the safety-critical systems domain, and its goals are to achieve, in the supply of safety-critical computer systems:

- Better informed application of safety engineering practices;
- Improved choice and application of computer-system technology;
- More appropriate research and better informed evaluation of research.

In pursuit of these goals, the Club seeks to involve both engineers and managers from all sectors of the safety-critical community and, thus, to facilitate the transfer of information, technology, and current and emerging practices and standards.

Through its seminars and newsletter (three issues per year), it facilitates the communication of experience among industrial users of technology, the exchange of state-of-the-art knowledge among researchers, the transfer of technology from researchers to users, and feedback from users to researchers. It facilitates the union of industry and academia for collaborative projects and provides the means for their publicity and the reporting of their results.

The benefits will be more effective research and a more efficient and successful adoption and use of technology. Indeed, one of the features of the Club is that it provides a vehicle for the communication of the progress and results of the research projects mentioned above. Indeed, although the collaborative projects had not yet been formally contracted, they all participated in a poster session at the Club's inaugural meeting in July 1991. This publicized their objectives and introduced other interested parties to the projects.

1.3 INDIVIDUAL AWARENESS AND RESPONSIBILITY

There is the cliché that quality cannot be painted on later, it must be built in. It is the same with safety. More and more managers, engineers and other staff are coming to realize that building in anything requires not just working to a set of rules, but genuine professionalism. And while a company can and should create a professional ethos and, indeed, demand professionalism, it is individuals who do, or do not, demonstrate it.

In all cases, workers have a duty of care, and this is emphasized in the UK in the Health and Safety at Work Act. In safety-critical projects, this responsibility is enhanced. The learned societies have always defined minimum standards expected of their corporate members; but recently, two documents have emphasized the special responsibilities of engineers in the safety-critical field. In 1991 the Engineering Council published a discussion document on Engineers and Risk Issues [EC 91], 'with a view to encouraging a widespread debate on technical risk issues and what engineers can do to mitigate them...' The document proposes a ten point code of practice which includes not only a professional approach, but also an understanding of risk recognition and evaluation, and a familiarity with ethics and the legal framework encompassing an engineer's job. In 1992, the IEE published *Safety-Related Systems* [IEE 92a], a professional brief which offers engineers an explanation of the issues involved in safety-critical software systems.

There is a proposal that Chartered Engineer status should be a minimum requirement for engineers - at least those with responsibility - working on safety-critical projects. This would not guarantee competence, for that is an issue based on education and training as well as experience and attitude, but it would suggest professionalism - and one aspect of professionalism is an awareness of one's own limitations. Instead of attempting a task for which one is not competent, a true professional seeks expertise in the appropriate field; it may at first appear to cost more, but it is an economy in the long run - and it increases safety.

1.4   STANDARDS

1.4.1 The Need for Standards

Given the potential complexity of software systems, confidence in achieving safety is increased by separating the functions relating to the control of equipment and those relating to safety protection. Distinct, perhaps geographically distinct, control and protection computer systems may then be designed to provide these functions.

The control system's main purpose is to govern the operation of the equipment under control (EUC). But control implies safe control, so a number of safety activities will be designed into this system. However, the more functionality there is in a system, the greater its complexity, and it is well known that complex software contains so many logical paths that exhaustive testing could not be carried out in a finite time. There is therefore always a finite chance of malfunction. The protection system is therefore provided as an added layer of safety assurance.

It is a principle of traditional safety-critical systems that the protection system be kept simple and free of unnecessary functions. The EUC may fail, or the control system may malfunction, but the protection system is designed and expected to detect these occurrences and take preventive measures to ensure that the system does not enter a non-safe mode or, if it does, to take corrective action so as to return it quickly to a safe mode. The safe mode may be shut-down, or it may be a fully or degraded operational state.

In industries, such as Nuclear, where electromechanical safety-critical plant has been in operational for many years, this separation of functions has been traditional. The introduction of computer systems some years ago into various aspects of control preceded by a long time their use in the safety-protection systems. The latter remained electromechanical until it was considered that computers had achieved a certain maturity and demonstrated consistency in reliability. Nevertheless, control and protection are still kept distinct, and it is a fundamental principle that protection systems are kept simple.

In many other industries, such as medical, software was often introduced for the first time in a new product, rather than to replace existing electromechanical equipment. The result is that there is not always this separation of systems: operational control and safety protection are entrusted to the same system - with various designs of fault tolerance being included in order to achieve the desired levels of reliability and availability. As shown above, however, such a system is, by definition, more complex, and it becomes increasingly so as more functions are added. It is therefore more difficult to make or prove safe. Only the rigorous application of methods, techniques and standards will provide the levels of confidence required by certification bodies, users, and the public.

This is discussed, from the point of view of the medical field, in the chapters by Fox and Barber in Part Three; and a brief discussion is given below of progress in standards in the safety-critical domain generally.

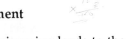

1.4.2 Standards Development

Awareness in software engineering leads to the development of standards. Greater awareness leads to their use in the work place. Standards define what must be done, and, usefully, they provide a yardstick (a 'standard') against which to check if it has been done - i.e. against which to measure quality.

Generic standards are broad standards, covering a domain, which define good practice and show what more specific sector or company standards should include. The HSE documents [HSE 87] were generic, but they not only served as guidelines on content, they also had the necessary effect of stimulating the development of sector-specific standards in gas engineering, instrumentation, control and automation, lift manufacture, and other sectors.

Then, in 1991, the Ministry of Defence issued its Interim Defence Standards 00-55 and 00-56 [MOD 91a and MOD 91b]. These are worth discussion, and they are considered in other chapters of this book, in particular that by Geary.

Meanwhile, the European Workshop on Industrial Computer Systems, Technical Committee No. 7 (EWICS TC7) had been carrying out pre-standardization work and developing guidelines on safety-critical software since the mid-1970s. This work, published in three books [Redmill 88, Redmill 89 and Bishop 90], has been used in various international standards and also as a basis for company standards.

Now Working Groups 9 and 10 of the International Electrotechnical

Commission's (IEC) Study Group 65A are in the final stages of producing true international standards [IEC 91 and IEC 92] for software-based systems in safety-critical applications (see Section 1.5 below).

That technical and professional awareness has improved in the last few years is illustrated by the facts that the imminence of these two standards is already a talking point in the UK and that their contents are awaited with some eagerness. Indeed, draft copies have found favour with those who have seen them, and other standards, for example in the road transport sector [Drive 91], are already benefiting from their principles.   If these standards are well publicized and widely used, with the professionalism and discernment which should result from greater awareness and more focused education and training, confidence in our ability to achieve systems of high safety integrity will be greatly enhanced.

1.5   RISK AND SAFETY INTEGRITY

When safety is based on reliability, with the fall-back being to shut the plant down, there is clearly a built-in trade-off between safety and availability. The plant is always safe if it is unavailable. Yet the users of the plant want its functionality - and never more so than today, when competitive forces and a demand for quality service lead customers to seek both safety and availability of service and companies trading these off against each other do so at their peril.

There are also instances when a shut-down and restart may themselves be expensive, as in the case of a nuclear power plant; and there are cases in which safety cannot be won by simply ceasing operation, such as on an airliner in flight.

To achieve the combination of safety and availability which customers, plant operators, and designers all want, and recognizing that total safety cannot be guaranteed, safety technology has taken a step towards a deeper analysis and understanding of the risk involved and towards the concept of 'tolerable risk'.

Working Group 10 of the IEC's Study Group 65A, in its draft standard [IEC 92], emphasizes the need to define risk and safety integrity levels and to identify a tolerable risk in designing or certifying a system (see the chapter by Bell in this book).

Risk is defined as the product of the consequence of a hazardous event and the frequency, or probability, of its occurrence. Thus, a risk may be reduced by decreasing either the event's frequency or its effect. A safety-critical protection system (see Section 1.4.1 above) is intended to reduce the probability of a hazardous event.

It is pointed out in the draft standard that the tests applied in regulating industrial risks are similar to those applied to daily life: one chooses to refuse to take the risk if it is unacceptably large, to accept it if it is negligibly small, or to reconsider strategy or tactics if it lies somewhere in between.

The concept of 'tolerable risk' implies the need to analyse and quantify the risk in any given situation, and to show that it is sufficiently low to be acceptable to society. What is actually considered tolerable reflects society's attitude, and determining it involves numerous factors, including politics, technology, need, availability of information, histories of accidents, and others. When a technology is new and in vogue, large risks may be accepted; later, after a disastrous accident, scepticism may cause even minor risks to be refused.

To aid risk assessors, the draft standard [IEC 92] suggests that numeric risk levels are classified into risk classes. A Class A risk is intolerable; a Class B risk is undesirable, and tolerable only if the risk reduction is impracticable or the costs grossly disproportionate to the improvement gained; a Class C risk is tolerable if the cost of the risk reduction would exceed the improvement gained; a Class D risk is a negligible risk.

One means of reducing risk is by providing safety functions via control and protection computer systems. It is then crucial that these functions are reliably performed, whatever else may go wrong, and the concept of 'safety integrity' is applied to such safety-critical systems. Safety integrity is defined in the draft standard as 'the likelihood of a safety-related system satisfactorily performing the required safety functions under all the stated conditions within a stated period of time'. Safety integrity is quantified, and safety integrity levels, both for systems and their software, are set so as to cater for the wide range of risk reductions which safety-critical systems are required to achieve. The opportunity is thus provided for determining numeric safety criteria against which assessors may measure the acceptability of systems.

1.6 EDUCATION AND TRAINING

1.6.1 Developers

To achieve the professionalism in individuals referred to earlier, as well as adequate competence for the job in hand, there is a need for a review of the education and training of safety professionals.

The development of software-based safety-critical systems requires the combination of the two disciplines of software and safety engineering. Safety engineering has traditionally been found in industrial practice, is only now beginning to enter academic domains, and is only infrequently familiar to software engineers. Likewise, safety engineers are not typically trained or experienced in software development.

Study groups of the BCS and the IEE have been active in attempting to derive standards and outline syllabuses for the education and training of engineers involved in safety-critical system development. Both professional bodies have presented reports on the subject [BCS 90 and IEE 92b] and, though there is a long way to go before there are standards in place, the awareness is there and work is in progress.

The trend is towards a three-tier structure in the education of software safety engineers. The first tier is general and applies to all engineers; the second is more detailed and applies to all engineers involved in safety-critical projects; the third consists of a range of modules, of Masters Degree level, each applicable to a particular sector and to the engineers working on safety-critical projects in that sector. Thus, every active safety engineer would receive the training described in both of the first two tiers as well as at least one module from the third tier.

The development of the syllabuses of the numerous modules will take some time, but the infrastructure is beginning to be put in place. Indeed, an MSc degree course on Safety-Critical Systems is already being planned by the University of York and may well be on offer in 1993.

The next question to be tackled is whether engineers involved in safety-critical projects, or, indeed, all safety professionals, should need to be individually accredited before being eligible for such work. Such a move would certainly lead to increased confidence in safety-critical software engineering.

1.6.2 Systems Operators

Computer control has brought about a major redistribution of the workload of many system operators, for example in the cockpits of aircraft: the traditional preponderance of manual tasks has given way to a mentally-based workload. In the airline industry, a number of accidents have been blamed on a failure in the communication between pilot and computer, and the question has been raised of whether training has kept up with this shift in workload. If pilots are not trained and practiced in interpreting the mass of data which appears on their screens, they and their passengers are endangered. And, 'practised' is important here: there's plenty of time to resolve queries when all is well, but only seconds when the plane is in distress.

In the medical field, it will be much the same for anaesthetists when software-based systems control the 'routine mechanical functions of administration of the anaesthetic agent, controlling or assisting ventilation, monitoring appropriate patient variables and providing good records of all relevant surgical events and patient responses' - as discussed by Packer [Packer 90] who goes on to say that 'If the computer can handle these manipulative tasks, the anaesthetist can devote more time to monitoring and assessing patient conditions. Such a division of labour has the potential to improve patient safety.' But then the anaesthetist's job will be a different one, requiring different training which fits him not only for monitoring under routine conditions, but, importantly, for quick detection of abnormal conditions, rapid analysis, and instantaneous emergency action, perhaps involving interaction with the computer.

And so it is in all industries. Computerization introduces not only a new means of control, but also new functions and a new work structure. It creates changes in the organization which it is designed to support. If safety is to be achieved, these changes need to be recognized early, planned for, and introduced formally and in a structured manner. Training must be provided for all operators, at all levels, *before* they are in charge of live operation.

1.7   CONCLUSIONS

This chapter has introduced some of the non-technical issues relevant to the development of safety-critical software. Software quality is, of course, important. However, safety is a system issue and a human factors issue rather than merely a software issue. In the end, however, total safety cannot be guaranteed, so it is important to calculate and understand the risk involved in a given circumstance and define a 'tolerable risk'; then, safety does not depend arbitrarily on the quality of the software, but on a deeper study of potential hazards and their likelihood. Nor does it depend on an arbitrary, and perhaps ill-founded, belief in absolute safety, but on a firmer-based confidence in a given level of safety.

While it has been impossible to discuss all the topics mentioned in this chapter in detail, each has been introduced and appropriate references given. Many of these references are to the reports of studies which have recently been carried out, to standards under development, and to recent initiatives, so it will be apparent to the reader that the importance of safety is not underestimated by the software profession - and, more generally, the engineering profession. Each issue mentioned in the chapter is constantly under review and, indeed, the subject of research.

Much of the research in progress consists not only of collaborative projects involving both academia and industry, but also the support and participation of government departments and the professional bodies. Both the Institution of Electrical Engineers and the British Computer Society have carried out studies into the education and training necessary to equip engineers for safety-critical work, and the Engineering Council has issued a draft code of practice for engineers involved with risk issues.

The use of software already enhances safety in many applications, but questions remain not only about the level of safety achievable when software is employed but also about the ability to prove that a system is safe. The work in progress is aimed at improving risk management and increasing confidence in software in the future.

1.8 ACKNOWLEDGEMENTS

Parts of this chapter are extracts from two earlier papers [Redmill 92a and Redmill 92b]. Acknowledgment is made to Microsystem Design and to the Institution of Electrical Engineers.

1.9 REFERENCES

[BCS 90]   British Computer Society: "BCS Safety Critical Systems Group Report of the Education Working Party." BCS Report, September 1990.

[Bishop 90]   Bishop P G: "Dependability of Critical Computer Systems - 3: Techniques Directory." Elsevier Science Publishers, 1990.

[Drive 91]   Drive Safely: "Proposal for a European Standard: The Development of Safe Road Transport Informatic Systems." Report of DRIVE Project V1051, Draft 1, August 1991.

[EC 91]   The Engineering Council: "Engineers and Risk Issues - An Embryo Code of Practice." Engineering Council Discussion Document, 1991.

[HSE 84]   Health and Safety Executive: "Guidance on the Safe Use of Programmable Electronic Systems." Draft Document in 3 parts, HSE, 1984.

[HSE 87]   Health and Safety Executive: "Programmable Electronic Systems in Safety-Related Applications." Two documents: 1 - "An Introductory Guide"; 2 - "General Technical Guidelines", HSE, 1987.

[ICSE 90]   Inter-Departmental Committee on Software Engineering: "SafeIT." Two documents: 1 - "Overall Approach"; 2 - "Standards Framework", ICSE 1990.

[IEC 91]   International Electrotechnical Commission: "Software for Computers in the Application of Industrial Safety-Related Systems." SC65A/ WG9 Draft Document, November 1991.

[IEC 92]   International Electrotechnical Commission: "Functional Safety of Electrical/Electronic/Programmable Electronic Systems." SC65A/ WG10 Draft Document, Version 5, January 1992.

[IEE 89]   Institution of Electrical Engineers: "Software in Safety-Related Systems." A Report Prepared by a Joint Project Team of IEE and

BCS, IEE, October 1989.

[IEE 92a]   Institution of Electrical Engineers: "Safety-Related Systems - A Professional Brief for the Engineer." Issue 1, IEE, 1992.

[IEE 92b]   Institution of Electrical Engineers: "Educational and Training Requirements for Safety Critical Systems." Public Affairs Board Report No. 12, January 1992.

[ISO 87]   International Standards Organisation: "ISO 9001: Quality Systems Model for Quality Assurance in Design/Development, Production, Installation and Servicing." ISO, 1987.

[ISO 90]   International Standards Organisation: "ISO 9000-3: Guidelines for the Application of ISO 9001 to the Development, Supply and Maintenance of Software." ISO, 1990.

[MOD 91a]   Ministry of Defence: "Interim Defence Standard 00-55/Issue 1 - The Procurement of Safety Critical Software in Defence Equipment." MOD, April 1991.

[MOD 91b]   Ministry of Defence: "Interim Defence Standard 00-56/Issue 1 - Hazard Analysis and Safety Classification of the Computer and Programmable Electronic System Elements of Defence Equipment." MOD, April 1991.

[Packer 90]   Packer J S: "Patient Care Using Closed-Loop Computer Control." Computing and Control Engineering Journal, 1, pp. 23-28, 1990.

[Redmill 88]   Redmill F J: "Dependability of Critical Computer Systems - 1." Elsevier Science Publishers, 1988.

[Redmill 89]   Redmill F J: "Dependability of Critical Computer Systems - 2." Elsevier Science Publishers, 1989.

[Redmill 92a]   Redmill F: "Quality ++ for Safety-Critical Systems." The Real-Time Software Engineering Conference, Wembley Conference Centre, March 1992.

[Redmill 92b]   Redmill F: "Computers in Safety-Critical Applications." Computing & Control Engineering Journal, 3(4), July 1992.

2

Issues in the development of safety-critical systems

John McDermid

2.1 INTRODUCTION

The aim of this chapter is to set out, on a broad basis, the key issues in developing safety-critical systems, when software is a major element. The aim is not to go into technical detail, but rather to draw out the key difficulties in developing such systems and to indicate the primary 'weapons', in both a technical and managerial sense, which we have at our disposal for achieving and demonstrating safety.

The chapter assumes relatively little prior knowledge of safety issues, although it does assume that the reader is generally familiar with current software engineering concepts and methods. Thus the chapter should be seen as an introduction to the issues for someone unfamiliar with the area, and as a 'scene setter' for other chapters in the book. It focuses on development issues, but briefly considers certification.

We start by discussing what is meant by safety and the term 'safety-critical system'. There is no 'universal' definition of these terms, so the aim is primarily to give an understanding of the concepts, whilst minimizing purely terminological discussion.

2.1.1 What is a Safety-Critical System?

There are many definitions of safety, and sometimes a distinction is made between systems being safety-critical and safety-related, dependent on the degree of harm they can cause. We present here a treatment of the concept of safety which allows the degree of harm to be considered as an independent factor, and we view all systems which can influence safety as being safety-critical.

We take the view that safety is concerned with *absolute* harm, that is irremediable or irrecoverable damage [Burns 92]. The damage can be to individuals, to property, or to the environment. However we observe that the 'opportunity' for causing harm depends on *context*, that is the situation in which the system is placed. One example where the same system can be used in more than one context is a syringe pump (see Note 1) which may be used to give medication on a ward, or to give anaesthetics in an operating theatre. Although failures in either situation can be life-threatening, the opportunity for harm is (in some regards) less in the operating theatre as there will normally be continuous monitoring of the patient's vital signs, and this is not true on a ward.

Computer systems, and hence software, can only influence safety if they are used to control some physical process which can lead to harm. In order to relate the concept of safety to computer systems, we introduce the notion that computer systems offer *services* to the controlled equipment - that is, they operate in order to (try to) satisfy some goal in the management of the equipment which the computer system is designed to control or influence. We use the term *controlled equipment* although we recognize that the computer system may not have full authority for controlling the equipment. The International Electrotechnical Commission (IEC) uses the term Equipment Under Control (EUC).

We can consolidate these concepts, and introduce a few new ones, to present a definition of the concept of a safety-critical service:

> A service is judged to be *safety-critical* in a given context if its behaviour could be sufficient to cause the controlled equipment to inflict, or prevent the equipment from inflicting, absolute harm on resources for which the organisation operating the service has responsibility.

The early parts of this definition follow from the earlier discussion. However, we introduce the distinction 'cause, or prevent' to cater for systems whose purpose is primarily one of protection, e.g. nuclear reactor protection systems.

Further, we introduce the notion of the organization operating the system and their responsibilities, for a number of reasons. First, there are safety requirements even for systems that are meant to be dangerous, e.g. weapons; without introducing the notion of responsibility, we could not produce a coherent definition, i.e. we could not distinguish doing harm as intended from doing harm to those whom the system is intended to protect. Second, the nature of the responsibility derives from the context, as well as the service offered by the system, and the definition allows us to capture this notion. In practice there are different sorts of resources and types of responsibility which we have to consider. For example:

- Staff of the organization operating the controlled system (this is a legal responsibility, through the Health and Safety at Work Act in the UK);
- Environment and the public (this may be a social or moral responsibility, although in some cases it will also be a legal responsibility).

We have presented a broad definition in order to capture these important concepts and distinctions.

It is now simple to indicate what is meant by a safety critical system:

A *safety critical system* (SCS) is one that has at least one safety-critical service.

While the discussion above has made this definition applicable only to computer systems, it would be very easy to generalize this to any form of system. Software within a computer system is viewed as being safety-critical if it is instrumental in providing a safety-critical service.

Based on the above definitions, we can say that:

A system is *safe* if it cannot (is acceptably unlikely to) cause absolute harm, or fail to prevent it when it is intended to do so.

However, we also note that there are two sorts of safety, and hence safe systems:

- *Intrinsic* safety - a system is intrinsically safe when there is no possibility of it causing, or failing to prevent, absolute harm;
- *Engineered* safety - this term applies when a system has been designed to minimize risk, or reduce it to an acceptable level.

There are relatively few, if any, intrinsically safe systems, although some systems fall into this class if we ignore misuse. (An example might be a feather duster.)

In practice we are primarily concerned with systems which we have to engineer to achieve acceptable levels of safety, and this is the focus of the rest of the chapter. In practice the degree of authority which the system has, especially where there are human operators, will affect the degree of criticality of the system, and the difficulty of engineering safety. Authority is an important notion, because difficulty often arises in deciding the balance of authority between computers which are relatively reliable and humans who are relatively good at handling unanticipated events, but space does not permit a full analysis of the issues.

These definitions enable us to draw out some important aspects of the notion of safety. First, the definitions explicitly acknowledge the role of *judgement*. That is, they recognize the fact that it often requires expert judgement to determine what aspects of computer behaviour (failures) can cause, or fail to prevent, harm due to the complex causal chains which exist in sophisticated systems and equipments. Similarly, value judgements must be made when we are concerned with issues of social responsibility. While the definitions do not necessarily help make these judgements, they do acknowledge their relevance and importance.

Second, the definitions acknowledge that safety is not an absolute property, that we need to assess systems against their scenarios of use, and that we need to take into account what sort and what degree of harm can arise from using the system. This is important as, in many cases, we are willing to use dangerous systems because of the benefits which accrue from their use. This opens up the issue of social valuation of risk [Jones-Lee 87], although we do not have space here to discuss in detail the difficult issues of willingness to accept risk and valuation of risk.

2.1.2 Content of the Rest of the Chapter

The remainder of the chapter is concerned with the key difficulties of engineering safety and outlining the characteristics of techniques for engineering safety. Section 2.2 deals with key difficulties, and Sections 2.3 and 2.4 look at the achievement of safety from a technical and project managerial perspective, respectively. Section 2.5 outlines the main elements of a methodological approach to achieving safety. Finally some conclusions and a summary are presented.

2.2   KEY DIFFICULTIES

It is widely appreciated that developing safety-critical systems is a difficult task. The aim in this section is to indicate reasons why the task is so difficult, as a precursor to the discussion of more detailed technical and managerial problems and solutions in Sections 2.3 and 2.4 respectively.

The most general point, which we cannot stress too much, is that safety is a *systems* issue - and we cannot consider *just* hardware or software in isolation. While this is well-understood in industry, it is perhaps less well-appreciated by those with an academic computing background (and hard for them to adapt to, as many of the disciplines involved are beyond their experience). For the sake of brevity we focus here on the computing aspects, but there are several books (e.g. [Hitchins 92]) which discuss the systems engineering issues at length (although safety is not a major focus).

It should also be stressed that engineering safety does not imply the need to achieve correctness (*vis à vis* some specification). A system may be incorrect, and unreliable, but safe because its failure modes are not hazardous. Similarly a system may be correct, but unsafe, due to errors in the specification. We stress this point, as it is a fairly common misconception that reliability and correctness are *necessary* precursors to safety. The reasons why safety should be seen as a distinct concept should become clear in the following sections.

We discuss here two problems of principle:

- Systems have to be safe even in the presence of failures;
- Absolute safety is an unobtainable goal and we always have to consider when we have 'done enough' to achieve acceptably safe operation.

While there are other difficulties, these seem to be two of the over-riding issues which colour the whole of the development and assessment process.

2.2.1 Safety in the Presence of Failures

The most striking difference between most 'non-critical' systems and safety-critical systems is that the non-critical systems are only required to work when 'all is well', but safety-critical systems must work even in the presence of failures. Although this is simple to state, and it seems almost trite, it has a pervasive influence on the whole development process as we need to consider the failure modes and failure rates of all components of a system, at all stages in the development process. There are many techniques introduced specifically for analysing the failure properties of systems (see Section 2.3), but we are more concerned here with the general problems introduced by the need to respond to failure.

In practice we distinguish a number of different responses to failure, more specifically, responses that can occur following failure of system components without compromising safety of the controlled equipment (more strictly, people in the environment, etc.):

- *Fail safe* - the system can bring the controlled equipment to a safe condition or state: for example, reactor shutdown by a monitoring and protection system;
- *Fail operational* - the system must continue to provide service if the equipment is not to be hazardous; for example, many control systems such as a flying control system for an aircraft (the so-called fly-by-wire).

The implication of the term 'fail safe' is that there is a safe state that can be reached easily, and with high reliability (see Note 2). For example, with many classes of electro-mechanical protection system, a safe state can be reached simply by opening a switch (relay). Solenoid valves and similar devices are used which, when de-energized, open (or close), thus stopping the process which is being monitored. This style of protection is also tolerant to power failures. It should be noted that introducing computers into this 'simple' situation is not without difficulties as we require power to stay on for the processors to close the system down. So we are, already, making some engineering compromises.

The 'fail operational' class really represents those systems for which there is no easily reachable safe state, or for which full control is required for some time before a safe state can be reached. In the case of a flying control system, especially for an aerodynamically unstable aircraft, loss of the computers at any point during flight could be catastrophic, and there may be no viable mechanical back-up, or reversionary mode which can be used until the aircraft lands (see Note 3). Here the engineering trade-off has been that, for the overall performance (and perhaps therefore the safety) of the whole equipment, one particular part will be made fail-operational, and hence will have to be built to the highest integrity levels.

In reality these are not distinct classes of system, but rather they represent points on a spectrum - a reactor protection system typically has to keep working for about a day after a reactor shutdown while the residual heat is being pumped out. Similarly, even flying control systems only have to remain operational until the aircraft can be landed. However, it is clear that the closer the systems are to the fail safe end of the spectrum, in the sense that simply stopping doing anything will cause the system to enter a safe state, the easier they are to design and evaluate.

In practice, the biggest problem is dealing with multiple (correlated) failures. The practice of developing safety-critical systems is such that relatively few systems fail due to single point failures. Instead, most incidents or accidents which do occur are the result of multiple simultaneous problems, often due either to unanticipated common mode failures, or hitherto unanticipated combinations of events. The difficulties arise from the sheer impracticality of analysing, or considering, all the possible failure modes and their combinations. In practice, simplifications have to be made, e.g. by assuming worst case failure behaviour rather than analysing real failure modes, but this only ameliorates the problems rather than eliminating them altogether.

It is worth making a brief comment about engineering safety in the presence of failures. Safety engineers often talk about integrity, or 'safety integrity'. Dictionary definitions say that integrity means 'freedom from flaws or corruption'. Thus, safety integrity means 'freedom from flaws or corruption which could compromise safety'. This is essentially a form of design correctness, but *vis à vis* hazardous failure modes, taking into account the unavoidable failure modes of the system components, sensors, actuators, and the like.

To achieve safety integrity, 'safety features' are introduce to detect component failures and to provide responses which prevent hazardous behaviour. Engineering safety means achieving safety integrity, but also achieving sufficiently high reliability of safety features that overall risk targets are satisfied.

2.2.2 Absolute Safety is an Unobtainable Goal

It should now be unsurprising to learn that absolute safety, in the sense that a system can never cause harm, is an unobtainable goal, at least for a very broad class of systems, if not for all. There are several factors here, one being that it is impossible to provide completely adequate specifications. This is true for engineering reasons - there are simply too many failure modes to consider. However there is also a philosophical problem - we can never know if we have covered all possibilities, i.e. that we have 'apprehended the world' correctly [Wittgenstein 69]. This difficulty has been noted by many workers in safety-critical systems, e.g. Leveson [Leveson 87].

In practice we can reduce the likelihood of safety-related failure although there are no guarantees of safety. From a methodological perspective, the aim is to have design and assessment practices (in the broadest sense) which reduce to an acceptable level the possibilities of accident in the systems they are used to produce and assess. More strictly, this means that the methods must facilitate reduction of risk to an acceptable level, and there are two different ways in which acceptability can be judged.

The requirement may be to reduce risk to a level which is deemed appropriate by some authority, e.g. a certification authority such as the CAA. In practice, such authorities may quote failure rate statistics rather than require demonstration of risk levels for the system, but they will have taken into account severity of failure in defining those failure rates (see Note 4). In other words, there is a level of risk specified and quantified, in some way, but no explicit cognizance is taken of benefit of using the system. In the air transport case, the statistical requirements are based on extensive historical information about aircraft safety. A similar situation exists in many other industries where safety requirements are derived over time, based on experience, gleaned from accident investigations, of the severity of particular sorts of failures.

Alternatively, the aim may be a trade-off between risk and benefit - and here one is in the business of making choices between two properties which are difficult to assess and quantify. An example might be the introduction of a robotic brain surgeon (see Note 5) which can carry out operations which no human surgeon can do, and perhaps may be more reliable than a human doctor. The issue then is one of weighing the risk associated with being operated on by an automaton against the benefits of a potentially life-saving operation. Here there may be judgements made about allowing the robotic device to be used at all, but the patient may also be able to exercise judgement, e.g. to refuse or accept the operation. Note that, in this sort of novel case, we are in a highly judgemental situation as there is no history of use of the systems upon which to base assessments of accident severity. There is thus the need to view risk from the point of view of uncertainty, not in 'frequentist' terms.

Perhaps a key issue as well is, who is accepting the risk. In the case of a brain surgeon, individuals themselves may be in a position to make the decisions about acceptability of risk - indeed it seems quite common for people to be willing to undergo quite hazardous operations and other treatment when faced with almost certain death if they do not. However, there are many cases where individuals are not really in positions to accept the risk themselves, either because they do not have the necessary technical knowledge, or because they do not have the necessary degree of control, e.g. over the cars that others drive, or the processes used by a chemical plant close to their homes. Thus, in such cases, the relevant licensing authority (if there is one) is acting as the agent of those who may be affected by any accident, or incident (see Note 6), and thus bears a considerable moral responsibility.

A further point is that, even if it were possible to produce 'perfect' specifications, and to build systems which were logically correct in terms of these specifications (at least the safety-relevant parts), they still would not be absolutely safe. Systems contain physical components and these will fail for a number of reasons, including mechanical wear out and memory corruption due to incident radiation. Any fault-tolerance mechanisms have their limitations, i.e. they cannot tolerate all possible failures and combinations thereof. Thus, the rate of failure of the system will be non-zero, and we must anticipate some risk of unsafe failure within the system's lifetime. In practice, we accept systems when they are 'safe enough' and this brings us on to the issue of evaluating safety.

2.2.3 Evaluation of Safety

It is common to state safety requirements in probabilistic terms, e.g. 'Failure mode X shall not occur at a rate of greater than 10^{-9} failures per hour'. While it is quite possible to show conformance to such requirements from extensive operational experience, it is now widely accepted that it is not practical, in general, to give a statistical evaluation of safety, based on test results, in advance of deployment [Butler 91]. More specifically, it is usually only practical to evaluate to approximately 10^{-5} failures per hour because of the length of time necessary to acquire the necessary test data.

In some cases statistical evaluation is practical. For example, the rate of 10^{-9} failures per hour might correlate to 10^{-5} failures per demand, where the demand rate is low, e.g. 10^{-4} demands per hour. If it is possible for the demand rate to be artificially increased, e.g. by simulating fault conditions, then such rates can be handled statistically. However, such 'speed-ups' are not usually possible for continuously-running, fail-operational, systems.

It should be clear from this brief discussion, and the recognition that 'absolute safety' is an unobtainable goal, that we need to determine the levels of risk we are willing to accept. In general, this evaluation needs to be carried out in the face of uncertainty, and without adequate data on which to produce statistical models (see Note 7). In this situation, acceptability of risk is a difficult socio-technical and socio-political issue, which we do not have space to discuss here. It is interesting to note, however, that economists, for example, have considerable experience in evaluating acceptability of risk under such circumstances, at least in certain fields such as road transport [Jones-Lee 87].

In practice, safety-critical systems are developed, evaluated and deployed, despite the fact that we cannot evaluate the safety levels statistically. In effect, we avoid or sidestep the difficulties by employing techniques to help us develop *assurance*, or confidence, in safety systems. In other words, we are using confidence, or assurance, in the face of inadequate knowledge and uncertainty as a 'substitute' for statistical knowledge. Although this is not statistically sound, there is considerable historical precedent for doing this in other engineering disciplines. We have previously argued that assurance derives from many facets of the process, and, in general, is based on understanding, or comprehension, of the artefact being produced and the process used to produce it , together with the level of diversity used in arriving at that understanding [McDermid 91a]. We use this notion as a basis of our discussion of achievement of safety, first from a technical, and then from a (project) managerial, perspective.

2.3   SAFETY AS A TECHNICAL ISSUE

In developing and evaluating safety-critical systems, we need to achieve assurance from a technical perspective, which means we must have:

- Understanding of the system, its environment, its workings, its failure modes, etc.
- Independent assessment (confirmation) of the design, implementation, failure analysis, etc.

We discuss ways of achieving (adequate) understanding, but first we consider the difficulties which have to be overcome in achieving safety.

2.3.1 Enemies of Safety

There are a number of problems to be overcome in developing and evaluating safety-critical systems which we refer to as 'enemies of safety'. There are, of course, many different classes of problem, and we have alluded to some of them above. Here we restrict ourselves to very general classes of problem which are likely to affect most systems (or systems developments) in some way or another. Put another way, when developing a safety-critical system it is extremely likely that it will be necessary for designers to address the following issues, to some extent.

The first issue is *specifiability*, i.e. the difficulty of producing, appropriate, adequate and effective specifications. There is considerable difficulty in eliciting requirements for safety-critical systems, for the reasons identified above, especially in knowing when all eventualities have been covered adequately. Philosophically, we can never be completely certain that we have covered all eventualities, and all we can seek to do is to try to reduce the uncertainties (risks) associated with the specifications to an acceptable level.

The most obvious issue is *complexity*, as this is a direct barrier to understanding, and hence is a major concern in the development of almost all safety-critical systems. This has long been recognized in traditional safety engineering disciplines, and effort is expended to achieve simplicity. However, this problem is perhaps less fully appreciated in software engineering, and there is something of a 'can do' mentality which accepts complexity as a challenge, rather than shunning it. There are difficulties resulting from this attitude which are apparent in many classes of system, e.g. luxury cars. Further, the increasing trend to automation also leads to integration between systems, and hence increased complexity (through vastly increased numbers of interactions), and some would argue that this is resulting in systems which are beyond our ability to design and assess adequately. Complexity is both a major problem and something of an enigma, as there are no easy and effective ways of measuring it (see Note 8). Thus, complexity is difficult to assess and control - and this is of course a management problem as well.

As was pointed out above, one of the major factors that leads to incidents and accidents is *unanticipated combinations of events*. Pragmatically this is a major concern, as most incidents and accidents which occur involve such combinations of events [Leveson 87]. By their very nature, such eventualities are very unlikely to be handled adequately (except by happenstance). The fundamental reason for this is that, if unanticipated combinations of events occur, this can invalidate any analysis which has been carried out, and hence the basis of the design (the design principles).

Another major source of difficulties is *human frailty*. All safety-critical systems are developed and operated by people, and people make mistakes which can lead to accidents. Such mistakes can be classified in various ways. One simple classification is to distinguish errors of:

● *Commission* - an act which transforms a safe (satisfactory) state into an unsafe of unsatisfactory state. Examples are introduction of errors in design; failure to follow defined procedures in operating the system (see Note 9);

from errors of:

● *Omission* - an act which fails to detect an unsafe (unsatisfactory) state, and thus allows it to remain in the system. Examples are overlooking flaws introduced in design so that they are not removed prior to implementation or even operational use; failure to understand the state of the controlled system and thus not taking appropriate actions to bring the controlled system back towards a safe state.

The analysis of human error is complex, and the above is necessarily a superficial treatment of the issues. Work by Reason [Reason 79] has provided a more comprehensive basis for analysing human error.

These issues identified above are all sources of problems in practice. Many of the problems are insurmountable, in the sense that they cannot ever be entirely overcome. The main aim in designing a system and in the software development process, however, is to minimize the risk that these problems may lead to unacceptable safety integrity of the system produced.

It would be possible to amplify each of the above points and, in some cases, to give quite detailed examples of situations where the above difficulties lead to incidents or accidents (where they were at least a partial cause of the accident or incident). For example, much has been written on human error, and ways of categorizing human error which is useful in considering (at least) the operational difficulties [Reason 79]. This is an important topic, and one which seems likely to increase in importance as interfaces to systems become more complex.

It is very instructive in developing safety-critical systems to consider the 'fault pathologies' leading to a particular accident or incident. We do not have space to do this here, but refer the interested reader to [AAIB 90] which is the report of the investigation of the accident at Kegworth. This is interesting and informative from a general perspective, but it also highlights one of the areas of difficulty for modern complex systems - that of ensuring effective man-machine communication, especially when an operator (pilot) is operating under stress, managing a system which has partially failed (see Note 10).

2.3.2 Approaches to Achieving Safety

In order to address the 'enemies of safety' outlined above, we need to deploy a number of techniques which can counteract, or ameliorate, these problems in achieving safety. These both cover specific design and analysis techniques, and also 'safety principles', i.e. concepts and ideas which guide the way in which a system is designed and assessed. We discuss some of the more important principles here.

The most fundamental principle is *simplicity*. This is the only real way to ensure understanding, or understandability, of the systems being produced. This is easy to state, but hard to achieve and control. It is also a broad concept. If we are to have assurance, we need simplicity in the system being developed, in the process used to produce it, and in its specifications. One of the major concerns regarding increasing computerization of safety-critical systems is not the use of computers *per se* but the increase in the complexity of the requirements which the use of computers makes possible. The only counter to this is to ensure that there is a simple and precise statement of requirements (e.g. a succinct axiomatisation of safety goals, if using formal methods - see Note 11), but this is usually where conflicts between operational performance and safety arise.

Where a system cannot be made intrinsically simple, it can be simplified by the use of appropriate *structure*. That is, we should divide the system into parts which are intelligible (simple) in themselves, and between which the interactions are also simple. Examples of ways of achieving good structure are:

- To provide separate safety systems, if possible; note that this is not always possible for fail-operational systems, but it normally is feasible for fail safe and protection systems;
- To provide 'firewalls' between system components, i.e. a facet of the design which prevents failures in one part of the design affecting another (some authors have suggested the idea of a safety kernel for software based systems [Rushby 89]).

Structuring is crucial. From a computer systems standpoint, the software and hardware system architecture is probably the most important aspect of structuring, rather than the lower-level structuring that occurs in modularizing programs.

The 'classical computer science solution' is to use *abstraction*. That is purposeful drawing away from, or omission, of detail, in order to gain understanding of complex systems. This, of course, remains a valid approach, but it is of limited utility for a number of reasons. Since we are concerned with systems which operate even in the presence of failures, we can only 'sustain abstractions' which respect the fault containment and management mechanisms (e.g. firewalls). The interfaces between components become more complex due to the interactions brought about by failures. The classical failure analysis techniques require detailed knowledge of the system, and cannot be based purely on abstractions, and so on. In summary, the need to treat failures is an 'abstraction breaker'.

A key principle is to make use of *mathematical rigour* - that is, to use rigourous mathematical models (and automation) to facilitate understanding of the system being produced and to reduce the opportunity for human failings (especially errors of omission) from leading to unsafe systems or unsafe situations. The most obvious guise for such mathematical rigour is the so-called formal methods, e.g. mathematically-based techniques for system and software specification and development. These techniques are beneficial, but again they have their limits [Barroca 92]. However, other forms of mathematical rigour should not be forgotten. It is possible to use mathematical techniques to analyse the timing behaviour of programs (specifically worst-case execution times) and to analyse the system-level scheduling properties so as to guarantee satisfaction of deadlines (within some failure hypothesis) [Burns 91, Puschner 89]. These techniques provide as strong a set of 'guarantees' about time-domain correctness as the more classical formal techniques do in the functional domain.

A vital aspect of the assessment of safety-critical systems is the process of carrying out *failure modes analysis* - that is, investigation of the behaviour of the system, including software, when some of the components of the system have failed.   This is crucial to showing that various sorts of requirement are met, and to understanding the behaviour of the system once failures have occurred. There are a number of standard techniques for failure mode analysis, and many of these can be applied to software-based systems.   Space does not permit a survey here.   There are few good accounts of these techniques, but [McDermid 92a] gives an overview of the techniques in a computing systems context.

Finally, it is crucial to ensure that there is *comprehensive validation* - both during development and in operation. As will be recalled, it is not practical to guarantee correctness of specifications. Thus, even if it were possible to guarantee adherence of systems to their specifications, we would need to validate the soundness, or appropriateness, of the specifications.   The validation process involves review, testing and, ultimately, operational use. Here monitoring of the system in normal operation and during incidents and accidents is required in order to detect and rectify flaws in specifications (hopefully before they lead to catastrophic failures).

Much more could be said about each of the above principles. Our aim here has been to indicate the important issues and to provide a small number of key references. The reader is referred to the rest of the book for more comprehensive (although not systematic and exhaustive) treatment of the issues (see Note 12).

2.4   SAFETY AS A MANAGERIAL ISSUE

Safety is at least as much a management issue as a technical one. For example, the court judgments seem to make it clear that the accident involving the Herald of Free Enterprise was primarily caused by management failings, amplified by some aspects of the design of the ship. Similarly, the accidents involving the Therac 25 (see Note 13) seem to have been brought about, at least in part, by failings in the management of the developers of the system, although there were, in this case, clear technical faults with the design and implementation of the computer systems, and this was not an issue in the Herald of Free Enterprise case.

Thus, safety is a management issue in the development and assessment process, and during operation. We focus here on the development process and, hence, on project management issues. As with the technical issues, the goal is to achieve assurance, and this means we need to have:

- Control over the process, e.g. design visibility;
- Documentation of the process, e.g. safety plans and hazard logs.

These are the primary ways of gaining assurance and facilitating independent confirmation of safety. As before, we start by considering the 'enemies of safety', i.e. the factors we have to overcome in trying to develop and assess safety-critical systems.

2.4.1 Enemies of Safety

The managerial enemies of safety are mainly concerned with aspects of human frailty, and the difficulties faced by modern industrial organizations. The following are some key issues which I have observed in my limited experience of unsatisfactory safety-critical systems developments. I do not pretend that this is an extensive analysis of human and organizational failings.

A crucial problem is often *unfamiliarity*. Project managers in industries developing computer-based safety-critical systems are often unfamiliar with software (and other forms of modern technology) and, in some cases, are even frightened of it. At best, this means that the provision of design visibility for managers is of no use without their having the necessary understanding, so their projects are not well run. This may lead to safety problems being overlooked. At worst, the project managers may make (design) decisions 'extrapolating' from their previous experience, and thus make inappropriate and, perhaps, dangerous choices, e.g. deciding on fault-tolerance strategies which cope well with random hardware failures but not with the specification and design errors which are the only failure sources for software. The author believes, but of course cannot prove, that one of the reasons for the increase in complexity of software requirements for safety-critical systems is an inadequate appreciation of the difficulties of developing and assessing software to the highest integrity levels, and the ramifications of increased complexity on safety (and cost) on the part of some (project) managerial personnel.

Managers have to function in the face of *conflicting pressures*. One of the most serious is the need to achieve safety at a price, or within defined project timescales. It is arguable whether or not such pressures should be allowed or accepted for safety-critical systems, but the reality is that they exist, and probably they affect almost all safety-critical systems projects.

At its starkest, managers may have to develop products to a keen and pre-defined market price. Exceeding the price by a small margin, e.g. 5 per cent, may lead to severely reduced sales (and perhaps a reduction in *overall* safety if competitor's products are inferior in this regard). This applies both to the manufacturing cost of the end product and the amortization of the development costs. Even where there are no firm prices or timescales, project managers are often faced with financially-based decisions which affect safety. As one can never be certain one has achieved acceptable levels of safety, one can always buy more confidence by spending more time and money on analysis, testing, and so on. There must always be a time when the manager says 'We've done enough', and it is usually the case that the sooner this is done, the greater the profitability of the organization.

There are many intermediate points on this spectrum. Common situations include the need to manage against fixed prices and timescales, or against performance bonuses or penalties associated with development timescales. In any event, managers will inevitably be faced with decisions which involve both safety and money, and the pressure will often be to save money at the *possible* risk of reduced safety. Of course, it is the difficulty of quantifying the possibilities which makes the decisions so difficult. There are extensive treatises on risk management, and some do address issues associated with safety-critical systems, e.g. [Cooper 87].

Another problem, which is perhaps less common, is *complacency or over-confidence*. Project managers place trust in people, processes, systems and tools without good cause. For example, they may assume that they can increase the complexity of systems while using the same processes and staff - 'They worked before, so they will work now'. A related form of problem is to assume that, because one built acceptable products before, one can do so now with new technology without the need to re-assess the risks. This is, to some extent, related to the issue of lack of understanding. If a manager does not adequately understand a technology, such as software, he may be prepared to accept the judgements of the 'specialists', without question and without appreciating the limitations of the technology or of the specialists' knowledge.

A further problem which project managers often have to face is that of *inappropriate standards*. Some of the standards to which the products and processes have to conform are inappropriate, in that they were conceived without cognizance of the issues introduced by computers and software, or they may simply be outmoded (see Note 14). As developers have the responsibility for achieving safety, and of conforming to standards, they may have to carry out one set of activities to achieve certification and another to achieve adequate safety. Inevitably this costs money and amplifies other pressures.   Some standards have been developed explicitly for dealing with safety-critical systems including software, e.g. the RTCA guidelines used in civil aviation [RTCA 85].

Some of the new standards are very challenging. The obvious examples are the Interim Defence Standards 00-55 [MoD 91a] and 00-56 [MoD 91b], which lay down very clear principles, but are beyond the state of the art (see Note 15). Project managers working to these standards have to decide (negotiate with the MoD) an appropriate way of conforming to the spirit of the standards, if not to the letter. This can be particularly difficult in a competitive tendering situation. Thus, the requirements for assessment or certification do not necessarily help, and they can be a hindrance.

Finally, a problem caused, or at least not prevented, by management is *over-reaching* - requiring too much complexity, too soon, given our understanding of the technology and equipments. This failing must be placed at the door of procurers, as well as developers. We have discussed this issue above, and it does not seem necessary further to amplify on the points.

2.4.2 Approaches to Achieving Safety

The project managerial difficulties are primarily related to people and organizations, and so are the solutions, or approaches to achieving safety. Again we focus on the development and assessment activities, although much of what is said here also applies to the operation of the system.

The fundamental issue is to use *good people*. Regardless of the technology used, deployment of individuals with the right attitudes and skills is the key to achieving safety. More strongly, the crucial factor in achieving safety is the choice of staff on the project. The technology used in terms of support tools and the like is primarily an issue of productivity, and the scale of system that can be handled, not one of safety.

The requisite skills and qualities of project personnel include relevant technical and interpersonal skills. The technical skills will be determined by the details of the project, specifically, the methods and tools used. While this is the factor that first comes to mind, it is perhaps the least important. At any rate, in the software engineering context, knowledge of the principles of specification, verification, testing, and so on are more important that knowledge of particular methods such as Z or VDM. Interpersonal skills go beyond the normal presentation and communication skills. They extend to the ability to work well in a team, to take a depersonalized view of one's work - to be pleased by constructive criticism that removes flaws from one's work, rather than being irritated or defensive, and so on. This also covers the attitude to safety (see below).

An often overlooked issue is knowledge of the application or problem domain. Software engineers will often detect flaws in specifications (and programs) based on knowledge of the application domain, not abstract knowledge of computer science. For example, incorrect gain in a control law definition will be detected using knowledge of the controlled system, not algorithm design. This indicates that teams need to be multi-disciplinary (see below), and also that software engineers need to have at least some understanding of the domain in which they are working (either learned on the job or through their academic education) in order to be able to communicate effectively as part of a multi-disciplinary team.

Assessments of the skills in UK industry suggests that there are not sufficient software engineers with the necessary skills and experience to work on the development and assessment of safety-critical systems. While much of the knowledge required relates to specific industries, there is a considerable body of material which can usefully be taught, independent of industry sector. The British Computer Society (BCS) set up a study to identify education and training requirements which are independent of industry sector, produced an outline curriculum, and identified some of the practical difficulties in putting such a training programme in place [McDermid 92b].

At the organizational level, the most important, and most elusive, factor in achieving safety is the establishment of a *safety culture* - running the organisation in such a way that safety is seen as a primary goal, and that consciousness of safety pervades all the development and assessment activities. There is no easy prescription for establishing such a culture, but there are some characteristics which can be identified. Safety cultures often reflect the ideas of 'ego-less programming' which avoid a parochial attitude to specifications and code. Similarly, adoption of a 'clean room' approach, which includes the restriction that a programmer is not allowed to test his own code, will be indicative of a safety culture. In the author's experience a safety culture is most likely to be found in an industry which has long been used to developing safety-critical systems, and where software has been adopted simply as 'another technology' to be used in the production of systems.

A further organizational factor is the provision of an appropriate balance of skills and individuals on a team. Developing and assessing safety-critical systems is an inherently multi-disciplinary activity. Getting the right mixture of software engineers, control engineers, cognitive psychologists (for assessing user interfaces), and so on, is crucial to achieving safety. No amount of technology and tools will make up for deficiencies in this regard. Building up such teams is another difficult activity, as it is necessary to make the teams 'gel', and there is a strong link to the development of a safety culture. Little has been written on such subjects, but DeMarco and Lister's advice on team building [DeMarco 87] is useful as well as entertaining.

A key project managerial tool in safety-critical systems development, as in other software engineering projects is defining an *effective process* - that is, selecting appropriate stages, phases, review points, methods, tools, hazard logging procedures, etc., to achieve the project's technical objectives while maintaining visibility and control over the technical work. Defining processes is a complex task, see for example [Rook 91]. Rook discusses process definition in the context of general software engineering, rather than safety-critical systems, but many of the principles apply. We discuss processes in some detail in Section 2.4, but briefly consider two critical issues here.

As with any other development project, productivity, if not ultimately quality, depends on *effective tools*. This means tools which are good for their role in the process and trustworthy in themselves. This latter point is important. In many cases, e.g. a loader, the tools will be trusted to preserve the safety integrity of the programs used in the safety-critical system. Also, analysis tools, e.g. those that show that deadlines will be met, can, if flawed, indirectly lead to hazardous operation of a system. Thus, the establishment of a process containing tools which are, in themselves, trustworthy, is an important managerial issue. This is becoming an important topic, and the Interim Defence Standards 00-55 and 00-56 require a hazard analysis of toolsets and development of tools to the same standards as the application in which they can directly affect safety.

The evolving draft standard DO-178B (see Note 16) takes a very different attitude towards tools, essentially placing trust in the effective pre-operational testing of the system to uncover flaws in tools. This illustrates one of the difficulties mentioned above where major standards present diametrically opposed requirements. A satisfactory stance on this issue has to be established for each project, but the community as a whole needs to reach a greater consensus on the issues of tool integrity.

In any development, it is necessary to have effective procedures for *quality control* - both within the project team and independently. Independence is important to minimize the possibilities of problems being overlooked as a result of 'groupthink' where all members of a group think the same way, because some ideas have become the accepted wisdom, and the underlying principles are no longer questioned. With safety-critical systems, it is common (and good practice) to establish an independent quality assurance (QA) team or, more precisely, a group concerned with independent safety auditing to avoid such problems relating to the safety properties of the system, and to check through important activities such as safety analyses. Such a team is usually referred to as carrying out IV&V (Independent Verification and Validation). The merits of having an IV&V team should be manifest. The provision of such a team is also mandated by some standards.

A managerial issue which impinges on the design process is *design for assessment* - carrying out the development with the aim of facilitating independent assessment, or certification. While this may seem like a technical issue, it is largely managerial as it is concerned with ensuring that the necessary documentation is produced to facilitate independent assessment, and this is the responsibility of management.

The suggestions above address some of the managerial issues, but not the problems of over-reaching current capabilities and establishing requirements which are too complex. Avoiding these problems requires enlightenment. In particular, it requires a considerable breadth and depth of knowledge on the part of developers and procurers - specifically the management in such organizations. Once the engineering process is started and detailed design is underway, it is not normally possible for individual engineers to perceive the overall complexity, or to do anything about it. Thus, the problems must be avoided at the beginning, and 'at the top'. Again, this is a 'people problem'. We need people with the right skills and experiences at the right levels in the organization, in order that appropriate and balanced decisions are made. Such people are rare, and this suggests a need for both appropriate education and training throughout a career. Again this is easier said than done, but perhaps one of the criteria one should look out for in an organization developing safety-critical systems is its attitude to such issues of education and training. There is little publicly available material on training programmes, but perhaps the BCS ISM, and its safety-critical systems sub-stream, is the best model available [BCS 91].

A further, and final, organizational matter relates to the financial issues which were discussed above. There is no 'correct' approach here, but achieving an appropriate balance between the pressures of profitability and safety requires 'long-termism' rather than the 'short-termism' engendered by current styles of corporate financial management and the influence of the City. Of course, companies must organize themselves so that they survive in the short-term, but it is necessary to weigh issues of short-term profitability against the long-term effects of inadequate safety (ultimately on the company as well as on the customers for, and users of, the company's products), and there will be situations where profitability should be sacrificed to safety.

Much more could be said here about procurement policies, accounting practices, and the like, but space does not permit a full discussion of these complex, and semi-political issues.

2.5   A METHODOLOGICAL APPROACH

It is of vital importance to have a methodological approach to the complete development and assessment process when producing safety-critical systems. This is not to say that it is impossible to produce safe systems with an *ad hoc* development - rather that such a process offers no way of *knowing* that adequate levels of safety have been achieved, nor the basis for convincing anyone outside the development team, e.g. a certification authority, that safety has been achieved. We do not have space to discuss the establishment of effective development processes in detail, but we can draw out some key issues.

2.5.1 Process Definition

As indicated above, one of the most important aspects of a methodological approach to achieving safety is to have a *definition of the process* - a document recording the key facets of the process, including stages and phases, and particularly identifying and specifying safety-specific activities. Without an explicit process definition, we have no effective basis for managing the project, nor for demonstrating that (adequate levels of) safety have been achieved. A process definition is roughly equivalent to a project plan, plus a quality plan, plus a resourcing schedule for a project. The development of process definitions has been discussed in detail [Rook 91]. The aim here is to draw out some safety-specific issues.

The project plans will identify activities which are only required because the system under consideration is safety-critical. These include hazard analysis, failure modes and effects analysis, establishment of integrity levels for system and software components, and so on. Other non-standard activities will be the independent assessments. The definition should say what techniques will be used, identify the requisite skills and experience of the staff involved, identify resource levels, and so on.

Other aspects of the process definition include the *establishment, or definition, of key roles*. This means identifying the responsibility and authority of safety-specific roles, e.g. a safety authority, and an independent safety assessor as required by the Interim Defence Standards 00-55 and 56. Role definitions should cover responsibilities, e.g. ensuring that particular standards are adhered to, authorities, e.g. signing off particular classes of deliverables, reporting lines, and so on. This is similar to normal project management practice, but focused on safety-related roles. A safety-specific issue might be the identification of the roles involved in reviewing particular documents to ensure that the right balance and mix of skills and knowledge are brought to bear in assessing the document.

The process definition also defines the *choice of development technologies*. That is the use of particular techniques, e.g. formal methods, for particular activities and components, as demanded by the appropriate integrity level. Generic standards, such as those developed by the International Electrotechnical Commission, may be relevant sources of information as they recommend different technologies for different integrity levels, and they are intended to be application domain independent.

Finally, the process definition should identify *applicable standards* - that is, standards which are mandated or have been chosen by the developers (these may be company, national or international standards).   The identification of standards is important as it guides and constrains the other aspects of the process definition, e.g. the establishment of roles.

There are other issues to be covered, but the above should illustrate the scope and nature of the process definition. Process definitions should not be written and forgotten; they should evolve as the project proceeds, reflecting necessary changes in procedures, roles, and so on. As with all other aspects of project documentation they should be subject to review. This leads us on naturally to documentation.

2.5.2 Safety Documentation

The project *software safety plan* is similar to a software QA plan in that it defines some key aspects of the project. Specifically, it should be thought of as the written definition of the process as identified above. Thus it will cover issues such as:

- Roles, organization and responsibilities;
- Process certification, i.e. the means of ensuring adherence to a process definition;
- Tool support and approval (qualification);
- 'Bought-in' software and sub-contract management;
- Safety engineering practices, such as:
  - Software hazard analysis;
  - Identification of safety-critical modules;
  - Controlled maintenance and evolution.

A more extensive discussion of the content of a software safety plan is under development by the IEEE, as draft standard P1228 [IEEE 92].

The software safety plan documents the development and assessment processes. There are two important and related parts to the documentation which are products of that process - the *hazard log* and the *safety case*. The hazard log forms the basis for, and index into, the safety case.

The *hazard log* is a record of hazards associated with the system under development, which is maintained throughout the development and assessment process and is preserved into operation and maintenance, where it is added to if necessary. It is established by a preliminary hazard analysis activity during the project's initiation phase. At this stage, the log will identify hazards typically associated with systems (controlled equipment) of the nature under consideration, but will contain little that is specific to that particular system. For example, the hazards typically associated with an aircraft flying control system will be well-known, and entered into the log at project initiation.

The log will be expanded during requirements specification, covering major hazards associated with the system, given those particular requirements. Thus, for a flying control system, the hazards will be refined, given knowledge of the control laws, the operational and performance characteristics of the aircraft, and so on. The log will be further expanded during design, detailing further hazards manifest at this level. However it is progressively more unlikely that hazards will be identified as we proceed through the development process, unless failure modes are discovered which can cause hitherto unanticipated hazards (see Note 17).

The hazard log is added to in maintenance, if this is shown to be necessary through incidents or accidents, although it is, of course, hoped that this will not be the case, i.e. that all potential hazards will have been identified much earlier.

The *safety case* is the documentation of the reasons *why the system is believed to be safe to be deployed* and it reflects the design and assessment work carried out in the development process. In many situations, the safety case (or a summary thereof) will be the major deliverable to the certification process or to an independent assessment. The safety case should contain the hazard log and arguments why the anticipated operation of the system, given the anticipated inputs and failures, will not lead to the identified hazards. In practice, the arguments will reflect design information, reliability calculations, safety analyses, and perhaps proofs of program properties [McDermid 92c]. The hazard log acts as the index as it should be possible to find the safeguards against each particular hazard, and the reasons for believing them to be effective, by tracing from the hazard.

2.5.3 Summary

The above discussion has inevitably been very brief. At the risk of trivializing the discussion, the safety aspects of the development process can be summarized as follows:

(i)   Identify potential hazards;
(ii) Design and verify the system to show that the hazards will not (are sufficiently unlikely to) arise;
(iii) Analyse possible failure modes and show that safety is maintained even in the presence of failures - this is a key aspect of validation;
(iv) Control the development process and produce documentary evidence so that it is manifest that you have done (i), (ii), and (iii) properly, both in absolute terms and against any relevant standards.

The hazard log is the result of task (i). Aspects of the design (task (ii)) will appear in the safety case, but task (iii) is the primary source of information for this. Task (iv) is concerned with management, and it will use the software safety plan as a basis for monitoring and controlling the development process.

2.6   CONCLUSIONS

This chapter is quite long. Yet it is rather superficial in some respects, for example, little has been said about certification or maintenance, both of which are important topics. Similarly, little has been said about the details of safety-relevant techniques, e.g. fault tree analysis and formal methods. The aim, however, has been to set out a broad overview of the issues relevant to the achievement and assessment of safety, and to set the context for the rest of the book. It is also hoped that the discussion herein will enable other general material on software engineering, e.g. that in [McDermid 91b], to be interpreted in the context of safety-critical systems.

Much of the rest of the book is more technical and detailed in nature, although it does not provide a complete and uniform coverage of all the topics relevant to the development and assessment of safety-critical systems. By contrast, we have dealt with some of the broader social and (project) managerial issues, and have given an overview of the technical and managerial approaches and techniques, focusing on problems and principles, rather than particular methods. The intention has been to provide general information which will help in forming judgements about the utility and relevance of particular techniques and technologies. Thus it is hoped that Sections 2.2, 2.3 and 2.4 will provide guidance which is of general, and fairly long-lasting, utility.

It seems appropriate to conclude by returning to a very general issue. How do we decide when a system is safe to be deployed? There are technical, managerial and social issues here, but a major point we have emphasized throughout the chapter is that much of the trust stems from the people involved in the development. Over-stating the point in order to make it, we should decide whether a safety-critical system is safe to be deployed by considering the people and organization first, and the technical issues second.

2.7   NOTES

(1)   A device which pumps fluid from a syringe according to some pre-set rate. Modern syringe pumps are microprocessor-controlled, i.e. a processor and its software control the rate at which the fluid is pumped from the syringe and deal with various other functions, for example, displaying the rate of flow to operators.

(2)   Note that this does not contradict the earlier point about safety not being synonymous with reliability. This refers to the reliability of a particular safety feature.

(3)   At present, commercial aircraft do have some reversionary modes,

e.g. a simple mechanical control in the A320, but this is not the case for some military aircraft, such as the EFA.

(4)   Risk is normally defined as the product of failure rate and severity (e.g. the number of lives expected to be lost). However, it is often difficult to quantify such issues, and this leads risk to be associated with uncertainty. In developing safety-critical systems, this view of risk is perhaps more appropriate.

(5)   This is not a hypothetical situation. Work is being carried out on just such a system.

(6)   An accident has the obvious interpretation of an event involving loss of life, injury, damage to the environment, etc. An incident occurs when some undesirable circumstances arise where margins of safety are reduced, e.g. loss of one engine on an aircraft, and some positive action (perhaps by an operator) is required in order to prevent the occurrence of an accident. In practice it can be difficult to draw clear distinctions between incidents and accidents, and to tell when one becomes the other.

(7)   There are some who would argue that we should not produce systems where we do not have the relevant statistical information. While this point of view is not without merit, it would imply a form of stagnation, as we would then never introduce new safety-critical systems which do not have historical precedents on which we could base evaluations of safety.

(8)   There has been a lot of work on software complexity measures, but it is quite widely accepted that these are not adequate and in many cases are misleading. Complexity is really a psychological issue, and we do not have good measures of the relevant cognitive processes.

(9)   Again, this is a factor in some real incidents and accidents, e.g. Chernobyl.

(10) This accident exhibits a number of the above properties, but complexity and interaction difficulties seem to have been paramount.

(11) The fundamental requirements for the SIFT (Software Implemented Fault Tolerance) system were expressed in less than ten axioms.

(12) The topics covered reflect the programme run by the DTI Safety-Critical Systems Club during 1991 and 1992.

(13) A radiation therapy machine which was responsible for the deaths of

six people through overdoses.

(14) There are also a lot of them; a figure of 147 has been quoted! Inevitably they contradict one another, and this further amplifies the project manager's difficulties in reaching sensible, and defensible, decisions.

(15) The author believes that the principles underlying the standards are sound. The difficulty, especially with Def Stan 00-55, is that they require the application of techniques which are currently beyond the state of the art for large-scale systems. Thus, it is necessary both to determine the extent to which it is possible to comply with the standards now and a way of migration towards more complete compliance later. The MoD have, as yet, provided no guidance on this.

(16) RTCA/EUROCAE DO-178A [RTCA 85] is the guidance document used in the development of software for civil aerospace applications. DO-178B is a revision of DO-178A which is currently in draft form.

(17) This is fairly improbable, and is most likely to arise if a common-mode failure is identified which can lead to an overall system failure mode which was previously thought to be incredible.

2.8 REFERENCES

[AAIB 90]   Air Accidents Investigation Branch: "Report on the Accident to Boeing 737-400 G-OBME near Kegworth, Leicestershire on 8 January 1989." HMSO, 1990.

[Barroca 92]   Barroca L M and McDermid J A: "Formal Methods: Use and Relevance for the Development of Safety-Critical Systems." Computer Journal, Vol. 35, No. 5, 1992.

[BCS 91]   British Computer Society: "Industry Structure Model (Release 2)." BCS 1991.

[Burns 91]   Burns A: "Scheduling Hard Real-Time Systems: A Review." Software Engineering Journal, Vol. 6, No. 3, pp 116-128, 1991.

[Burns 92]   Burns A, Dobson J E and McDermid J A: "On the Meaning of Safety and Security." Computer Journal, Vol. 35, No. 1, 1992.

[Butler 91]   Butler R W and Finelli G B: "The Infeasibility of of Experimental Quantification of Life-Critical Software Reliability." In: Proceedings of Software for Critical Systems, ACM, 1991.

[Cooper 87] Cooper D and Chapman C: "Risk Analysis for Large Projects." Wiley, 1987.

[DeMarco 87] DeMarco T and Lister T: "Peopleware." Dorset House, 1987.

[Hitchins 92] Hitchens D K: "Putting Systems to Work." Wiley, 1992.

[IEEE 1992] IEEE: "Software Safety Plans." IEEE Draft Standard P1228, IEEE, 1992.

[Jones-Lee 87] Jones-Lee M W: "The Political Economy of Physical Risk." Journal of the Society of Radiological Protection, Vol. 7, No. 1, 1987.

[Leveson 87] Leveson N G: "Software Safety: What, Why and How?" ACM Computing Surveys, Vol. 18, No. 2, 1987.

[McDermid 91a]McDermid J A: "Towards Assurance Measures for High Integrity Systems." In: Proceedings of Reliability '89, UKAEA National Centre for Systems Reliability and Institute for Quality Assurance, pp 3A/1-3A/9, 1989.

[McDermid 1991b] McDermid J A (ed): "Software Engineer's Reference Book." Butterworth Heinemann, 1991.

[McDermid 92a]McDermid J A: "Safety Analysis for Real Time Systems." In: Proceedings of NATO ASI on Real-Time Systems, W Halang (ed), 1992.

[McDermid 92b] McDermid J A (ed): "Education and Training for Safety Critical Systems Practitioners." In: Software in Safety Related Systems, B Wichmann (ed), Wiley 1992.

[McDermid 92c]McDermid J A: "Safety Cases and Safety Arguments." In: Proceedings of CSR Conference on Software Safety, Luxembourg, April 1992.

[MoD 91a] Ministry of Defence: "The Procurement of Safety Critical Software in Defence Equipment." Interim Defence Standard 00-55; Directorate of Standardization, Glasgow, 1991.

[MoD 91b] Ministry of Defence: "Hazard Analysis and Safety Classification of Computer and Programmable Electronic System Elements of Defence Equipment." Interim Defence Standard 00-56; Directorate of Standardization, Glasgow, 1991.

[Puschner 89]   Puschner P and Koza C: "Calculating The Maximum Execution Time Of Real-Time Programs." The Journal of Real-Time Systems, Vol. 1, No. 2, pp 159-176, 1989.

[Reason 79]   Reason J: "Actions not as Planned: The Price of Automatization." In: Aspects of Consciousness, G Underwood and R Stevens (eds), Academic Press, 1979.

[Rook 91]   Rook P and McDermid J A: "Software Development and Process Models." In: Software Engineer's Reference Book, McDermid J A (ed), Butterworth Heinemann, 1991.

[RTCA 85]   Radio Technical Commission for Aeronautics: "Software Considerations in Airborne Systems and Equipment Certification." DO-178A, RTCA, 1985.

[Rushby 89]   Rushby J M: "Kernels for Safety." In: Safe and Secure Computing Systems, T Anderson(ed), Blackwell, 1989.

[Wittgenstein 69]   Wittgenstein L: "On Certainty." Blackwell, 1969.

3

The JFIT safety-critical systems research programme: origins and intentions

Bob Malcolm

3.1 BACKGROUND

The research programme of the Joint Framework for Information Technology (JFIT - a collaboration of the Department of Trade and Industry (DTI) and the Science and Engineering Research Council (SERC)), has a number of genealogical lines. Apart from the general evolution of computer-based system technology, and software technology in particular, there was a specific spur, in 1986, in the shape of the ACARD Report on *Software: A Vital Key to UK Competitiveness* [ACARD 86]. That report contained some contentious suggestions for approaches to the development of safety-critical software-based systems. It also suggested that the Institution of Electrical Engineers (IEE) should lead a study into the subject. At the time, the IEE made an initial position statement, together with a draft summary guide to the subject.

In its response to the ACARD Report, the IEE maintained that software should not be treated in isolation; that 'safe software' is a meaningless concept. Software may well play a significant role in the safety of a system, and there are indeed potential safety-related problems specific to software, and software-specific techniques which may ameliorate some of those problems. Nevertheless, the safety-related aspects of software should, in general, be considered in the context of the system of which it is a part. It is but one element of design which must be set alongside overall system specification, design, construction, and operation.

The IEE then established a working party, drawn from a wide range of industry sectors, to study the subject in greater depth. The British Computer Society (BCS) was invited to participate in the study; and the Department of Trade and Industry both participated in the study and made a financial contribution to its support.

Around the same time as the ACARD Report, there were a number of other initiatives. The International Electrotechnical Commission issued draft international standards [IEC 89a, IEC 89b]; the Health and Safety Executive issued guidelines for programmable systems [HSE 87a, HSE 87b] and was working on their extension to encompass software; the UK Ministry of Defence issued draft defence standards [MOD 91a, MOD 91b]; and the European Community issued its Product Liability Directive. So much activity generates as much confusion as clarification. The ambition of the IEE-BCS study was to try to bring together representatives of all interests and achieve a consensus on the way forward.

The official objectives of the study were to survey regulatory practice and trends in a range of application areas and sectors of industry, in order to provide a firm basis from which to propose options for improvements. The potential role of certification was specifically addressed, and the position with respect to liability and insurance requirements investigated.

The working party delivered its report in 1989 [IEE 89]. The report was directed to two types of professional engineer - those familiar with safety engineering practices in their industrial sectors, but who were facing the introduction of computers into their systems, and those familiar with software engineering but unfamiliar with safety engineering. It was a summary of the important issues, not a text book - though it did contain many references to other sources of information - and much of its material has been revised and re-published in later work [IEE 92, Malcolm 92].

The report also contained recommendations on the way forward for the profession, for the regulatory authorities, and for government. There were many such recommendations - for awareness, dissemination of information on safety concerns arising from emerging technology, standards, competence requirements, and safety-assessment reports. Perhaps the key recommendation was for pan-sector harmonization of safety engineering practices. It was agreed that such harmonisation should be achieved on an international basis, as all standardization of any significance is internationally based for each industry sector. The conclusion was that it was in the UK's interest to take a leading role in such standardization.

Finally, the report identified research which should help to put 'engineering judgement' on a firmer footing, and to cut through some of the arguments - such as the 'formal methods debate' - which bedevil technical discussion.

Shortly after the IEE-BCS Report was published, the DTI and SERC were considering their future programme of research, to follow on from the

Information Engineering Advanced Technology Programme, itself a successor to the Alvey Programme. It was decided that instead of a single all-embracing IT research programme, there should be a range of smaller, more focused programmes to tackle specific subjects. At the top of the priority list from the Systems Engineering community was the recommendation for a Safety-Critical Systems research programme.

A £35M, 5-year programme was then planned [Malcolm 90], starting from the recommendations of the IEE-BCS report. The programme was approved by the Secretary of State for Trade and Industry in April 1990 and launched in September 1990. Proposals were submitted in January 1991 and the first grant for a project was offered in July of that year.

3.2 SAFETY?

The research programme follows the International Electrotechnical Commission in taking a broad definition of 'safety' - one which includes the risk of widespread environmental damage and economic loss, as well as danger to human life and limb.

3.3 SYSTEMS OR SOFTWARE?

During the debate in recent years over the way in which to treat software in safety-related systems, it has been said many times that 'safety is a systems issue'. This is entirely accepted and its recognition is embodied in the objectives of the programme. However, it should be remembered that the search for harmonization across industrial sectors had its origins in the search for a common approach to the introduction of software into a wide variety of types of application system. The drive for harmonization has in turn identified the absence, in many sectors, of an explicit rationale for existing practice.

So there are at least four targets of the research in this programme:

(i)   How should we produce, and manage the production of, safety-related software in particular situations?
(ii)   Can we find a common approach?
(iii)   What is the rationale for present tradition and practice in a variety of sectors?
(iv)   How can we harmonize the various traditions in such a way that a common approach to software can be incorporated?

Nevertheless, taken together they amount to the question with which we began, namely: How should we handle software in safety-related systems? Even though some projects might not address software - or indeed any specific technology - explicitly, all projects should contribute to the solution of this problem.

3.4   RESEARCH SUBJECTS

The programme addresses a very wide range of issues. In addition to the exploration of improvements in specific technologies and techniques, there is the search for understanding and unification of criteria and techniques for safety assurance. For example, what is the basis for present practice? Where do sectors fundamentally differ and why? How common can they be? Can we characterize systems so that they and their appropriate procedures and techniques can all be fitted into a common framework, so as to facilitate harmonization across industrial sectors?

The detailed requirements, summarized here, are contained in the Research Workplan [Malcolm 90]. It is not the intention of the workplan to prescribe particular items of research. Instead, some indication is given of the range of technical problems which we know must be addressed - though not necessarily all in this research programme - and the range of research themes which might contribute to their solution. In neither case is it likely that they are complete, and they are not intended to be definitively constraining. The aim is to encourage lines of enquiry rather than exclude them. It is then for potential participants to devise interesting and innovative projects which tackle the main aims of the programme, as described earlier.

The workplan sets out three main groups of research topics - technologies, human factors, and 'unification'. However, this grouping is purely for presentational convenience. It is expected that many projects will span research interests in more than one group, and in all cases projects should consider whether they can benefit from, or contribute to, work from other areas.

3.5   TECHNOLOGIES

'Technologies', as used here, encompasses many aspects of process, product, and their evaluation. A software design technique would be considered to be technological; so would organizational techniques and procedures relating to parts of the overall process; so would support tools. The relationship between these different facets of development is also of interest. For instance, techniques for design should be influenced by their suitability for assessment and for fault diagnosis.

Whatever our concerns about safety, we must always work within budgets, and in the knowledge that absolute certainty is as unreachable as absolute zero. So cost-effectiveness is important. Any technological proposals for the future must take this into account.

To assess the cost-effectiveness of new technology, we must compare its cost-effectiveness with that of the old. This is related to the desire to understand better the contribution of existing technology and practice. While we must not be complacent, and while we recognize some of the outstanding problems, existing engineering practice has nevertheless served us well. If we can understand it better, to the extent that we can compare it for cost-effectiveness with new approaches, then maybe we will be able to put its positive contribution on a more rigorous footing.

Many of the projects which have been approved so far are, as expected, concerned with developing and improving upon current software design technology. There are also, though, some encouraging investigations of alternative approaches, such as domain-specific languages and component sets, rule-based systems, executable specifications, and machine learning. There are strong engineering hunches that some of these new technologies may be 'safer' than existing technologies. But in the absence of any rigorous justification, there is a danger that they will be precluded by emerging standards. So, in what circumstances is the use of the more avant-garde technologies best justified, and how?

Simplicity, intelligibility, and traceability are all believed to be important. 'Separation of concerns' is often said to help. This may be seen as one of the benefits of parametric packages and subsystems - such as the general-purpose programmable process-controller - in which reasoning about the assurance of a system is separated from reasoning about the generic package or system, reasoning about the parameterisation or programming, and reasoning about the combination. Interest in such approaches is developing in parallel with an emerging interest in the mathematical methods community with 'compositionality' - both of components and of elements of logical reasoning. Will it at last be possible to provide a rigorous basis for such separation of concerns? Is this the way to think about rule-based systems - as separating reasoning about the application-specific rules from reasoning about the generic inference engine?

3.6   HUMAN FACTORS

Human factors issues encompass all aspects of human involvement in systems, from conception to operation and beyond. Ultimately, humans, whether operators, maintainers, designers, or software programmers, are *always* the weakest links in the chain - or, to be more precise, the weak tail of the chain in, say, a Fault Tree Analysis.

There has been some work on human dependability in safety-critical systems, but the majority of this work has been concerned with the dependability of humans involved in existing, built, systems - the operators and maintenance staff. There is much less work on the dependability of humans involved in design and specification, and in particular on the dependability of communication between them.

There is interaction between technological developments and human factors - not just with respect to the 'usability' of new techniques. Certain technological developments may well contribute to safety, but it is important to consider their impact on human factors (in the broad sense used here) and on the whole system, rather than just a local 'improvement'. 'Displacement', whereby the human fallibility problem is pushed elsewhere - and perhaps made worse overall - must be avoided.

In all cases, it is not sufficient simply to identify a problem. In addition to understanding the problem better, we seek guidance on what to do about it, such as recommendations on appropriate forms of design language and management structure, preferably supported by an explanation in terms of contribution to a safety argument.

And, despite making it clear that we intend human factors to be concerned with much more than just the human-computer interface, there is doubtless much HCI research still to be done on safety-critical systems design.

3.7   UNIFICATION

Existing practices are often based on either explicit or implicit expert judgement. This may be an inevitable element of all safety engineering. If so, how should we control it? How should we integrate such qualitative assurance with quantitative measurement, and with logical analysis? How can we 'unify' these different elements of assessment?

Can we go further? Can we generalize? An ambition of the programme is to encourage research into ways in which to select, on a more sound basis than tradition, engineering judgement, or evangelism, appropriate developmental approaches for particular application scenarios.

The main focus of unification may well be the 'safety argument' such as some industries currently require, and as has been recommended for all safety-related systems [IEE 89]. (The safety argument is sometimes called a 'safety case' and sometimes a 'safety justification'.) Quantified Risk Analysis (QRA) and Probabilistic Risk Analysis (PRA) are specific approaches to the construction or support of a safety argument.

Can the sound engineering principles and rules-of-thumb which underlie many existing practices be identified, perhaps formalized, and their value, perhaps in terms of contribution to a safety argument or to a quantitative assessment, be exposed?

Attempts to deal with unification are likely to require contributions from the so-called 'soft' sciences, of psychology and sociology, as well as from the 'hard' sciences and technologies of engineering and computing.

Again there is a link between unification and technological research. If we succeed in making some advances in unification, then we should be able to use the emerging unification techniques for assessment of the impact of a particular technological development on overall system safety and its assessment and assurance. And, on the other hand, given a rigorous approach to assessing the contribution of technology to the overall safety argument, we should be able to direct the development of technology to better effect.

3.8   STRUCTURE OF THE PROGRAMME

There are three main elements: a few large projects (up to £3M costs); a score or more of smaller projects (less than £1M and typically £0.5M); and a 'community club' - the Safety-Critical Systems Club. The programme is intended to be predominantly industrially-oriented. This is reflected in the balance of funds, with £14M from DTI for industrial organizations, and £4M from SERC for Higher Educational Institutions (HEIs). Industry should recognize that, whereas industrial organizations may 'own the problems', academia may be harbouring potential solutions.

All projects should have at least one industrial member, together with either an academic partner or another industrial partner.

The smaller projects are intended to address specific research topics, some of which have been alluded to above in discussion of the technical issues. But they would also benefit by addressing some of the wider concerns of the programme, such as consensus building.

An important role for the larger projects is their contribution to consensus building through cross-sectoral working. Suppliers to different markets should work side by side, comparing and contrasting approaches to development, assessment, and regulation, to try to accommodate them within a common framework. They should aim for an appropriate mix of partners to achieve this with, if possible, an involvement of a regulatory authority, a small company, and a software supplier. As these large projects are intended to be influential within the industry, they will require the proper commitment of opinion-forming individuals and organizations in realistic developments, in realistic environments, which will demonstrate the viability of the approaches taken in these projects.

There is no prior allocation of research topics to either large or small projects. While it is reasonable to expect the larger projects to concentrate on practical problems, such as procedural harmonization, or technology evaluation, this should not constrain them from addressing the deep research issues - especially those of unification, for which these projects may well provide a sound experimental basis. Similarly, the smaller projects should consider the aspects of this programme other than specific research items - especially the desire to involve as wide a community as possible. Organizations from sectors other than the obvious high-technology industries would help to achieve that spread, help to ensure the wider applicability of the programme's results, and, by bringing their different perspectives, help directly to achieve those results.

3.9   THE SAFETY-CRITICAL SYSTEMS CLUB

This community club is expected to have a major role in the achievement of consensus. It is the primary means of dissemination of intermediate and final results of the programme, and a sounding board for them; it is the forum in which workers in very different areas can compare notes; it is the focus for newcomers to the safety-critical 'scene', where they can quickly find out who knows what about what.

3.10   RELATIONSHIP BETWEEN THE RESEARCH PROGRAMME AND SafeIT

SafeIT [DTI 90] is the umbrella title for a range of government-initiated activities coordinated by ICSE(SRS) - the government Interdepartmental Committee on Software Engineering (Safety Related Systems Working Group). The emerging SafeIT strategy has four main themes, which are:

- Research;
- Technology transfer;
- Education and training;
- Standards.

The present collaborative research programme addresses the research theme, whereas the Safety-Critical Systems Club addresses some of the technology transfer ambitions.

Other SafeIT programmes in support of the strategy, perhaps tackling particular themes or subjects within the themes, may be announced in the future.

3.11   FIRST-PHASE PROJECTS

From the proposals submitted in January 1991, sixteen projects were given technical approval. Categorization of these projects is somewhat problematic, given the rich mix of subjects to be addressed. However, the following are illustrative.

- Stage in the lifecycle - specification, design, etc.;
- Application sector(s);
- Technical theme - technology, human factors, unification;
- And sub-theme - human dependability, human-computer interaction.

Unfortunately, there are more dimensions than can be represented on a simple sheet of paper. Furthermore, many of the projects address a variety of concerns, and cannot be neatly categorized in this or any other way. This is, in fact, an indication of success in achieving interlinked coverage of the desired topics. But it still leaves the problem of summarizing that coverage.

The approach taken here is to categorize the projects by the way in which they address the 'bridging' problem in system design. This is the bridging between the application problem owner's intent for a computer-based system and the realization of that intent in an operational system.

3.12 A BRIDGE FROM INTENTION TO REALIZATION

The *intent* is what we would like the system to do, whether or not we know what that is. (See Annex A to the IEE-BCS Report [IEE 89] on *'ideal operation'*.) Our cognitive model of the world and the intended system within it comprises our *conceptualization* of our intent. We then try to describe this conceptualization in a *specification*.

Thereafter, the specification is transformed ('refined' being a questionable notion - see later) into other representations more suitable for design and construction. Now, different forms of representation, and different approaches to transformation, are likely to have differing efficacy in supporting reasoning about the conceptualization, and in communicating it to another human, or to a machine. Furthermore, that efficacy is likely to depend not only on the type of system but also on the nature of the application domain and the environment in which it is operating.

Consider the specification of a robotic brain-surgery system (they do exist!). The conventional approach to specification and design might be to bring in a 'systems analyst' ('requirements engineer' in today's parlance?) who would ask lots of questions of the brain surgeon; go away; come back with a very thick specification; ask the brain surgeon to 'sign it off' even if it meant nothing to the surgeon; go away again; come back some time later (and later and later ...) and eventually ask someone to 'accept' the 'finished product'.

Who would know *what* the system would do, and what relationship it would bear to the intent? The system *might* include some of the things which the surgeon wanted but did not ask for, as long as the developer thought to ask about them. It would be unlikely to embody the requirements embedded in domain assumptions which neither had thought about.

Perhaps, instead, our brain surgeon is a computer enthusiast who volunteers a Turing tape for the computer system? That would be a perfectly precise specification, with the semantics completely defined. But would it *really* be a good representation to facilitate reasoning about whether the system would do what the surgeon intended, and whether that was the right thing to do?

We need an approach which is more satisfactory than the sloppy first of these, and more realistic than the second. So how *can* we best bridge that gap between intent and realization?

3.13 TOP-DOWN STRUCTURED DESIGN?

Twenty years ago, the best way of bridging the gap was thought to be the use of third-generation languages coupled with top-down structured programming and structured design methodologies. This was certainly an improvement over the spaghetti-like assembly-code of thirty years ago. But the approach turned out to present major problems for both purchasers and suppliers, which many are still facing today.

First, the purchaser, at the top of the design tree, who was asked to approve thick volumes of high-level design specifications. The developers then said that, thereafter, there would be mere 'refinement' and mere 'implementation' - implicitly a near-automatic, and therefore reliable, process. Unfortunately, we later discovered that the labelled boxes of the high-level design notations could contain some surprises. Despite having contractually 'signed off' the specifications, customers turned out to be less than happy with their delivered systems - the developers' realizations of those labelled boxes. Many bitter contractual battles have ensued. Worse, by thinking that we *had* solved the problem with what we *thought* was a common communication medium - the labelled boxes - we made matters worse by misleading ourselves and our customers, thus storing up trouble for the future.

The supplier ran into difficulty during the process. That 'mere refinement' turned out to be a mixture of requirement refinement and design refinement. Important aspects of functionality had to be introduced way down deep in a hierarchy of code. Understanding what it all did was meant to be easy, but it was not. Understanding of where and how to make changes was supposed to be easy, but it was not. The development overruns, and the inflexibility of the systems in the face of need for change, have been expensive and embarrassing for both purchaser and supplier.

In fact, the purchaser's problem and the developer's problem are two sides of the same, more fundamental, problem.

3.14 FORMAL METHODS?

Ten years ago, we found a new hope - the use of formal methods, based upon mathematical logic. Unfortunately, the genuine benefits of mathematical techniques have become obscured by early hype and the haze from the subsequent war of words. Untrue claims that it is possible to 'prove systems safe', and misleading claims that it is possible to 'prove correctness' have not helped. There has been, as a consequence, considerable confusion over what is or is not possible and/or sensible.

The arguments have ranged from the practical - whether the techniques are manageable on a large scale, whether there are sufficient skills - to the philosophical - whether all 'proofs' are fundamentally unsound. However, there are even more fundamental concerns for safety-related systems.

The mathematical techniques require the expression of specification in a well-defined mathematically-oriented notation. This then allows manipulation of the representation of a mathematical nature. Such manipulation enables the 'proof' of some properties of the specification itself, such as some aspects of self-consistency. It also enables proof of consistency of the design with the specification (if, in addition, we express the design in the formalism).

However, we usually wish to go beyond reasoning about self-consistency, to reason about the 'correctness' or appropriateness of the specification itself. Indeed this is often held out as the great promise of such techniques. To do this, it is the connotation in our heads, induced by the notation on paper, rather than the 'mathematically precise' notation itself, that enables us and even prompts us to reason about the important aspects of the specification.

This turns upon the representative value of the notation, and of the expressive power of particular representations in the notation. Many software design methodologists use a by now famous example of a lift (elevator). It is interesting to test the efficacy of their methods by replacing all references to 'lift', 'floor', 'up' and 'down' by arbitrary strings.

There is a further problem, concerned with the extremely 'flat' (apparent, if not actual) structure of most formal specifications. This makes human communication difficult at all times, and negotiation of change particularly difficult. A number of schools have begun to address the problem with a variety of structuring techniques, many with the newly fashionable object-oriented flavour. The catch-word for this subject of study is 'compositionality', though it is still early days, and the jargon has not yet settled down in a way which clarifies whether this refers to composition of components within an architecture, composition of parameterizable components and their parameters, or composition of pieces of reasoning about a system and its environment, possibly connected to composition of components. Whatever the name, and whatever the precise scope of the studies, the theoretical work in this area promises to be exciting and of direct practical relevance to the assessment of development paradigms.

3.15 A BRIDGE OVER SHIFTING SAND?

In addition to bridging the gap during initial specification and design, we would like to minimize traffic on the bridge between intent and realization, despite subsequent changes in intent (and even in the form of realization, perhaps, as technology moves on). A representation which requires complete re-verification and re-validation, for instance, after a minor change to the requirement, is simply not practicable.

We need a form of modularization which localizes the effects of change, minimizing propagation of changes, and thereby minimizing consequent additional rework. Even more importantly, it could well be that such a modularization will also facilitate reasoning about validity in the first place.

There are some prospects: for instance, a representation which is executable clearly requires less error-prone transformation by human designers than one which requires intermediate stages of design and verification. The intermediate error-prone stages are avoided not only during initial development, but during all subsequent stages.

More generally, we try to build the bridge using several spans, in such a way that we achieve 'separation of concerns'. The intention is threefold:

- To minimize the complexity of reasoning and re-reasoning;
- To ensure that individuals are operating, as far as possible, entirely within the scope of their own competence, uncluttered by worries about things outside their own fields;
- To enable individuals to partition even their own thinking in time, minimising muddling interactions between partitions.

One classical way to achieve some of these effects is to use bigger conceptual components. In software engineering, we used to think, as in top-down structured design, that any old conceptual components would suffice. We talked glibly - and very frequently - of 'abstractions'. But we have since found that *any* abstractions will not do (see 'Structured Design' above). Individuals may devise their own design abstractions as they go along, to partition their own thinking (the third objective above), but this may be the least important requirement. For the first two and probably more important objectives above, especially for safety, where persuasion and 'convincingness' are very significant, the semantics of those abstractions must be shared by all involved parties.

As in other domains, we bridge the gap with higher-level standard components, standard architectural structures, and standard interfaces between them. They might be specific to an application domain - such as application-specific languages and reference architectures. They might be generic to a class of application domains - such as expert system inference engines. Or they might be entirely generic - like the spreadsheet or word-processor. In all cases they provide a more powerful virtual machine, building a bridgehead from the computational domain to the application domain, and minimizing the bridge-building work for particular applications.

Then, when we come to reason about whether a particular application system will do what we want it to do, we want, in a sense, to be able to take the virtual machine for granted. We want to be able to assume that the virtual machine programmer, in making the mapping from the application domain, 'knew' the computational domain on to which he was mapping. (This, of course, is precisely what we do *not* have with the layers of abstractions in 'top-down structured design'.)

So far, though, these ideas have, for the most part, been expressed only informally. To those familiar with this approach, such as the process industries with their 'process management systems', this has not been a problem: such systems have worked reliably for many years. But there is a gulf between them and those who come from the bespoke embedded system software engineering community, from which community came the desire for 'proof'.

There has been little work done to bridge this different gap - between the communities and their approaches. As will be seen later, there are some projects in the programme which are addressing this problem. More generally though, there is an emerging interest in the formal methods community, as exemplified by the interest in 'compositionality' discussed above.

3.16   FIRST-PHASE PROJECTS: CONTRIBUTIONS TO BRIDGE-BUILDING

Of the projects which have received approval so far, it is encouraging to find that the philosophical considerations outlined above are being realized in a number of areas.

The perspective of 'bridging', between intent and realization, does allow a common, if crude, characterization of these projects. Some are looking at how to strengthen some of the spans; some are trying to determine which are the weak spans, and which the strong, and *why*; some are trying to reduce the number of spans required; some are looking at totally new types of bridging structures - like changing from multi-span brick arches to modern single-span suspension bridges.

One mechanism, in which modularization is best matched to the needs for both reasoning and change in the domain, is the domain-specific language, perhaps coupled to parameterizable standard components. This is also a way of increasing the 'common ground' in communication between application engineers and system development engineers. This approach is the subject of a number of projects in sectors such as mining engineering, gas-turbine engine management, the process industries, and, in a recent suggestion, for active suspension on motor-racing cars.

Executable specification is one way of 'reducing the number of spans'. This approach is to be tried in an automatic medical screening system, in an approach based on functional programming.

For 'new structures' - new *forms* of bridge - perhaps the most obvious example, and the most contentious, is the application of 'Artificial Intelligence' (AI). To really put paid to the myth that AI is good for only off-line applications, one project is attempting to improve upon the control of helicopter flight. The design of the multi-mode control algorithms for helicopters is extremely difficult. It is hoped that a rule-based system will be quicker to develop, provide much greater design visibility, and yield all the other benefits of separation of concerns first mooted, so contentiously, in the workplan. Moreover, this project is also investigating the use of machine-learning to derive the rules directly from pilot–monitoring, in order to tackle the specification problem - which is particularly error-prone in systems like this which are based on human physical and mental coordination skills in a way which is notoriously difficult to articulate.

Other AI-related projects include one which is looking at formalizing the reasoning about the correctness of medical diagnostic systems, and another which combines AI and domain–specific languages via an expert system which generates the signalling language code for railway signalling.

Each of the projects which has been approved so far will now be described briefly.

3.17   THE PROJECTS

MORSE is one of the large cross-sectoral projects. It aims to support re-use so as to maximize the benefits to be derived, in a safety-critical environment, from the use of generic components. The approach to be explored is based on object-orientation, which has much support as a paradigm for re-use. In addition though, the team intends to put the method on a formal footing, using the RAISE tools and techniques (arguably the leading formal methods development to come from the ESPRIT programme).

Failure Modes and Effects Analysis is a technique which is widely practised for evaluation of hardware reliability. The application of the same concept to software dependability would be highly desirable, but, given the 'systematic' nature of software failure, this is problematic. The FASGEP project intends to tackle this difficult problem of analysis of error introduction and removal, with a view to the development of a technique which would facilitate both within-project dependability assessment, and more general evaluation of development techniques and tools.

SafeFM is a project which seeks to explore ways in which to introduce formal methods into practical development and assessment environments. The intention is to approach the problem from both directions - integration of existing techniques with formal methods, and development of a new approach to the use of formalism based on 'provably coherent system specifications'. All of this is to be done in a way which is driven by the need to make real-world safety arguments - for which the project intends to explore the possibility of more formal approaches. A further objective of the project is to develop models for the quantification of software, so as to assess the benefits of the recommended techniques. The results will be published in public-domain guidelines.

In the process industries, much use is made of a particular kind of special-purpose computer known as a 'Programmable Logic Controller'.

Through tradition and practice, specialized techniques have evolved which are both understandable to the application engineer (important in order to ensure that the PLCs are doing the right job), and have a structure which facilitates reasoning about their correctness. However, these techniques do not have any sound basis and are, furthermore, becoming very difficult to manage as the complexity of systems increases. SEMS-PLC is another large project which brings together users and suppliers from a wide range of sectors to put PLC design techniques on a more sound and secure footing for the future.

CONTESSE, another of the large cross-sectoral projects, will produce definitive guidelines on testing: its value in different situations and its cost-effectiveness in relationship to other approaches to gaining confidence in systems and software. The team is particularly strong, with a very practically oriented representation from a range of industrial sectors, including aerospace, transportation, oil and gas production, defence, and power generation.

SCRECS is one of the smaller projects based primarily on an application need arising in a single sector - engine management and control. The technological development in this project is directed towards the use of a modern generic technology, Object-Oriented Design with Ada, to reproduce their traditional approach based on a 'home-grown' domain-specific language and component set. The results could be of use in many other sectors, and the prospects for such wider dissemination will be investigated.

'Reliable Vehicle Software' is a rather unusual project. Members of the Society of Motor Manufacturers and Traders have formed a club, MISRA (the Motor Industry Software Reliability Association) to undertake and commission research. The intention is to establish, for the first time, common standards for the UK automotive sector. These will be compatible with the emerging international (IEC) standards, which are the latest drafts of the references already given [IEC 89a, IEC 89b]. The research comprises a number of sub-projects, each addressing software safety problems specific to automotive engineering, from a need for resilience in a noisy electrical environment to software-based control engineering problems.

ROBUST is a project which aims to develop design standards, guidelines, and support tools and techniques for the development of robotic systems in safety-critical environments, from surgery to nuclear engineering. The field of safety-critical robotics is especially interesting, since it forces explicit recognition of the modelling of the real-world assumed by all systems and the need to structure these models - thus bringing to the surface the issue of 'separation of concerns'. It also forces recognition of the need to apportion responsibilities between human and machine. The major deliverables of the projects will be a Safety Methodology Handbook and a database of hazards in advanced robotic systems.

SAFESYS is a 'club-based' project. About 10 companies are expected to contribute significant funds to 'buy into' the research, comprising at least two 'sub-projects'. These sub-projects are intended to address problems which are sufficiently different that, through comparison and contrast, it will be possible to add flesh to the skeleton of the proposed SafeIT 'standards framework' - enabling selection of an appropriate mix of tools and techniques for particular application problem types. The club will provide a broad base of application problems to be addressed, along with strong industrial direction and built-in dissemination.

SAFESA is a medium-sized project to develop criteria and techniques, for the assurance of computer-based structural analysis in fields as diverse as aircraft and civil-engineering. The aim is to reduce dependence on extensive testing, which is costly, time-consuming, and unreliable. A significant feature of the project is the intention to develop a generalized framework for validation, which will accommodate off-line and on-line software from a variety of application sectors, each with their specific requirements. This will be of great interest to mathematical modellers, beyond the immediate field of structural analysis, and the project will make particular efforts to establish the wider applicability of the results.

'SSI Tools' is a project concerned with the Solid State Interlocking systems for railway signalling. It seeks to capitalize on the idea of separation of concerns, using and integrating a range of novel technological developments. The intention is to use an expert system to transform from geographic data, coupled with railway signalling 'rules', to the 'code' used for railway signalling, which is itself then 'compiled' for use on an application-specific virtual machine. Essentially, the project will develop an application-specific architecture which maximizes the generic, proven elements of a system - whether components or tools.

Flight control for helicopters is a particularly difficult safety-related problem, with multiple concurrent control modes giving pilots a very high workload, risking excursions beyond the desirable flight envelope. Efforts have been made to introduce 'carefree handling', but the management of flight control via conventional software algorithms has proved difficult. The ISSAFE project will investigate the possibility of using rule-based systems and, moreover, attempt to elicit the rules by machine-learning from real pilots. The problems for validation of the software so produced, and the certification of aircraft using it, are technically interesting - and hard. Whatever the outcome, the results of the research will be of interest in many other application areas. If successful, the effect on take-up of such AI techniques could be significant.

SADLI is a project to investigate the potential for the development of automatic cervical cytology (cancer screening). The technological interest lies particularly in the proposed use of 'functional programming' both to increase assurance in the final system and to reduce costs at the same time, through, in effect, executable specifications. The results will therefore be of wide interest in other sectors.

The SCSET project brings together a range of systems engineering companies to pool their efforts in an investigation of their mutual needs for a tool-set for safety-critical applications development. Their approach is to examine the whole range of activities involved in such developments; decide on the best mix of human contribution and automation to minimize unnecessary and error-prone human intervention; establish criteria for tool-sets which provide the automation; then commission an appropriate set of tools. The tool-set criteria will be put in the public domain and offered to the standards community.

DECSAFE brings together a most unusual mix of organizations, to tackle the difficult but fascinating and rewarding challenge of verification and validation of expert-system based Decision Support Systems (DSS), with a view to legally-acceptable certification. Part of the solution is believed to be a DSS generator which embodies the principles which the team hope to uncover and articulate. This could have significant commercial impact.

3.18 SUMMARY

The introduction of computer-based sub-systems into safety-critical systems has come at about the same time as moves to establish harmonized international system safety standards. Through posing questions as to what should be generic and what should be domain-specific, these two developments have interacted to stimulate considerable thought about the nature of generic safety principles and, more generally, about the 'right' way to manage complexity. These concerns led to the IEE-BCS Study of Software in Safety Related Systems, to the recommendations of that study for research, and to priority within the DTI-SERC JFIT initiative being given to research into safety-critical software-based systems. The consequence is the present programme of research.

There are unlikely to be any quick and easy answers: the questions themselves are very difficult. The concentration on software has forced attention on design and specification issues which, in many sectors, have received little attention to date. Even where engineering practices have been found do address design issues - such as HAZOP studies - their extension to software, even by analogy, is by no means clear.

Then, where there are in place software development practices which have proved reasonably effective for some time - such as those used in process management systems - there is at present no sound, rigorous, basis upon which an argument for their safety can be based.

On the other hand, where there are techniques which are intended to enhance the safety of software, the way in which they should be incorporated into safety engineering raises some extremely difficult technical - even philosophical - issues. The interfacing and integration of the absolute reasoning techniques of logic with much that must necessarily be subjective and qualitative elsewhere in safety management, is a case in point. Should one, as some recommend, insist on the use of such absolute techniques wherever possible because such absolute assurance is necessarily a good thing, however localized and however it affects the connecting and surrounding aspects of assurance? Or should one follow others in dismissing the techniques as being of unquantifiable value when modified by surrounding arguments and, therefore, worthless in, say, a probabilistic risk assessment?

The confusion is compounded by the big differences between safety engineering practices in different sectors. These are not just technological, terminological, and procedural: they embody different philosophical approaches to safety. One of the strategic aims of the research programme is therefore to bring different sectors together, both in the programme as a whole and even within cross-sectoral projects. The intention is that, by comparing and contrasting their approaches, the reasons for their differences will become more apparent, as will their similarities and the ways in which they could be brought closer together. This understanding should then provide a proper basis for harmonization.

In order to resolve the software techniques debate, a second strand in the strategy for the programme is to bring together not only different sectors, but diverse specification and design techniques. Then, again through comparison and contrast of the very different ways in which they address the design problem, industry will come to understand better what new techniques can contribute in what way to what kind of application, and, most importantly of all, why.

Early indications are that these ambitions are successful, with at least some of the hoped-for diversity of both industrial sectors and technological approach (though there is still scope for extending the coverage). It is to be hoped that their dissimilarities and their multi-dimensional overlaps will induce the 'comparison and contrast' which has been sought. The necessarily over-simplified presentation of the projects should be used only as a starting point, to begin to establish a conceptual framework within which to position one project with respect to another.

Only those projects which have emerged from the initial call for proposals have been described here. It is hoped that, in the second phase of the programme, it will be possible to address some of the areas not covered so far. Apart from involving additional industrial sectors, especially the process industries, priority will be given to the technical themes other than software technology, which tends to dominate at present. In particular, projects will be sought which address the construction of safety arguments - which promises to be the vehicle with which the problem of 'unification' will be tackled, and human factors - and particularly human reliability during specification and design.

The diversity achieved so far has already shown itself both in conflict and in co-operation. Initial conflict is not uncommon in collaborative projects and, however painful it may seem to the participants at the time, it is usually a precursor to healthy cross-fertilization. Overt co-operation between projects is not always so evident, so early, since projects are usually concerned in their early days with making progress according to their own plans, using their own approaches. However, already the mix of problem-owners, from a variety of sectors, and solution-providers, is having its intended effect, with joint meetings between projects taking place, even before contracts are signed, to discuss whether solutions being tried in one sector might be appropriate for another.

One encouraging sign already coming from the research programme is a shift in emphasis among those involved - from concerns over particular techniques and tools to a deeper understanding of underlying principles. The particular must be still managed in the short-term, if only because commercial reality will not wait for research results. But the general facilitates much improved communication within the community and provides a much firmer basis for standardization and for further work.

To the benefit of scientific progress, a second encouraging sign is the relinquishment of preconceptions, with less strident position-taking, and more muted, more thoughtful, discussion - at least among those involved in the research programme.

So far, the discussion has been concerned with the particular problems of safety-critical systems. However, the interest in safety, and the role of software within safety-critical systems, has, in turn, stimulated some deeply philosophical discussions about the nature of software more generally, and about the nature of the way in which software 'should' be developed. These studies may well have an impact far beyond just safety-critical applications. The principles of 'confidence' in a system, and 'convincingness' of arguments about the confidence which one may have in a system, are by no means restricted to safety-critical applications. They apply to dependability in a much more general sense: to the *effectiveness* of security measures, to quality, and particularly to that bug-bear of discussions about quality - fitness for purpose.

The distinguishing feature of all these concerns is that they imply that mere contractual 'conformance to specification' is not always sufficient. Safety, however, has the special property that it is not possible, as it is with some other attributes, to hide behind the contract. One cannot escape from consideration of whether the system will do what it should in the real world. To quote from the IEE-BCS Report [IEE 89]:

> *It might be argued that the specification is our best understanding of the requirements, and that its errors and ambiguities are not our concern. That may, perhaps, be the legal, contractual, position with some products and on*

> *some bespoke projects. But the engineering challenge is to meet the subset of the requirements concerned with safety, in the real world, regardless of the specification.*

For a quarter of a century, the software engineering world has emphasized the separation between the real world requirements and their formalization in a specification. For at least at long, and despite exhortations that specifications should be 'clear, concise, and unambiguous', there have been contractual haggles over whether specifications properly captured the intent of customers. Maybe, with safety, where this is not simply a matter of commercial bargaining, we may at last, as a community, rethink our whole approach to the capture of requirements and their specification.

3.19 REFERENCES

[ACARD 86]   Advisory Council for Applied Research and Development: "Software: A Vital Key to UK Competitiveness." An ACARD Report, HMSO, 1986.

[DTI 90]   Department of Trade and Industry: "SafeIT: The Safety of Programmable Electronic Systems: A Government Consultation Document on Activities to Promote the Safety of Computer-Controlled Systems." Part 1: Overall Approach, Part 2: Standards Framework. DTI, May 1990.

[HSE 87a]   Health and Safety Executive: "Programmable Electronic Systems in Safety-Related Applications: 1 - An Introductory Guide." HMSO, 1987.

[HSE 87b]   Health and Safety Executive: "Programmable Electronic Systems in Safety-Related Applications: 2 - General Technical Guidelines." HMSO, 1987.

[IEC 89a]   International Electrotechnical Commission: "Software for Computers in the Application of Industrial Safety-Related Systems" (proposal for a standard). IEC SC65A/WG 9, June 1989 (Document number SC65A/WG9/45).

[IEC 89b]   International Electrotechnical Commission: "Functional Safety of Programmable Electronic Systems: Generic Aspects. Part 1: General Requirements" (proposal for a standard). IEC SC65A/WG10, Oct 1989.

[IEE 89]   Institution of Electrical Engineers and the British Computer Society: "Software in Safety-Related Systems" (A Report Prepared by a Joint Project Team.) IEE, 1989 (ISBN 0852963 91 2).

[IEE 92]   Institution of Electrical Engineers: "Safety-Related Systems: Professional Brief." IEE, 1992.

[Malcolm 90]   Malcolm R E: "Workplan for the JFIT Safety Critical Systems Research Programme." Department of Trade and Industry, 1990.

[Malcolm 92]   Malcolm R: "Software in Safety-Related Systems: Basic Concepts and Concerns." In: Bennett P A (Ed.) "Safety Aspects of Computer Control", Heinemann-Butterworth, 1992.

[MOD 91a]   Ministry of Defence: "Requirements for the Procurement of Safety Critical Software in Defence Equipment." Interim Defence Standard 00-55, MoD, April 1991.

[MOD 91b]   Ministry of Defence: "Requirements for the Analysis of Safety Critical Hazards." Interim Defence Standard 00-56, MoD, April 1991.

PART TWO
REQUIREMENTS AND SPECIFICATION

4

Natural language processing for requirements specifications

Benjamin Macias and Stephen Pulman

4.1 INTRODUCTION

The purpose of this chapter is twofold: to provide a brief review of the basic techniques used to process natural-language expressions by computer; and to suggest some possible applications of these techniques in the area of requirements specification for safety-critical systems.

The work reported here is taking place in the context of the MORSE project (see Note 1), a fact which influences both the choice of examples and the precise approach to natural language processing (henceforth NLP) adopted.

In this project, we are using a general-purpose NLP system developed by SRI International, Cambridge. This NLP system, CLARE, contains a domain-independent system known as the Core Language Engine (CLE) to carry out general linguistic processing of English sentences. CLARE also contains a rich set of tools for customizing to new applications, and for carrying out the 'contextual reasoning' (a term explained below) which is involved in many interactive NLP applications. Both CLARE and the CLE have been applied to a variety of tasks, such as building an experimental translation system for English-Swedish, and creating an interface to a database. We do not have space here to give a description of CLARE to any degree of detail; readers may refer to [Alshawi 91], and [Alshawi 92] for more information and further references.

4.2   INTRODUCTION TO NATURAL-LANGUAGE PROCESSING TECHNIQUES

4.2.1 Natural-Language Processing Systems

Natural-language processing (NLP) systems are, generically, computer programs that use data sentences in a natural language such as English. Typical examples include a translator of sentences from one language into another, a generator of messages in English, or a program that allows a user to query a knowledge-based system such as a database, in English, instead of using a specialized query language.

NLP is conventionally divided into two main areas: understanding, or the problem of how to extract the meaning of natural-language sentences; and generation, the study of how to produce sentences conveying a specific message. In other words, the core task of an NLP system is either to translate an input English sentence into its 'meaning', or to take a 'message' and derive an English expression from it. In this review, we will identify such 'meanings' or 'messages', associated with the content of an English expression, with the uniform notion of 'logical form' (LF). These translation processes can then be pictured schematically in Figures 4.1 and 4.2.

CLARE is designed to perform both of these tasks, and uses for them the same sets of linguistic rules. To constrain our review of the basic NLP techniques to a manageable size, we will limit ourselves to describing the process of extracting the meaning of English sentences. Although the task of generation involves some problems of its own, the reader can think of it in very general terms as being similar to understanding, but applying the rules involved in extracting a logical form in reverse order.

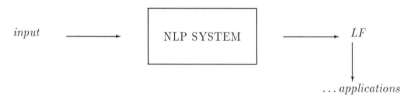

Figure 4.1: Translating an expression into its meaning.

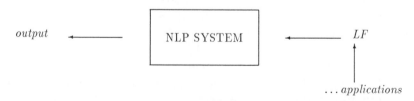

Figure 4.2: Deriving a language expression from its logical form.

4.2.2 Structure of an NLP System

A common approach to the design of an NLP system is to separate the task of understanding into a series of steps, each one associated with a different aspect of the problem. This division corresponds in the main to the distinction found in linguistic theory to distinguish the various kinds of organizing principles of language, such as morphology, syntax, and semantics.

This methodological division naturally results in computer systems that consist of a number of semi-independent modules, each containing the knowledge that corresponds to a different source of knowledge. The input sentence is processed by each of these modules sequentially, so that the output of one module corresponds to the input of the next one, with an LF as the final result.

An NLP system must also contain a lexicon of English words and their meanings.

A system such as CLARE has the following modules, listed in order of application (see Note 2):

(i)   Morphology: containing rules of word formation;
(ii)   Syntax: rules of parts of speech;
(iii)   Semantics: the meanings of the parts of speech and their combinations;
(iv)   Contextual reasoning: context-dependent aspects of interpretation like reference of pronouns, resolution of ellipsis, and choosing between ambiguous interpretations.

There are various motivations for this approach. Sequential processing is, from a computational point of view, the easiest way to understand the behaviour of what are often complex systems; with this organization, the user can sometimes help to guide the system to process a sentence. A modular organization has also well-known advantages from a software-engineering point of view: modular systems are easier to program and test, and the encapsulation of application-specific components encourages portability. As we will try to convey below, a core NLP system capable only of strictly linguistic analysis must encode nevertheless a surprisingly large amount of knowledge. By making this part of the overall task separable, we can use the same modules in quite different domains. After all, the rules of English apply to sentences about gas installations just as much as to sentences about the properties of landing gears. Finally, by maintaining separate modules for each linguistic-specific aspect of the process, we can incorporate new results from linguistic research in a more direct manner.

We now give a brief descriptions of the main modules of an NLP system, indicating their tasks and some of the computational problems at each step.

(a)   Morphology

In order to extract the meaning of a sentence, we first need to know how to categorize each of the words of the input sentence, i.e. to assign to each word a label from a set of nouns, verbs, adjectives, particles, punctuation marks, and so on.   For example (see Note 3), consider the following sentence:

> Authorization is required before the transfer of propane from the trucks can commence.

We will have to use the information that 'transfer' is a noun in order to conclude (and eventually comprehend) that 'the transfer of propane' is a noun phrase. Clearly, the first element required is a lexicon containing information about English words and their meanings. However, more is needed that just a very long list of words, namely the ability to match derived words with their base forms, deducing at the same time the information conveyed. In the sentence above, for example:

(i)   The word 'trucks' is a noun derived from the noun 'truck'', and the ending + s is used in English to indicate plurality. Hence, the phrase 'the trucks' is about a set of more than one truck.

(ii)   The word 'required' is the participle verbal form of the verb 'to require'. Participles in English are formed by adding the ending + ed to the base verb form, and this word has the simplified spelling 'required' (and not 'requireed').

(iii)   The word 'acknowledgement' is a noun derived from the verb 'to acknowledge', composed with the nominal suffix + 'ment'.

CLARE has a comprehensive set of the rules necessary for English. Notice that the output of morphological analysis is not usually unique, but may contain alternatives equal to the product of the number of labels of each word. In the sentence above, assuming that 'transfer' has three possible labellings, and 'can'' two, the morphological analyser will produce at least six different hypotheses of how to label each word in the sentence. This information will be taken by the syntactic component as input.

(b)   Syntax

Unfortunately, we cannot derive the meaning of a sentence by considering only the meaning of each of its words. We must also take into account the relation that words have to each other in a sentence; that is, we must parse it, that is, find its grammatical structure. For example, we can say that a sentence such as:

> The operator must authorize every transfer.

has schematically a grammatical structure like:

{{the operator} {must authorize {every transfer}}}

Syntactic rules code exactly this kind of information about sentence structure.

CLARE contains a very large syntactic component, with a coverage that includes the most common constructions of English. In addition, CLARE contains some useful specialized capabilities, such as an extensive treatment of dates, and the possibility to handle idioms. Nevertheless, exhaustive coverage has proved elusive, limiting applications to date to the most ordinary constructions of a language. These limitations must be borne in mind when devising applications of NLP techniques.

In the case of our example sentence, CLARE will produce the following analysis (slightly simplified):

```
[[s_np_vp_Normal-2,
  [[np_det_nbar-3,[[lex-4,the],[lex-5,operator]]],
   [vp_v_comp_Normal-6,
     [[lex-7,must],
      [vp_v_comp_Normal-8,
        [[lex-9,[authorize]],
         [np_det_nbar-10,[[lex-11,every],[lex-12,transfer]]]]]
        ]]]]]
```

The parsing process allows the elimination of some of the combinations generated by the morphological analysis (e.g. by identifying 'every transfer' as a noun phrase, the possibility of 'transfer' being a verb in the imperative will be ruled out), but it is also the case that new alternatives are often generated at this stage. This is because many constructions have more than one parse, usually corresponding to different possible readings. For instance, a phrase such as 'the detection of a gas leak in the reception and storing area' can either mean detection in: {the reception} and {storing area}, (i.e. two distinct areas), or: the {reception and storing} area (i.e. just one area).

Similarly to the process of assigning lexical categories to words, it often happens that many possibilities usually not envisaged by a human reader are generated by a machine analysis, revealing ambiguities and vagueness in seemingly clear sentences. Unfortunately, languages are structured in such a way that relatively small sentences can produced dozens or even hundreds of analyses. This creates the problem for an NLP system of how to choose the most appropriate analysis (something which people usually do without conscious effort). This is one of the most difficult problems in NLP research, and we return to some of its implications below.

(c)   Semantics

Although this might not be immediately apparent, the syntactic structure underlying sentences is necessary in order to work out the compositional semantics of a sentence. So the next stage of processing takes as input the syntactic analysis or analyses produced by the parser, and, together with the lexical information contributed by each word, derives an initial logical form representing the sentence's meaning. For instance, if the input is a simple affirmative English sentence, this process will commonly extract a main actor from the subject noun phrase, a main predicate from the verb or verbs, and a list of affected objects from the complement phrases of the main verb. Using these rules, CLARE might derive the following LF for our example (again, in a somewhat simplified form):

```
authorize(term(exists,C,event(C,pres,must)),
   term(the,A,operator(A)),
   term(every,B,transfer(B)))
```

At this stage (which we call 'quasi-logical form' or QLF), several pieces of information necessary to interpret the sentence appropriately have not yet been determined. This expression can be paraphrased approximately as saying that 'the relation of authorization holds (in some fashion) between one or more events, an operator, and every transfer'. It is usually the case that spelling out exactly in what respects the sentence says that this relationship holds requires consultation of the context and various types of reasoning.

The semantic component must contain rules to extract a QLF for each of the many variations allowed by the syntax of English to convey meanings: passives, negatives, interrogatives, their combinations, and so on. Most of these QLFs will contain constructs that need further resolution. The 'reference resolution' phase of interpretation tries to produce candidates to 'fill in' these constructs so as to arrive at a complete proposition: the message conveyed by that utterance of that sentence in that particular context.

(d)   Reference Resolution

Some of the QLF constructs that require contextual reasoning for their resolution are:

*   Quantifier scope. When a sentence contains several quantifier phrases, their relative scope has to be determined. For example, 'every truck is controlled by an operator'' can mean that each truck has its own operator, or that there is a single one with overall control. Spelling out

these alternatives and choosing between them requires complex reasoning.

- Reference determination. In a sentence like 'the truck must connect to it', we need to determine which truck is being referred to, and exactly what 'it' is. Depending on what the context is, different entities may be involved.

- Vague relations. In a phrase like 'truck pump connection', the relations between the entities mentioned are left vague. The phrase might mean 'the connection between the truck and the pump', or 'the connection on the pump on the truck', or even 'the connection on some other entity for the truck's pump'.

We refer to all of these phenomena as requiring 'reference resolution'. The process of reference resolution usually suggests many possible candidate interpretations for a particular sentence. It is then a further task to decide which of these candidates is the correct one for the sentence in that particular context.

Making this decision requires reasoning about the context. Ultimately, to do this satisfactorily needs complete and explicit knowledge and understanding of a domain, the intentions of the participants, and so on. Representing the kind of information that is needed for this is extremely complicated and presupposes a solution to many of the classical problems of Artificial Intelligence. For this reason, systems that carry out this kind of reasoning currently only do so in the context of very limited domains, domains which are restricted enough for it to be realistic to build a complete axiomatization of them. It is, at the current state of the art, not possible to build general-purpose reference resolution mechanisms.

Nevertheless, heuristic techniques can be used in a general-purpose NLP system to control the combinatorial explosion and narrow down the search for an interpretation. In general terms, the idea is to define a mechanism that rates the alternative analyses at each stage according to their *a priori* plausibility, and instruct the system to consider only those analyses whose rank is above a certain threshold (see Note 4). By adopting these heuristics, we can indicate which readings to prefer. In conjunction with this, if the application in question is an interactive one, we can often involve the user in confirmation that the appropriate analysis has been selected. This is in many ways a safer alternative, although it might make the use of NLP a little tedious in some circumstances.

There is thus something of a conflict between domain-specific and general-purpose systems. Domain specific systems are in principle much more accurate in tasks like disambiguation, but require labour-intensive customization. General-purpose systems are less accurate, but can operate with little or no customization, relying instead on their heuristics.

4.3   THE USE OF NLP TECHNIQUES
IN FORMAL SPECIFICATION TASKS

In the previous section we stressed that ambiguity is a pervasive, if often undetected property of natural languages. This is an important factor to bear in mind when thinking about requirements specifications. Anecdotal evidence suggests that a large number of problems in building systems that have the behaviour required by their initiators arises not in the implementation phase, but in the requirements phase. It is plausible to speculate that a large proportion of these errors are the result of ambiguity or vagueness in a specification.   The very fact that human beings are superbly efficient at resolving ambiguities, so much so that they frequently fail to notice them at all, should alert us to the possibility that not all ambiguities are being resolved correctly. Normally, the 'correct' reading of an ambiguous sentence is contextually much more plausible than the alternatives. Under these circumstances, the alternatives may not be noticed. However, if two readings are almost equally plausible, then the reader may choose a different interpretation than was intended by the writer. If this misunderstanding goes unnoticed, as it almost certainly will when the ambiguity was not apparent, trouble may be round the corner.

Having seen some of the problems behind the extraction of LFs from sentences, we will now discuss some possible applications of NL techniques in the writing and checking of requirements specifications for safety-critical or other systems. Some of the applications described here are part of our actual MORSE project work plan, while others are of a more conjectural nature. In both cases, the reader must keep in mind that we are restricting ourselves to tasks that we believe are realistically achievable with current technology, and that we are, with the exception of one or two of the later suggestions, primarily emphasizing the role of domain-independent NLP techniques. More ambitious applications of NLP in this area may be possible, but they would require sophisticated domain modelling which might be too labour-intensive to be profitable.

4.3.1 The Production of Easily-Readable Specifications

We will first review the application of NL techniques to control the vocabulary and style of natural-language specifications. The main focus here will be on the use of a number of techniques aimed at controlling the user to draft specifications that are easy to understand, ranging from the type of vocabulary used, to the overall style of writing. When more than one person is involved in the specification, or it takes place over a long period of time, these techniques can also be useful to enforce a consistent style throughout a project, and support its administration.

(a) Use of a Controlled Vocabulary

The first aspect of writing specifications that can be enhanced by an NL system relates to the set of words and expressions that a user employs when drafting specifications. For a given application, it is to be expected that both the vocabulary and the associated meanings will be, if not entirely fixed, at least reasonably limited. Furthermore, it is to be expected that all the users agree on their meaning. A simple NL system, using just some morphological and syntactic analysis techniques can be written to define a controlled vocabulary, and to ensure that the users employ only this vocabulary to define specifications. By ensuring that every definition consists of words in the authorized set, or known morphological variations of them, we can encourage all users to use words and expressions consistently while writing specifications. A more complete interface can also be used to restrict the task of adding words and expressions to a 'super-user'; this would help the administration of the project and add some control to the process (see Note 5).

The words in the controlled vocabulary presumably reflect the most important concepts used in the specifications, and could also be used automatically to generate indices and lists of cross-references. This could be very useful for the administration of the project, especially when large specifications (which can sometimes run into the hundreds of pages) are being developed. Cross-referencing in particular can aid consistency: whenever some concept is referred to, if other references to it are immediately made available, it is much easier to see if all these references are mutually consistent. However, accurate cross-referencing requires at least a modest degree of linguistic analysis. For example, one would want references to the 'pump operator' to be cross-referenced to 'operator of the pump' but probably not to things like 'inoperative pump'.

(b) Enhancing a Simple Style of Writing

A more sophisticated use of NL techniques involves the development of programs to analyse and criticize the style of a given text. In these applications, the goal is not only to check that every input sentence is grammatically correct, but also that it agrees with a set of pre-determined criteria. These criteria will typically try to produce documents that are clear and simple to understand.

For example, an organization writing user manuals will try to enforce a style of writing consisting of simple, direct sentences, which could contain style rules of the following kind:

(i)   Favour affirmative sentences over passive ones;
(ii) Mark noun phrases with several noun-noun compounds as inadequate;

(iii)   Do not use reduced relative clauses;
(iv)   Avoid the use of many qualifying phrases;
(v)   Penalize sentences that are too long.

These criteria can then be used by a general-purpose syntactic analysis system to score each sentence and assign a rating that reflects its complexity. Hopefully, these constraints will enhance the author's strategy for organizing information, and will result in documents that are easier to read and comprehend.

It is important to note that these rules will often refer to syntactic characteristics that can only be provided by some sort of syntactic analysis and will presumably be developed on top of an NLP system that performs full syntactic analysis (see Note 6). In general, the more sophisticated the linguistic analysis performed, the more discriminating and informative will be the stylistic monitoring.

4.3.2 Reducing the Ambiguity of NL Specifications

As we have seen, a main problem of translating English sentences into LFs which reflect their meaning is the problem of finding the intended interpretation among a potentially large number of possibilities. Moreover, people are usually unaware of them during production or interpretation of sentences.

We intend to experiment with CLARE in automatically profiling various equivalent descriptions of tasks and specifications. Each of them will be analysed by CLARE and given a score depending on the degree of syntactic and semantic uncertainty of the sentence. This score is available as the result of applying the general-purpose heuristics for ranking analyses that were described earlier. The goal is to have a tool that helps the specifier to obtain expressions that are unambiguous. By using the over-eagerness of the system to find unsuspected vagueness and unintended readings in all but the simplest sentences, we can turn what in some circumstances is a weakness into an advantage, and help the production of clear, precise specifications.

We give an example (due to H. Alshawi) of how such a system could operate. Assume that an input sentence such as:

> The transfer of propane from the trucks can only commence after authorization from the DC.

is proposed to the system as an initial specification. CLARE will proceed to analyze it, and will return a score grading its degree of ambiguity. The user can then be invited to re-phrase the original in various ways. Successive refinements of the initial proposal will be proposed until a minimally ambiguous statement is found with the help of the system. Such a process could proceed as follows (a high score means low ambiguity):

(i) The transfer of propane from the trucks can only commence after authorization from the DC. Score = 65 %.

(ii) The DC authorizes every propane transfer from a truck before the start of the transfer. Score = 70 %.

(iii) DC authorization is required before the start of the transfer of propane from the truck. Score = 73 %.

(iv) Only the DC can authorize a transfer. All transfers of propane from the truck must be first authorized. Score = 75 %.

This process of refinement must be carefully tailored to ensure that the information contained in the original sentence is preserved throughout. The system must be designed to provide enough feedback to avoid problems. In the next section, we will suggest how this may be done.

4.3.3 A System to Control the Information in an NL Specification

So far, we have reviewed possible contributions of NLP techniques to the production of syntactically clear specifications. In this section, we will approach the same problem in a slightly deeper manner. We will sketch ways of applying NLP techniques to help the user see the information conveyed by an input specification written in English. Ideally, this information can be employed to organize a statement in such a way that it contains precisely the information one needs to derive a formal specification (i.e. a complete but non-repetitive statement). At a very abstract level one can think of this as a translation problem: a translation from conversational English into a completely explicit sub-language of English.

As argued earlier, one of the challenges of using CLARE in the context of formal specifications is the study of general NL techniques to produce good analyses without a detailed model of the universe of discourse. The application presented here does so by requiring the user to provide all the information necessary to carry out the contextual reasoning required to understand fully and disambiguate the sentence. Suppose that the user proposes the following sentence as part of a possible specification:

> A reservoir will be chosen to be loaded, and the outstation will check all the input values.

The system can begin by pointing out that, before a successful analysis is produced, the user must completely determine the entities referred to by the phrase 'the input values'. The user then tries a more specific description:

> A reservoir will be chosen to be loaded, and the outstation will check the input values of every reservoir.

A complete LF can be extracted, but the program might have to make assumptions that are marked as having a high cost. For example, the verb 'to check' might be allowed to have an NP as complement, but it would prefer a 'that sentence'' (see Note 7):

'The sentence "Check the input values of every reservoir" is possibly underspecified, try "Check THAT ..." '

The user finds that in fact an important piece of information is missing, one indicating what to check for. The next attempt is:

A reservoir will be chosen to be loaded, and the outstation will check that the input values of every reservoir equal zero.

A further analysis of this LF might discover that there are two unconnected statements, suggesting that either a relation is being missed or that there are actually two unconnected sentences that would be better if written separately. The user realizes then that there is indeed a causal connection missing between the two sentences, so he suggests:

After a reservoir has been chosen to be loaded, the outstation will check that the input values of every reservoir equal zero.

The consideration of this LF can point to the fact that there is a main event related to the choosing of the reservoir, but the potentially crucial information specifying who or what chooses the reservoir is missing. The user then corrects the sentence and types:

After a reservoir has been chosen by the operator, the outstation will check that the input values of every reservoir equal zero.

This sentence fully describes the action of choosing a reservoir, but, inadvertently, the purpose of the action has been deleted. If the system keeps track of the information contained at each step, it can detect this problem and prompt the user:

'The event associated with "to choose" is less specific than before; previous qualifying "to be loaded" is missing'.

The user rereads the next-to-last sentence and suggests this time:

After a reservoir has been chosen to be loaded by the operator, the outstation will check that the input values of every reservoir equal zero.

The system has no further suggestion, and the process finishes.

4.3.4 Designing a 'Claims' Language

Claims languages are English-like artificial languages for expressing various types of security function as part of a requirements specification. These languages are deemed to be useful because they completely constrain what can be said in them (like a technical language), but can be read by a non-specialist. They are intended to show links between claims, reduce ambiguity, and facilitate the evaluation of the claims being made in the specification.

These languages must be used with care: they are restricted, but it does not automatically follow that everyone understands a sentence written in such a language in the same way. A constant theme in the previous section has been the unlimited amount of ambiguity and vagueness in all but the simplest of sentences. This suggests that we are likely to find the same problem in the current application, resulting in specifications that can be read in more than one way by different users.

An NL application can usefully be applied to criticize such languages, supporting the designer of the Claims language, and helping in the definition of a language for specifications that allows only unambiguous statements (see Note 8).

Before we explain in detail how to do this, we need an example application within which to frame the discussion. Assume that we are engaged in the production of an artificial language to draft the specification of a series of events - possibly subject to conditions - in the domain of gas storage applications. To achieve this goal, we would like to define a grammar to produce sentences such as:

> The outstation will check and open the reservoir input valves.

and

> The reservoir output valves will be closed depending on the operator's criteria.

We first write some simple rules to generate a sentence of the first type (see Note 9):

> [1.1] event_spec = entity_spec + 'will' + list_actions_spec +entity_spec
> [2.1] entity_spec = 'the outstation'
> [2.2] entity_spec = 'the reservoir input valves'
> [2.3] entity_spec = 'the reservoir output valves'
> [2.4] entity_spec = 'the operator's criteria'
>
>   ...
>
> [3.1] list_actions_spec = action_spec
> [3.2] list_actions_spec = action_spec 'and' list_actions_spec
> [3.3] list_actions_spec = action_spec 'or' list_actions_spec
>
>   ...

[4.1] action_spec = 'check'
[4.2] action_spec = 'open'
[4.3] action_spec = 'close'
[4.4] action_spec = 'be closed'

...

With them, we can produce the first sentence by applying the rules above to transform an 'event_spec' into a sentence. At each step, we will take the leftmost 'spec' and replace it according to some rule, as we did in the sub-section on Syntax above:

event_spec (rule 1.1)
entity_spec + 'will' + list_actions_spec + entity_spec (rule 2.1)
'the outstation will' + list_actions_spec + entity_spec (rule 3.2)
'the outstation will' + action_spec + 'and' + list_actions_spec + entity_spec (rule 4.1)
'the outstation will check and' + list_actions_spec + entity_spec (rule 3.1)
'the outstation will check and' + action_spec + entity_spec (rule 3.2)
'the outstation will check and open' + entity_spec (rule 2.2)
'the outstation will check and open the reservoir input valves'

If we want to extend the grammar to include sentences of the second kind, we need to add only the following rule:

[1.2] restricted_event_spec = event_spec + 'depending on' + entity_spec

With this, and following essentially the same steps (Rules 1.2, 1.1, 2.3, 4.4, 2.4), we obtain the second sentence. There are some problems, nonetheless. Inadvertently, we have opened the possibility of generating sentences such as:

The reservoir output valves will be opened and closed depending on the operator's criteria.

which is ambiguous, that is, it can be interpreted as meaning:

The reservoir output valves will be opened depending on the operator's criteria, and the reservoir output valves will be closed depending on the operator's criteria.

or:

The reservoir output valves will be opened, and closed depending on the operator's criteria.

The second interpretation leaves it open that the valves may be opened without reference to the operator's criteria.

An NLP system can be envisioned to identify this kind of problem first, then code the grammar using rules such as the ones above, and generate a representative set of sentences from the grammar. Then, it would input this set of sentences to CLARE, which would produce as many analyses as possible for each example. If the grammar generates potentially ambiguous specifications, we will be able to detect this by finding that CLARE has identified valid sentences (i.e. sentences that were obtained by following correctly the rules of the artificial language) with more than one analysis, which are therefore ambiguous.

4.3.5 Translating English-Like Specifications into a Semi-Formal Specification

We continue with an example of a more difficult application. For this, we will assume that we have a specification, written perhaps in a custom-made artificial language. This specification will be divided into three fields of preconditions, actions, and postconditions, and will describe some operation in the form of a simple series of actions. Suppose that one such specification is (see Note 10):

- Preconditions: the operator has indicated whether liquid or gaseous transfer will take place, and the target reservoir has been identified. Inlet valves A and B are closed.
- Actions: The outstation will open the inlet valve of the target reservoir. The status of the valve is checked. Truck earth connection is made. The operator presses the start button Z.
- Postconditions: The reservoir is loaded.

We have in mind the following application: a system to translate this specification into a target expression in some semi-formal specification language (SL) (see Note 11). As we will argue, this problem seems to bear considerable similarity to the one of creating an NL interface to a database. In the database query task, a contextual reasoning cannot be avoided, and a great deal of effort has to be expended in writing axioms that connect the linguistic concepts used to the relevant fields and keys of the database relations being queried. An appropriate SQL or other query language expression has to be inferred from the LF representing the content of the original English question (see Note 12). Often, the result of the query is translated back into English to help the end user understand the answer (see Note 13).

Before continuing, it will be useful to give a more complete description of our example. Assume that we want the system to translate the specification above into a notational specification of the following sort:

PRE:
      indicate_transfer_value(OPERATOR_37,kind_transfer);

        in(kind_transfer, { LIQUID, GASEOUS });

        indicate_reservoir(OPERATOR_37,target_reservoir);
        valid_target_for_loading(target_reservoir);

        closed_inlet_valve(A);
        closed_inlet_valve(B).
ACT:
        do_open(OUTSTATION_1,INLET_VALVE_1,target_reservoir);
        do_check_status(INLET_VALVE_1,OK);
        do_connect(CONNECTION_45);
        do_press_button(OPERATOR_37,Z).
POST:
        full(target_reservoir).

In this example, predicates and existentially-quantified variables are in lower-case, constants in capitals. The task of the system here would be, first to translate each sentence into its logical form, and then to map the logical form into the database query proper.

To carry out the second task, the main difficulty is to translate the elements constituting the query into the corresponding ones in the database. As the user of the system might not be aware of the exact nature of the database, this can be a serious problem. For example, notice the difference in the following levels of representation:

    'Truck earth connection is made' (input sentence)
    make(truck_earth_connection) (LF)
    do_connect(CONNECTION_45) (DBQL)

The task that needs to be completed before translation of this sort is possible is quite a large one. It would be likely to be cost-effective to invest in this type of labour-intensive knowledge engineering only when a large number of specifications within a particular limited domain are being produced.

4.3.6 Generation

So far, we have concentrated on the possible applications of NLP techniques that relate to analysis. In this section, we will point to some ways in which NLP generation techniques can help to produce, revise, and store formal specifications.

(a)   Paraphrasing Specifications

The first task that can be supplemented by generation techniques is the production of natural language specifications without hidden or understood relations. As we have indicated above, CLARE contains a variety of mechanisms to deal with under-specified sentences, with elliptic and indirect references, vague relations, and so on. CLARE can also generate natural language expressions from logical forms, so it is possible to produce sentences in English that exactly correspond to the meaning of the underlying logical form (see Note 14).

One application could be designed to produce paraphrases of input sentences, filling in any under-specified aspects of them, and then helping the user to choose an adequate specification. This would enhance an original specification in two different ways. First, it would help the user to draft specifications in a more natural language; for example, using pronouns, or under-specified referents. Second, it could help to bring to light unconscious assumptions made at the moment of writing the specification.

We give two examples of how this process could be carried out. Suppose that the user types in the following sentence:

> The operator will then connect the hoses.

The system can then reply by producing a full paraphrase, in this case one in which the referents 'the operator' and 'the hoses' have been fully identified by the surrounding context (see Note 15):

> The input sentence can be paraphrased as: 'OPERATOR_37 will then connect HOSE_11 and HOSE_12'.

A slightly more complicated example suggests how to help the user identify and correct an incomplete specification. In this case, the user types in a sentence such as:

> The operator will then connect the hoses and the truck earth connection XS1O1 will be made.

After analysis, the system can inform the user that the sentence has three possible readings, depending on the resolution of the term representing the missing agent making the connection that was referred to in the first part of the sentence. Using the generation component, the system can then produce each of the paraphrases, ranked in order of preference (see Note 16):

> The input sentence is ambiguous, and can be paraphrased in three different ways; choose the correct one:
>
> 'Most favoured interpretation: "OPERATOR_37 will then connect

HOSE_11 and HOSE_12, and OPERATOR_37 will make the TRUCK_CONNECTION_XS101."

'Second possible interpretation: "OPERATOR_37 will then connect HOSE_11 and HOSE_12, and the OUTSTATION_11 will make the TRUCK_CONNECTION_XS101."

'Least likely interpretation: "OPERATOR_37 will then connect HOSE_11 and HOSE_12, and the RESERVOIR_4 will make the TRUCK_CONNECTION_XS101." '

The user can then either mark one of the paraphrases as the one intended, or proceed to write a more informative specification.

(b)   Generating NL Descriptions from SLs

Another application of generation techniques can be the generation of entire paraphrases of specifications written in an SL. As before, one purpose of this application is the generation of paraphrases that can be read to verify that the specification has the intended meaning. More ambitiously, it could become the kernel of a larger system designed to produce automatically reports in English of a formal specification. With such a system, there would be only one 'true' specification, written in an SL, and all other versions, written in an artificial language, in a form of restricted English, or as a full English text, would be produced automatically by the computer. This approach would eliminate the compatibility problem caused by having different specifications used simultaneously by separate groups of people, as they would be using different paraphrases of the same specification. Of course, the ambiguity problem arises here too: we have to be careful that a sentence expressing the content of one logical form cannot also be understood as expressing another. One way of partially solving this problem is to use only a subset of the rules that are necessary for the description of English, generating only a small and relatively unambiguous subset of it.

The following example continues the one above in the section on 'Translating English-like Specifications into a Semi-formal Specification'. There we considered the translation of one small specification into another, written in a fictional SL. Here we will consider the creation of a system to produce a text in English that corresponds to the SL specification.

As the example will show, the generation of text presents some problems that do not arise when generating isolated sentences, because the system must produce sentences which make clear - hopefully in a natural manner - the way in which the different entities and actions relate to each other in the specification.

A viable solution involves the use of pronouns, as they naturally occur, supplemented with some notation to describe exactly what entities in the discourse universe are referred to by the referential expressions in the text. Before we sketch a text generated by this hypothetical NLP system, we introduce the following conventions:

(i)   Entities that correspond to well-defined entities in the discourse universe will be written in capitals (e.g. OPERATOR_37, A, ONE);

(ii)   Specific definite noun phrases will be used to signal salient entities in the discourse universe;

(iii)   The sign '=number' will indicate co-referential expressions, i.e. correspond to the same entity ([the operator]=3 ... [he]=3).

Using this notation, our system could generate the following text to re-express the SL specification:

> Specification of PROCEDURE_15 (where   'the operator'' is OPERATOR_37, and 'the connection' is CONNECTION_45):

Preconditions:

> (i)   the operator must identify a [kind of transfer]=1
> (ii)   [it]=1 must be either liquid or gaseous
> (iii)   [the operator]=3 must identify a [target reservoir]=2
> (iv)   [it]=2 must be a valid target for loading
> (v)   the inlet valve A must be closed
> (vi)   the inlet valve B must be closed

Actions:

> (i)   the outstation will open [the inlet valve ONE]=4 of [the target reservoir]=2
> (ii)   [the operator]=3 will check that its=4 status is OK
> (iii)   [he]=3 will establish the connection
> (iv)   [he]=3 will press button Z

Postconditions:

> (i)   [the reservoir]=2 must be full.

(c)   SL Specifications as DBs

As we suggested above in the section on 'Translating English-like Specifications into a Semi-formal Specification', the process of translating a natural-language specification into a formal language resembles the process of deriving a query to a database from a sentence in English. In this last example of generation techniques, we will further explore the idea of treating SL specifications as a kind of database.

Let us assume that we have a system capable of deriving an SL equivalent of an English expression, and also of producing English sentences of SL statements. With these elements in place, we can employ the entire specification as a database, and use it dynamically to query the specification in order to answer questions about it.

With such an interface, the user could directly interrogate the database as follows:

> (question) what is the result of procedure 15, assuming that 'the result' corresponds to the set of postconditions of PROCEDURE_15? Answer: The target reservoir must be full.

> (question) who identifies it?
> 'Assuming that "it" corresponds to the target reservoir,
> and the specification is of PROCEDURE_15,
> answer: OPERATOR_37 must identify the target reservoir.'

> (question) which valves must be closed before the actions?
> 'Assuming that the specification is of PROCEDURE_15,
> answer: The input valves A and B must be closed.'

> (question) can procedure 15 be used to transfer solids?
> 'Answer: No.'
>
>   ...

4.4   SUMMARY

This chapter has introduced the basic ideas behind general techniques to process natural-language sentences, and explored some possible applications of them to help the writing of precise, clear and unambiguous formal specifications in English.

The emphasis has been on the presentation of domain-independent techniques to comply with the objective of the MORSE project, namely the study of reusable techniques in formal specification tasks.

Many of the techniques presented here are complementary rather than exclusive, and, used together, could significantly enhance the use of natural-language in this area.

In terms of the inherent difficulty of the various applications which we have sketched, in general we started with the simplest and worked up to the most complex. There are two types of complexity involved: the degree of linguistic processing required by an application, and the degree of domain modelling required. Linguistic processing gets more complex and non-deterministic as we go from morphology through to semantics. Applications get more complex and labour-intensive the more that the precise resolution of linguistic properties like reference or disambiguation depends on non-linguistic factors such as those that would be captured in a domain model. Given this fact, we feel that in the short term at least it is most worthwhile to explore those applications that involve general-purpose, domain-independent, linguistic processing.

4.5 NOTES

Some of the material contained in this paper describes joint work with Hiyan Alshawi, SRI Cambridge. In particular, the original ideas for the applications described in the section on 'Reducing the Ambiguity of NL Specifications' is due to him. He also contributed with comments and criticisms that improved the overall quality of this paper.

(1)   Methods for Object Reuse in Safety Critical Environments: a collaborative project under the DTI Safety Critical Systems initiative. The current partners are LLoyds Register, BICC Transmitton, West Middlesex Hospital, Dowty Controls, and Cambridge University.

(2)   We are simplifying considerably in the interest of legibility; readers are encouraged to consult the source documents.

(3)   Unless otherwise stated, our examples will either be direct quotes from [Banks 91], or possible variations of them in the same context.

(4)   CLARE contains such a mechanism to handle preferential readings, and implements a number of preferences (see [Alshawi 91], Chapter 5).

(5)   This could of course take place within a more general MIS to administer and document the entire development process: definitions, changes, amendments, etc.

(6)   For more on systems of this kind, see [Heidorn 82], or more recently - and using a formalism similar to the one in CLARE - [Douglas 92].

(7)   We will use single quotes to denote the system's response.

(8)   Note that, in contrast of the applications described before, this one is not geared towards eliminating ambiguity directly at the object level (i.e. the level of concrete specifications), but at the level above, the one where specifications are described.

(9)   We use the conventions introduced in the section on Syntax.

(10)   This example is a modified version of a real one.

(11)   The specification language used here does not directly correspond to

any real one; we informally introduce one only for the purposes of this and subsequent examples.

(12) The reader can consult [Perrault 86] for an introduction to this subject.

(13) CLARE has been successfully used to create an NL interface (see [Rayner 92]).

(14) See [Alshawi 91], Chapter 6.

(15) We indicate with capitals identifiers that refer to well-identified individuals in the discourse.

(16) The ranking would depend on similar criteria to the ones used to analyse a sentence. In this example, the first preference to resolve the elliptical reference would be to 'the operator' because it is the most recent entity and can be substituted without violating any constraints. The last substitution of 'reservoir', on the other hand, would break a sortal constraint that restricts the ability to make truck connections to animate entities, and would thus be only marginally possible.

4,6   REFERENCES

[Alshawi 91]   Alshawi H et al.: "CLARE, A Contextual Reasoning and Cooperative Response Framework for the CORE Language Engine." Second SRI International Tech. Report, November 1991.

[Alshawi 92]   Alshawi H (Ed.): "The Core Language Engine." MIT Press, 1992.

[Banks 91]   Banks R: "Transmitton Case Study, Requirement specifications." MORSE Project, Doc. Id. MORSE/TRANSMITTON/RJB/1/V1. 1991.

[Douglas 92]   Douglas S. and R. Dale. 1992. "Towards Robust PATR." Proc. International Conference on Computational Linguistics (COLING), pp 468-74, Nantes, France, August 1992.

[Heidorn 82]   Heidorn G E, Jensen K, Miller L A, Byrd R J, and Chodorow M S: "The Epistle Text-Critiquing System." IBM Systems Journal, 21, pp 305-26, 1982.

[Perrault 86]   Perrault C R and Grosz B: "Natural-Language Interfaces."

Ann. Rev. Comp. Sci. Vol 1. pp 47-82, 1986.

[Rayner 92]   Rayner M. and Alshawi H: "Deriving Database Queries from Logical Forms by Abductive Definition Expansion." 3rd. Conf. on Applied Natural Language, 1992.

5

ViewPoint-oriented development: applications in composite systems

Anthony Finkelstein, Jeff Kramer and Bashar Nuseibeh

5.1 INTRODUCTION

This chapter describes an organizational framework for the development of heterogeneous, composite systems. Such systems deploy different technologies and require diverse expertise for their development. They employ a number of development participants who adopt different development strategies and use different representation schemes to describe their respective domains of interest or responsibility.

Safety-critical systems are a special class of heterogeneous, composite systems whose development has traditionally relied on closer adherence to structured methods, stricter quality control and the occasional use of more time-consuming and expensive formal methods. Closer inspection however reveals that such systems have in fact a limited number of safety-critical aspects or components. The framework described in this paper facilitates the description of such components by allowing the use of specialized representation schemes, such as formal methods, for individual component descriptions. Thus, additional development effort may be devoted to particular components rather than entire systems.

The framework presented facilitates the description of system development participants, their roles in the development process, and their views of a problem domain. It employs coarse-grain objects, called *ViewPoints* [Finkelstein 92], that represent 'agents' having 'roles in' and 'views of' a problem domain. These ViewPoints are loosely coupled, locally managed encapsulations, integrated via many inter-ViewPoint consistency relations and transformations. ViewPoints may be used to describe both safety-critical components and the services which they contribute to the overall system.

The chapter provides a description of ViewPoints from the perspective of the software engineer, whose duty it is to elicit system requirements and to develop the system in a potentially distributed setting. A prototype, integrated ViewPoints' support environment, called *TheViewer*, developed at Imperial College, is also briefly presented.

5.2   VIEWPOINTS

Large system development projects typically consist of a number of participants, engaging in the partial specification of system components. These participants frequently employ different notations and development strategies to produce descriptions of different (or the same) problem domains. To model this scenario we define a ViewPoint as 'a loosely coupled, locally managed object, encapsulating partial knowledge about the system and domain, specified in a particular, suitable representation scheme, and partial knowledge about the process of development'. A ViewPoint encapsulates this knowledge in five so-called slots: style, work plan, domain, specification and work record. These are shown in Figure 5.1.

Each ViewPoint is associated with a particular development participant called the ViewPoint 'owner'. The ViewPoint owner is responsible for enacting the ViewPoint work plan to produce a ViewPoint specification, in the ViewPoint style, for the owner's domain of responsibility.

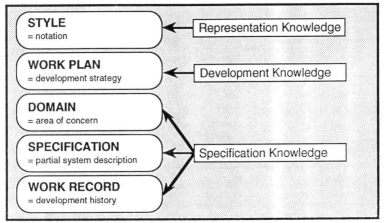

Figure 5.1: The five slots of a ViewPoint.

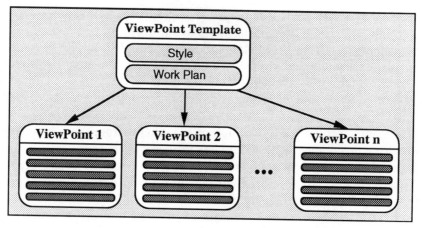

Figure 5.2: A ViewPoint template may be instantiated to produce many different ViewPoints for different domains.

Clearly, a number of ViewPoints may employ the same style (e.g. functional decomposition) and the same work plan (e.g. description of a top-down strategy), to produce different specifications for different domains. We therefore define a reusable *ViewPoint Template* in which only the style and work plan slots are elaborated. A ViewPoint template is in effect a ViewPoint type, whereby a single ViewPoint template may be *instantiated* to yield several different ViewPoints, and by extension several ViewPoint specifications (see Figure 5.2).

A software engineering *method* in this context is a collection of ViewPoint templates, representing the constituent development techniques of the method (see Figure 5.3). Customized methods, or combinations of methods, may thus be constructed by grouping together the relevant templates. The

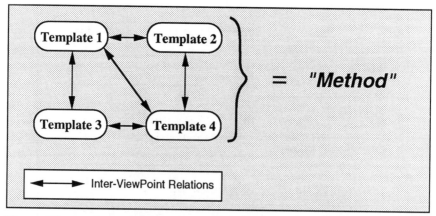

Figure 5.3: A software engineering method - a collection of ViewPoint templates integrated via a series of inter-ViewPoint relations.

binding of these templates is via *Inter-ViewPoint rules* that relate the style components of the various templates. These rules are effectively the method integration mechanism, and are used to check consistency between ViewPoints. Such inter-ViewPoint relations may also be used for checking the critical dependencies between various safety-critical components of a system.

ViewPoint templates are also strong candidates for reuse. One or more such templates may be used in different methods, and because they have been tried and tested, their reuse leads to more effective and robust methods.

ViewPoint oriented development also provides the opportunity for the reuse of actual specifications and designs. A ViewPoint (i.e. an instantiated Viewpoint template) encapsulates a specification and its development rationale for a particular problem domain. A single ViewPoint may thus contain the specification of a safety-critical component which may be used in other systems requiring that component.

ViewPoint development, management and reuse all benefit from automated support, and the next section describes *The√iewer* - a prototype environment providing such support.

5.3   TOOL SUPPORT

The√iewer is a ViewPoint support environment implemented in Objectworks/ Smalltalk Release 4. The start-up window shown in Figure 5.4 conveniently illustrates its scope. On the one hand, a 'method designer' is provided with the opportunity to design, describe and integrate ViewPoint templates that constitute a method. On the other hand, a 'method user' may instantiate pre-defined templates to yield concrete ViewPoints, whose specifications may be developed, checked and managed within the boundaries of a system development project.

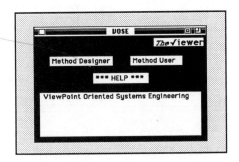

Figure 5.4: The start-up window of the Viewer.

5.3.1 Method Design

Method design takes the form of ViewPoint template description and integration. The constituent techniques of 'the method' are chosen, and then a template for each is elaborated. The *Viewer* provides a Template Browser to facilitate such activities, and two snapshots of this are shown in Figure 5.5. In the figure, a customized example 'method' is being defined. It consists of three graphical techniques: functional decomposition, object structuring and action tables. The functional decomposition template has been selected for this example. In Figure 5.5a, the style slot is being described, while Figure 5.5b shows part of the work plan description. The consistency relations and transformations between templates of the method are defined under the Inter-ViewPoint Checks section of the work plan (see Figure 5.5b).

For a selected template, the user may describe (a) the style, by clicking on the 'style' button, or (b) the work plan, by clicking on the 'work plan' button. The descriptions may be textual (bottom left) and/or graphical (bottom right). The 'Process Modeller' button provides tools for defining ViewPoint state transitions and context-sensitive guidance. Process modelling is a work plan activity.

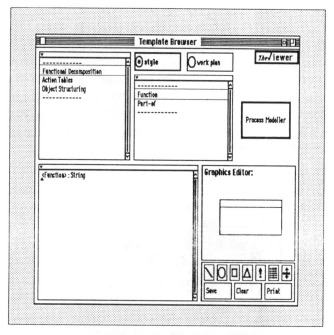

Figure 5.5a: A snapshot of the Viewer's Template Browser.

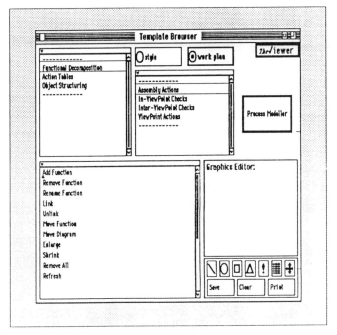

Figure 5.5b: A second snapshot of the Viewer's Template Browser.

5.3.2 Method of Use

(a) Development (Project) Management

A systems engineering project revolves around instantiating ViewPoint templates, developing ViewPoint specifications, and checking for consistency between them. A project under development therefore consists of a number of ViewPoints, instantiated from the constituent templates of the method on which the project is based. These ViewPoints are displayed in a ViewPoint Configuration Diagram, which tabulates ViewPoints instantiated from the same template in columns, and those relating to the same domain in rows.

TheViewer employs a ViewPoint Configuration Browser (see Figure 5.6) as the overall project management tool. This browser allows the creation of projects based on pre-defined methods, the instantiation of the methods' constituent templates, and the presentation of selected projects' ViewPoint configuration diagrams. A ViewPoint configuration diagram may be navigated by selecting the required ViewPoint and executing the required command.

The ViewPoint Configuration Browser also provides a number of ViewPoint monitoring and overall report generating tools.

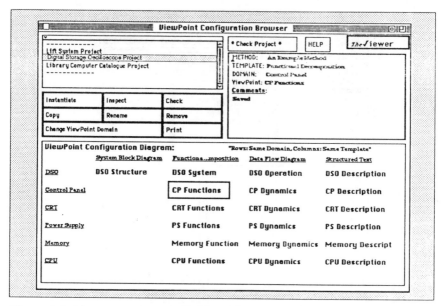

Figure 5.6: The Viewer's ViewPoint Configuration Browser. The list of projects created is shown in the top left window, and the panel of command buttons below it applies to the ViewPoint selected from the ViewPoint Configuration Diagram in the lower window. The 'Check Project' button produces the Project Analyser.

(b)   ViewPoint Development

Actual project development occurs in projects' various constituent ViewPoints using ViewPoint Inspectors (see Figure 5.7). Such tools are loosely coupled and potentially distributable; thus, several ViewPoint Inspectors may be active simultaneously, with different ViewPoint owners developing different ViewPoints concurrently.

The ViewPoint Inspector provides the mechanisms for editing and checking ViewPoint specifications - both internally and across other ViewPoints. Editing commands appear under the 'Assemble' button and are derived from the 'Assembly Actions' description in the corresponding ViewPoint template (see Figure 5.5b). Consistency checking may be performed by a rudimentary Consistency Checker (see Figure 5.8), and coarse-grain, context-sensitive method guidance is also available. The work record automatically keeps track of all actions performed on the specification, and the user may optionally annotate some or all of these actions to explain or provide a rationale for various design decisions.

5.3.3 Tool Integration

Within the ViewPoints setting, The Viewer facilitates tool integration and reuse. This is achieved by treating the problem of tool construction and

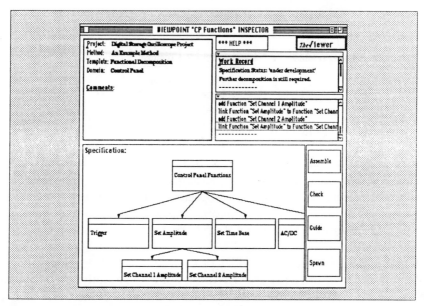

Figure 5.7: A ViewPoint Inspector. This window provides tools for the development of ViewPoint specifications. The tools include facilities for editing (assembling) specifications and checking their consistency. The figure shows a "typical" functional decomposition specification, with the work record in the two top right windows.

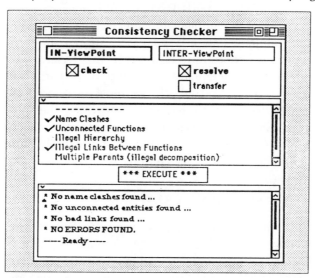

Figure 5.8: A ViewPoint Consistency Checker. The scope of the checks is selected by in- or inter-ViewPoint buttons. There are two modes of application: 'resolve' shows success or failure when checks are executed; 'transfer' passes on the necessary information to and from other ViewPoints to maintain inter-ViewPoint consistency. The list of appropriate checks is displayed and may be selected and executed individually or in two groups.

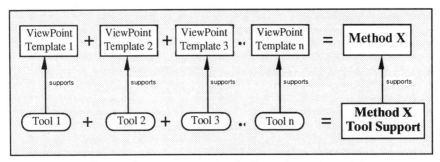

Figure 5.9: Method tool support. A 'method' is the union of its constituent development techniques (ViewPoint Templates); a 'tool' supports an individual ViewPoint Template. 'Method tool support' is the union of all the tools supporting the method's constituent ViewPoint Templates.

integration as a subset of the wider problem of method development and integration. The framework and *TheViewer* allow the addition of individual tools to support individual development techniques, which can then be integrated via the inter-ViewPoint relations specified by the ViewPoint templates.

A ViewPoint template encapsulates within its two slots (style and work plan) declarative information about the development technique which it describes. How this is supported by a CASE tool is left to the tool implementor. Different tool implementors may choose different algorithms, indeed different implementation languages, to support the same template. What these tools must conform to however, is the declarative information supplied to them by the templates they support. In particular, the inter-ViewPoint, and hence inter-Tool, checks must be picked up from the appropriate templates. These rules, which provided the mechanism for method integration, now also act as the tool integration mechanism. Method tool support is then treated as the union of the tools supporting the method's constituent templates (see Figure 5.9).

5.4   CONCLUSIONS AND FUTURE WORK

ViewPoint Oriented Systems Engineering (VOSE) acknowledges the inevitable role played by a multitude of development techniques in a single development project. ViewPoints encapsulate representation, development and specification knowledge within a single object. Further modularity is achieved by selecting ViewPoints that describe different problem domains. ViewPoints are bound together by inter-ViewPoint relations which specify dependencies and mappings (critical or otherwise) between system components. These relations represent the integration thread that passes through the configuration of system ViewPoints, which are otherwise entirely loosely-coupled and locally managed.

The VOSE object-based architecture offers considerable scope for reuse. Reuse is supported at the levels of both method design and method use. ViewPoint templates are the reusable components of representation and development knowledge during method design and construction. ViewPoints are the reusable components of specification knowledge during method use.

Methods are treated as a union of ViewPoint templates, and method tool support as the union of the individual tools supporting the methods' constituent templates. Tool integration is a natural consequence of the method integration provided by the VOSE framework via inter-ViewPoint relations and transformations. Further work is needed to explore how these relations and transformations should be described and used.

VOSE is a proposed integration mechanism for the ESPRIT II project REX [REX 89], and is under development at a number of European industrial and academic sites. A number of case studies [Nuseibeh 91] have been performed instantiating methods such as CORE [Mullery 85] and the Constructive Design Approach [Kramer 90] into the framework. Individual development techniques including SPEC Nets [Graubmann 90] and their simulators have also been described using ViewPoint templates, and specialized, high performance tools developed to support them [Graubmann 92a, 92b].

As part of the FOREST project [Cunningham 85], an object oriented requirements analysis method, VSCS [Castro 91a], for producing formal specifications in Modal Action Logic [Jeremaes 86] has been described in outline within the ViewPoint framework [Castro 91b]. VSCS guides the analyst through five loosely coupled stages utilizing informal, structured and formal representation schemes. These stages are reflected in the description of VSCS using ViewPoint templates.

Current research is focused on improving the structuring of large ViewPoint configurations to allow the scaling up of the framework to large, industrial developments [Kramer 91]. Moreover, a variety of notations and mechanisms for expressing and implementing inter-ViewPoint communication in a distributed environment are also being investigated.

5.5 ACKNOWLEDGEMENTS

The authors would like to gratefully acknowledge the contributions of their colleagues at the Distributed Software Engineering Group at Imperial College. Special thanks to Michael Goedicke and Peter Graubmann for their work on ViewPoints. This paper draws together work reported in [Finkelstein 92] and [Nuseibeh 92].

5.6   REFERENCES

[Castro 91a]   Castro J and Finkelstein A: "Elicitation and Formalisation with Structure." Deliverable Report NFR/WP2.1/IC/R/001/A, FOREST Research Project, Department of Computing, Imperial College, London, May 1991.

[Castro 91b]   Castro J and Finkelstein A: "VSCS: An Object Oriented Method for Requirements Elicitation and Formalisation." Deliverable Report NFR/WP2.2/IC/R/002/A, FOREST Research Project, Department of Computing, Imperial College, London, October 1991.

[Cunningham 85]   Cunningham R, Finkelstein A, Goldsack S, Maibaum T and Potts C: "Formal Requirements Specification - The FOREST Project." Proceedings of IEEE Workshop on Specification and Design, IEEE Computer Society Press, 1985.

[Finkelstein 92]   Finkelstein A, Kramer J, Nuseibeh B, Finkelstein L and Goedicke M: "Viewpoints: A Framework for Integrating Multiple Perspectives in System Development." International Journal of Software Engineering & Knowledge Engineering, Vol 2, No. 1, March 1992, pp 31-57.

[Graubmann 90]   Graubmann P: "Definition of SPEC Nets." REX Technical Report REX-WP3-SIE-008-V1.0, Siemens, Munich, Germany, July 1990.

[Graubmann 92a]   Graubmann P: "The HyperView Tool Standard Methods." REX Technical Report REX-WP3-SIE-021-V1.0, Siemens, Munich, Germany, January 1992.

[Graubmann 92b]   Graubmann P: "The Petri Net Method ViewPoints in the HyperView Tool." REX Technical Report REX-WP3-SIE-023-V1.0, Siemens, Munich, Germany, January 1992.

[Jeremaes 86]   Jeremaes P, Khosla S and Maibaum T S E: "A Modal (action) Logic for Requirements Specification." In Brown P J and Barnes D J (Eds.): Software Engineering '86, Peter Peregrinus, 1986.

[Kramer 90]   Kramer J, Magee J and Finkelstein A: "A Constructive Approach to the Design of Distributed Systems." Proceedings of the 10th International Conference on Distributed Computing Systems, Paris, France, 28th May - 1st June 1990.

[Kramer 91]   Kramer J and Finkelstein A: "A Configurable Framework for Method and Tool Integration." Proceedings of European Symposium on Software Development Environments and CASE Technology, Konigswinter, Germany, Springer Verlag, June 1991.

[Mullery 85]   Mullery G: "Acquisition - Environment." In Paul M and Siegert H: Distributed Systems: Methods and Tools for Specification, LNCS 190, Springer-Verlag, 1985.

[Nuseibeh 91]   Nuseibeh B A: "VOSE: An Interim Report and Case Study, Internal Report." Department of Computing, Imperial College, London, March 1991.

[Nuseibeh 92]   Nuseibeh B A and Finkelstein A C W: "ViewPoints: A Vehicle for Method and Tool Integration." Proceedings of International Workshop on CASE (CASE 92), pp 50-60, IEEE CS, Montreal, Canada, 6-10 July 1992.

[REX 89]   "REX Technical Annex." ESPRIT Project 2080, European Economic Commission, March 1989.

6

The FOREST technique for system specification and validation

Bill Quirk

6.1 INTRODUCTION

The application of reliable and high-integrity computing techniques is increasingly recognized as crucial to the development of safety-critical control systems in defence, aerospace, medical, nuclear, and other such fields. The use of formal mathematically-based techniques has been advocated for quite some time as the most promising way forward, but they have been somewhat slow to 'take off' in many industrial applications. A number of reasons have been proposed for this. One is that there is little assistance available in developing an informally stated requirement into a formally stated one. The process is seen as being a specialist human one, and, hence, expensive. A second reason is that the specification stated in logic is often perceived as being less useful than the informal, natural language version. A third reason is that the process of formalizing a specification is not seen to be particularly valuable. The potential of early analysis is either not recognized or not realized.

The FOREST project addressed all these points. In it, a proper systematic method has been developed to guide the requirements elicitation process and target it to the production of a formal logical specification. This has been described in the previous chapter, by Finkelstein.

In addition, within the FOREST project, a new logic has been developed, much richer than the popularly used First Order Predicate Logic. Finally, some powerful validation tools have been developed to exploit the advantages offered by having a formal representation. There has also been some consideration of the process of using the logic for the design process. This chapter will address these last three points.

6.2   FORMAL SOFTWARE DEVELOPMENT

The principal problem with an informal software development process is that little or no machine analysis is available until the coding stage. Verification and validation take place throughout the development procedure, but these are based on human 'eyeballing', 'code analysis', 'walk-throughs', and the like. Good though these have proved in practice, it is still widely acknowledged that the deep problems are the most difficult to detect, and these often persist until commissioning (or even beyond). Faults discovered late are the most expensive to repair: all the work involved in design, coding, testing, and integration has to be repaired. What is more, this all happens when the customer is jumping up and down wanting the system. If the requirement itself was lacking for whatever reason, then this too should be modified - but how often does this happen?

It is important to realise that formalizing a specification is not a goal in itself. The purpose is to improve the quality of the final system. This comes about because of the properties inherent in formality. Formal systems are mathematically-based theories with axioms and proof rules. Providing that the initial axioms are themselves consistent, and the proof rules can be shown to be sound, then the whole theory will be consistent. A good example is Euclidean geometry, which also happens to satisfy the following important property: the theory reflects reality (at least to a close enough approximation for most of us!). The theorems which can be proved themselves reflect truths which can be observed in the real world; for example the famous theorem of Pythagoras.

The FOREST formal approach attempts to improve on this traditional situation. The informal application concept is transformed into formal specification of those requirements, guided by a systematic method especially developed and targeted to the purpose. Once this formal specification has been achieved, powerful validation tools can be brought into play, thus allowing validation to proceed before any design work has started. With good tools support, the requirement can be analysed and developed with the customer until there is general agreement that the requirement, as gathered and understood by the producer, meets the real need of the customer; and this occurs before any further stages of the development process are undertaken. In a perfect formal world, these development processes would need no verification, since they would already be proven.

But even in the present real world, the development can be undertaken with increased confidence that the *right* system is being produced.

One of the most important considerations in specification is clarity of expression and, hence, ease of understanding. In formal systems, this implies that the logic underlying the method must provide a good abstraction for the relevant application areas. It has been stated that one reason for the decline of the Roman Empire was that their system of arithmetic was so complex that the taxes could not be calculated and thence collected efficiently. For example, is

MCMXLIV

- divisible by 2?
- divisible by 3?
- divisible by 5?
- divisible by CCXLIII?

If these examples are not convincing, consider setting programmers the problem of writing a program to implement a simple Roman numeral calculator. I warrant that the vast majority would translate the input numerals into decimal, carry out the calculation in that form and then translate the result back into Roman for output.

6.3   THE FOREST MODAL ACTION LOGIC

The FOREST project took First Order Predicate Logic and extended it with a number of modalities to enhance its expressiveness and power of abstraction [Maibaum 86].

6.3.1 Structural Axioms

The first extension developed by FOREST is the introduction of the concepts of Agents carrying out Actions. In the initial version of the logic, this was indicated by the form:

Pre => [Action, Agent] Post

The meaning of this is that if the precondition **Pre** is true then, after the **Agent** carries out the **Action**, the postcondition **Post** will hold. Axioms of this form allow the expression of general effects of actions on the state of the system. For example a lift system might have:

true => [pressed, button] lit

which expresses that in all cases buttons light when pressed. Since in this case there is no precondition, such axioms are usually shortened to the following:

[pressed, button] lit

The precondition is often referred to as the context in which the action occurs. A more sophisticated lift system might have buttons which normally light when pressed but only if the lift is not already at the floor in question. In this case, separate buttons would have to be identified and related to the floors; perhaps:

floor<>f => [pressed, f_button] f_lit

Presumably, the buttons are not supposed to be permanently lit once the first press action has occurred. Thus some other action axiom can be expected which cancels it. Typically, the light is extinguished when the lift doors open at the relevant floor; thus:

floor=f => [open, doors] NOT f_lit

These axioms define a simplified life history of the button lights. Clearly more detail would be required to achieve a realistic scenario: the status of the lights when the system was first switched on, the possibility of bulbs blowing, and subsequent repair. Such things as bulbs blowing are usually modelled by actions of an environment agent - God, if you will. The creators and repairers of systems are usually more immediately identifiable. But note the complexity of the axioms which starts to develop:

NOT blown(f_button) & at<>f => [pressed, f_button] f_lit
[f_button_break, god] blown(f_button)
[f_button_fix, repairman] NOT blown(f_button)

A more concrete example is the 'Martian Lander' described by Jahanian and Mok [JaMo 86]. This space vehicle landing system operates in one of two modes: normal or emergency.

When first turned on, it operates in normal mode and the pilot can control the vehicle attitude and velocity by controlling the thrust generated by the motor. This is implemented by an iteration of two phases. In the first phase, a sensor device is initiated to read the thrust demanded by the pilot, and a watchdog timer is set to interrupt 100 mSec later. Providing the read action is completed before the watchdog interrupts, the second phase is entered in which the demanded thrust is set and the first phase re-entered. If the read operation fails to be completed within the 100 mSec timeout period, the emergency operation mode is entered in which a second set of instruments is used to land the vehicle automatically.

This might be translated relatively simple-mindedly into FOREST in something like the following:

[turn_on, pilot] normal & phase=1 & NOT emergency

That is, when first turned on, the system is in its normal first working phase.

normal => [complete_read, sensor] phase=2

If the read operation is completed, the system proceeds to its second normal operational phase. This axiom says nothing about what the result would be if a read operation were completed in emergency mode and, as the specification fragment stands, the results of that are left unstated. This is not necessarily a failing. In the first place, there may be situations in which the desired result of an action has yet to be defined. Secondly, it may be that the likelihood of the action occurring in another context is considered either impossible or so improbable that it is not worth detailing what the possible effects might be.

[set_thrust, system] phase=1

Finally, once the thrust has been set, the system iterates.

All these axioms capture 'universal' truths about the system and are referred to as 'structural'. They state what the result of an action will be in certain contexts. Two of these are truly universal: there is no contextual precondition in the axioms. The second axiom of the 'Martian Lander' system states what happens when the read operation is completed in the normal mode of operation.

However, what these axioms do not detail is when the particular actions should, may, or should not occur. The rules governing the 'evolution' of the system have to be detailed separately and this separation of concerns is an important attribute of the FOREST approach.

6.3.2 Deontic Axioms

To determine when actions should or should not occur, the FOREST Modal Action Logic adds a second level, which are the concepts of permission and obligation. (The word 'Deontic' means 'pertaining to duty'.) The general form of such axioms is:

Pre => obl(Action, Agent)

Pre => per(Action, Agent)

Pre => ref(Action, Agent)

where the meanings are, respectively, that if the precondition **Pre** holds, then the **Agent** is obliged, permitted, or must refrain from performing the **Action**. This allows the expression of what causes actions to occur within the system, and, within this context, the system and its environment are treated identically.

At any time, an agent can only legitimately perform those of its actions for which it has permission. There may be times - contexts - in which many if not all actions of an agent may be forbidden, although, clearly, if all actions of all agents were not permitted, the system would be in deadlock. Examples abound: most passengers would be delighted if the pilot switched off the engines when the aeroplane had arrived at its destination terminal, but would be rather less at ease if the same action was taken in flight at 30,000 feet!

Obligation is a rather stronger concept. In the original logic, once an obligation had been incurred, that obligated action had to be the next action undertaken by the agent concerned. Other actions of other agents could occur and, indeed, the obligation could be revoked by another action. But as long as the obligation persisted, the agent could legitimately only do nothing - literally - or perform that action. In particular, an agent could therefore not have two obligations at any one instant.

Permissions are essentially long lasting. Once established, they remain until the consequences of an action are to remove them. Obligations are transitory. When incurred, they last until either they are revoked or the action occurs.

The Martian lander example might develop the following:

normal & phase=1 => obl(read//set_watchdog, system)

Here, the parallel combinator has been invoked to produce a new action for the system which both initiates the read operation on the sensor and sets the watchdog timer as a single atomic action:

[set_watchdog, system] obl(time_out, watchdog)

Now the watchdog is obliged to interrupt if it has been set. Notice that this does not quite fit the general pattern given above, but it saves writing three axioms:

[set_watchdog, system] watchdog_set
watchdog_set => obl(time_out, watchdog)
[time_out, watchdog] NOT watchdog_set

These three would become even more complicated after the next few axioms:

phase=2 => obl(set_thrust//reset_watchdog, system)
[reset_watchdog, system] NOT obl(time_out, watchdog)

Remember that if the read operation was completed, the phase was changed to 2. Clearly there is no intention of the watchdog timer interrupting if everything else is functioning correctly. Thus the obligation to time-out is removed, providing the read operation is completed before the time interval has expired.

[set_thrust, system] phase=1

And, finally, the system reverts to its first phase to iterate its normal operation.

Before leaving this example, it is worth sketching its development to the emergency mode of operation:

[time_out, watchdog] emergency & NOT normal

First, the time-out causes the transition from normal to emergency operation. There would then follow the axioms detailing the required behaviour in this emergency mode of operation.

6.3.3 The System Environment

The environment of the system has so far been ignored. How far out the system-environment boundary should be drawn is a matter of judgement. Should the system designer be included, the system builder, the system maintainer? Here, only the pilot is included. First, the pilot turns the system on, but only if she or he wants to:

per(turn_on, pilot)

Second, the pilot is allowed to use the system.

per(demand_thrust, pilot)

One could argue on whether or not the pilot can turn the system on again while it is still on. Is the mechanism to be a push button which can be repeatedly pressed, or is it an on-off switch? Can the pilot switch the system off again? These are areas for validation, addressed below, but there are several possibilities. Probably the harshest regime would be:

[turn_on, pilot] NOT per(turn_on, pilot)

However, this would deny any sort of reset possibility to the pilot. The first turn_on action would be the last normative turn_on action, and there would be no escape from an emergency should one occur. A more realistic scenario might be:

emergency <=> per(turn_on, pilot)

This allows the pilot to attempt a reset if an emergency arises, but outlaws such resets when the thrust controller is functioning normally.

It is dangerous to try to guess what a requirement should be, especially when one is not an expert in the particular domain under consideration. As explained below, completion of a partial specification or removal of ambiguities from a requirement is a validation issue. It is ultimately the customer's responsibility to decide what the real requirement is. But note that the FOREST approach using its Modal Action Logic allows the expression of partial knowledge and, as will be shown later, useful validation support can be provided even on such fragmentary information.

Finally, there is no definition in Jahanian and Mok [JaMo 86] of how the emergency status can be resolved; and no axioms are presented here to resolve it. However, it is likely (and, hopefully, for the well-being of the pilot) that it is possible to recover from such a state of affairs. It might be that there is a repair action that the pilot could take; perhaps being part of a more global system reset. Perhaps the attention of an engineer is required. Again, this is a question of where the system boundary is drawn. If there are 'no user repairable parts inside', then the pilot may have little interest in specifying the repair procedure. However, the space agency may well be interested in repair procedures - assuming the disabled craft can return successfully to a suitable depot. This is not an unimportant observation. Real requirements are the agglomeration of information from many viewpoints, many people, many interests, many responsibilities. A system boundary has, eventually, to be agreed, but it is now well agreed that drawing the boundary too closely only causes problems. No one specifies the whole world, and systems have to operate and be operated in the world. Setting the system boundary correctly is perhaps the art, rather than the science, in system requirements engineering.

6.3.4 Structuring the FOREST Logic

The first of these lander axioms highlights the so-called frame problem. It is necessary to make it explicit that the turn_on action does not (and cannot) itself cause an emergency. Deviating slightly from the description given by Jahanian and Mok, this axiom could be replaced with:

emergency=s => [turn_on, pilot] phase=1 & emergency=s

This would admit the possibility of turning on the landing system during an emergency detected from another component of the lander. The initial operating phase would still be established, but the emergency status would not be affected. Thus, interacting subsystems can be specified when and where appropriate. The same problem affects nearly all the lift axioms given previously. It was stated that a button lit if it was pressed when the lift was not at that floor, but it was not made explicit that the button would not illuminate if the lift was at that floor. Likewise, the effect of the doors opening at a floor on that button was defined, but it was not stated that the status of other floor buttons should not be changed by that action. One approach to this is simply to maintain that the only changes which do occur are those which are explicit or implied by the axioms stated; no other changes occur. Unfortunately, it is computationally complex to calculate these consequential changes, and this makes validation difficult. As already commented, the alternative of making everything explicit makes the axiom set excessively cumbersome. The solution is to move from a 'flat' logic to a structured one, and the most recent FOREST approach to this is now briefly described. Fuller descriptions are contained in [Ryan 90] and [RyFi 91].

The first fundamental idea is to allow agents to be declared and defined as basic building blocks. For example a lift system might have the fragment:

AGENT **button;**
LOCAL ACTION **press;**
SHARED ATTRIBUTE **lit;**
[press] **lit;**
END **button;**

The fourth line is the definition already seen, while the first three lines essentially form a declaration of the button. The action 'press' is declared as local because it is not intended that any attributes of any other agent will be modified by the occurrence of the press action. On the other hand, the attribute 'lit' has to be shared because the light is not to be extinguished by an action of 'button' but by an action of some other agent - in this case, as already known, the doors. Note however that the agent identifier no longer appears within the action modality, since it is now contained within the declared agent structure. There are subtle matters concerned with the differentiation of logic and specification language here, but this is not the place for the details.

One of the key concepts of the object oriented approach to programming is the recognition that complex systems often inherit properties from simpler ones, and often in multiplicities, and this constitutes the second fundamental concept. Thus, a lift system is likely to contain a number of buttons. These will be separate physically but share the same behaviour. In order to construct the panel of buttons within a lift cabin, one button for each floor and each button mimicking the one described above, the essentials of this are captured in the next fragment:

AGENT **panel;**
INCLUDES **button** VIA **1;**
INCLUDES **button** VIA **2;**

. . .

INCLUDES **button** VIA **n;**
END **panel;**

This fragment defines a panel of n buttons, one for each floor to be served by the lift; and the buttons are explicitly named as 1.button, 2.button, etc., up to n.button, by the expression 'VIA'. No further theory is developed here, although this is not the typical situation, as the next fragment illustrates:

AGENT **lift_cabin;**
INCLUDES **panel;**

INCLUDES **door;**

...

floor=f => [open] NOT lit(f.button);

...

END **lift;**

Even though the agent door is yet to be defined, the intention here is clear. The lift cabin includes (at least) a panel of buttons and a pair of doors. The lift cabin now has an inherited 'open' action from the included doors and, when these doors open in the context of a lift cabin, this action has the added effect of extinguishing the lamp in the relevant floor button.This extended logic also allows that the 'button lit' attribute can be localized, indicating that it is unaffected by any further actions of other agents which could have inherited the panel. This would ensure that only presses and opens could affect the illumination status.

Formally, this structuring is based on category theory and morphisms. This provides the necessary mechanisms both for the inclusion procedure and for maintaining the separation of names between separately declared agents or modules. Although, in the lift example, the included buttons are all different, there are situations in which the same structure has to be included in different parts of the overall structure; some of the controls in the lander may be linked to several different systems. As well as inclusion, the structured logic also allows the definition of server-client relationships. In this case, it is the server interface only which is included in any potential client, rather than the complete server. This hides the internal structure of the server, just as the internal details of a software procedure are hidden from a calling program. The details can be found in various FOREST reports.

6.4 VALIDATION IN FOREST

As already mentioned, formality is not a goal in itself. Rather, it is the ability to start the validation process early in the production cycle which is one of the key driving issues. Validation is an interesting process. Even within a formal framework, the validation process is not itself formal. It is all about human judgement, human interaction and human intuition. Automated support certainly helps; indeed, it is almost indispensable for large systems with serious safety responsibilities. But there is no possibility of answering the question 'Is this correct?' in the affirmative by totally automated techniques. Furthermore, there are good theoretical reasons why answering that same question in the negative can be guaranteed. The ideal of being able to prove incontrovertibly the consistency and completeness of a system is, unfortunately, pie in the sky.

The problem with completeness is easier to see. If an aspect of the system requirement is totally absent, then how is this to be detected? This is another aspect of the problem of embedding a system in its environment: where is the boundary? Or, maybe, for safety-critical systems, where is the emergency stop button?

The problem of consistency is more theoretical: it has been established that an attempted proof of something which is in fact false may never terminate. Thus, it is impossible to guarantee whether something really is inconsistent (i.e. wrong) or whether we have just not tried hard enough (or waited long enough).

The FOREST approach is to give the analyst powerful tool support to assist in this intensive process. While acknowledging the problems discussed in the previous paragraphs, useful consequences of specifications can be derived which certainly help in increasing confidence that the specification does meet the real needs of its user, or, alternatively, demonstrating that something is, indeed, awry.

Consistency is managed principally during the requirement elicitation phase. A network database has been integrated into the Structured Common Sense support to ensure that differences between the various viewpoints on requirements are at least made known to the analyst. A degree of automated 'fixing' has also been included although this is under the control of the user. This was an important decision, reflecting the fact that specifications are built up incrementally and, consequently, that trying to enforce absolute consistency all of the time would be totally counterproductive. Again, this approach is detailed in the previous chapter.

The two major validation tools are an animator and an automated deduction tool or theorem prover. The animator [Booth 87, CoCu 90] essentially implements a test-bed for the specification, in a way which is closely analogous to the use of a high-level debugger at code testing and integration time. The progress through the potential states of the system is under the control of the user who selects the sequences of permissible actions to be taken by the system. Actions which are obligated are highlighted and, although other agents may carry out their permitted actions first, obligations cannot be overruled. The animator can be instructed to continue carrying out obligations until no further ones exist - the equivalent of a 'stop at next interesting position' instruction. A number of other facilities are included, but the details are inappropriate here.

The major importance of the animator is that it puts validation firmly in the application domain rather than in that of the formalist or logician. Unlike the code debugger analogy already mentioned, a graphical interface can be produced so that the behaviour of the system under consideration can be mimicked or simulated in terms of that application domain, rather than merely having an indication of the system states in the form of a set of values. Despite the well known limitations of testing, this makes the validation potentially available to the domain expert in the terms of that expert. And no one is likely to be a better judge of whether or not a specification meets the real requirement than the domain expert.

Of course, the graphical interface has to be produced for each different application. However, it is easy to envisage that such interfaces could be generated at least partially automatically for given applications. One example which has already been used involved a mock-up of a railway signalling system which closely modelled a standard signal box control panel. Plant control rooms and air flight displays are also candidates.

As already stated, the other validation tool is an automated theorem prover [AtCu 91, CoCu 88, Kent 91]. Although usually considered a somewhat arcane occupation, the FOREST implementation is targeted at real industrial use. The approach adopted is based on the so-called Tableau method, a well established method for First Order Predicate Logic. This is essentially a proof by contradiction. For any postulated theorem, the prover tries to demonstrate that the negation of that sentence is inconsistent with the axioms of the specification.

Consider the following simple example. To prove

mortal(SOCRATES)

from the following pair of axioms

FORALL **x: human(x) -> mortal(x)**
human(SOCRATES)

First, the negation:

NOT **mortal(SOCRATES)**

is added to the axioms. Then, the first axiom can be re-written as:

FORALL **x: mortal(x)** OR NOT **human(x)**

and from this can be deduced:

mortal(SOCRATES) OR NOT **human(SOCRATES)**

The OR now causes the Tableau to split into two branches. On the first or left hand branch, there is a contradiction with the negation of the desired theorem:

NOT **mortal(SOCRATES)**

On the other branch, there is a contradiction with the second axiom:

human(SOCRATES)

Thus the negation of the theorem is inconsistent with the axioms and hence the validity of the theorem is established.

Because of the action and deontic modalities of Modal Action Logic, the basic Tableau method has to be extended. The developments needed are demonstrated in the following example, an extension of the previous one. This time, there are six axioms:

FORALL w: human(w) -> mortal(w)
FORALL x: in_heaven(x) -> happy(x)
FORALL y: good(y) -> [die, y] in_heaven(y)
FORALL z: mortal(z) -> per(die, z)
human(SOCRATES)
good(SOCRATES)

and the goal is to prove:

[die, SOCRATES] happy(SOCRATES)

Again, the desired result is negated, the first four axioms re-written as in the previous example and the same initial deduction made as of mortal(SOCRATES). In order to make progress, the action 'die' must be taken and, for this to be normative or allowable, permission for that action must be established. This is derived from the re-write and specialisation of the fourth axiom:

per(die, SOCRATES) OR NOT mortal(SOCRATES)

The right hand branch contradicts the initial deduction so the left hand branch, which contains the necessary permission, must be considered. At this point, the prover decides to develop the action and, to do this, it opens a new Tableau representing the changed system world or state. In this new Tableau, the axioms are still valid - they are valid in all states - and the post-condition of the action also holds. Thus:

in_heaven(SOCRATES)

can be asserted. However, the re-write of the second axiom is

happy(SOCRATES) OR NOT in_heaven(SOCRATES)

and both sides of this are contradictory: the first with the negation of the desired result, the second with the immediate consequence of taking the action 'die'.

The automation of such a proving technique does present problems. However, one of the properties of this procedure, as implemented in the FOREST toolset, is that it needs almost no guidance by the user - unlike most other theorem provers which require detailed operator interaction throughout the progress of proving a theorem. *Almost* none, because it is only necessary to set a search depth limit initially. Otherwise, the potential breadth of the proof space may never be investigated because the equivalent of an infinite loop may occur while going down a particular branch of the search tree. This choice of search depth is not final. If no proof is found at the selected depth, the prover will ask if the depth should be increased and then proceed accordingly.

Returning to the Martian Lander example, there is a safety requirement that the pilot cannot prevent the functioning of the thruster. The natural language requirement is not sufficiently detailed to ensure that the pilot cannot repeatedly turn on the thrust controller, say every 90 milliseconds, thus stopping the system entering its emergency automated mode of operation. To ensure that such aberrant behaviour cannot occur, more precision is necessary about the turn_on action. In detail, the reset must only be effective if the controller successfully interacts with the sensor - that is, the read operation gets a response. This can be achieved by the following axioms:

$$\text{emergency} => [\text{turn\_on, pilot}]\ \text{reset\_pending;}$$
$$\text{reset\_pending} => \text{obl(read, system);}$$
$$\text{reset\_pending} => [\text{respond, sensor}]\ \text{phase=2 \& NOT emergency \& NOT}$$
$$\text{reset\_pending;}$$

With these added to the specification, the safety theorem can be formulated as:

$$\text{reset\_pending} => [\text{read, system}]\ (([\text{respond, sensor}]\ \text{NOT emergency) OR}$$
$$([\text{time\_out, sensor}]\ \text{emergency));}$$

This states that after the pilot has attempted a reset during an emergency, either the thrust sensor responds to the read and the emergency status is cancelled, or the read action again times-out and the emergency status persists, leaving the automatic control activated. This is typical of the sort of formula that the theorem prover can establish. If a proof can be derived, then that proof is displayed. This is to ensure that the software has not itself failed and produced an invalid conclusion - an important consideration for a safety-critical validation tool.

6.5 CONCLUSION

Modal Action Logic has proved to be a very expressive medium in which specifications can be constructed. Many real industrial systems have been successfully described using this technique, and the usefulness of the validation techniques have been demonstrated.

Furthermore, the proof theory developed for this logic allows significant validation potential, even on only partially completed specifications - a not unimportant consideration since specifications are rarely fully complete! The combination of the action modality, the deontics, and the structuring principles provide one of the most powerful combinations for requirements specification and also assists both reuse of libraries of specifications and the general principals associated with object oriented approaches.

An associated systems analysis method has been developed and is described in the previous chapter. Further work has also been done in going from the logic, especially the new structured version, to an implementation [GoQu 91]. In all, FOREST provides an integrated approach to produce and manage the specification and design process.

6.6   REFERENCES

[AtCu 91]   Atkinson W D and Cunningham R J: "Proving Properties of a Safety-Critical System." IEE Software Engineering Journal, Vol 6 No 2, 1991.

[Booth 87] Booth J P: "Animating Formal Specifications." Harwell Report AERE-R12869, 1987.

[CoCu 88]   Costa M C and Cunningham R J: "Mechanised Deduction and Modal Action Logic." Alvey FOREST Report R5, Imperial College, London, 1988.

[CoCu 90]   Costa M C, Cunningham R J and Booth J P: "Logical Animation." Proc. Int. Conf. Software Engineering, Nice, 1990.

[GoQu 91]Goldsack S J and Quirk W J: "Design Issues in FOREST." FOREST Research Report WP1.R2, Imperial College, London, 1991.

[JaMo 86]   Jahanian F and Mok A K-L: "Safety Analysis of Timing Properties in Real-Time Systems." IEEE Transactions on Software Engineering, Vol SE-12 No 9, September 1986.

[Kent 91] Kent S J H: "A Deduction Calculus for Modal Action Logic with Action Combinators." FOREST Report WP3.R2, Imperial College, London.

[Maibaum 86] Maibaum T S E: "A Logic for the Formal Requirements Specification of Real-Time Embedded Systems." Alvey FOREST Report 3, Imperial College, London, 1986.

[Ryan 90]   Ryan M: "Structured MAL." FOREST research report WP1.R1, Imperial College, London.

[RyFi 91]   Ryan M, Fiadeiro J and Maibaum T S E: "Sharing Actions and Attributes in Modal Action Logic." Proc. Int. Conf. on Theoretical Aspects of Computer Science (TACS'91), Springer Verlag, 1991.

7

Requirements development for safety-critical systems - a total systems approach

Jeremy Clare

7.1 HOW SAFE ARE LARGE SYSTEMS?

There is increasing concern that large computer systems are hazardous to the individual and to the environment. The special problems of such systems should therefore be taken into account during their procurement.

In this chapter, *large systems* are those systems which have complex interactions with the world, are operated or used by many people, possess at least some unique characteristics, and take more than a year to procure. Examples include systems in air traffic control centres, power station control rooms, military command and control centres, and critical control centres such as aircraft cockpits.

Safety issues are those associated with the aspects of a system where any failure may lead to personal injury or death, or can lead to environmental damage.

Procurement is the consideration of all aspects of the acquisition of a system, including requirements analysis, specification, tender assessment, and award and project management.

So what are the special problems of large systems?

Firstly, because they are large and complex, it is very difficult for a single individual to understand all their aspects and issues. The problem becomes more than a 'single brainfull'.

Secondly, because they possess unique characteristics, we are unlikely to have procured one like this before. There will therefore be aspects which are novel, either because the technology has not been used before or because well established technologies are being used in a novel manner or in novel combinations. In such cases, we cannot be sure of foreseeing the nature or consequences of failure.

Thirdly, they include people. For most designers of systems, people are a problem. People are highly variable, they are adaptable, they do not seem to obey normal laws of physics or engineering, and, when they are 'operators', they are clearly 'unintelligent'. This impression is due to the fact that equipment designers are rarely operators or users of the equipment they design, and do not appreciate what is involved. The result is that, typically, the designer produces equipment to be operated by the 'ideal' user .

An ideal user is someone who understands the engineering constraints, the scope of functionality and the full extent of the 'requirements'. He or she probably does not want to do anything with the system other than make it work to its specification, so will not seek to use it to meet some external objectives such as production targets, return on investment, or military advantage.

7.2   SO HOW DO WE OVERCOME THESE PROBLEMS?

Firstly, we take a total systems approach, which considers the overall functionality of the system. This embraces both machines and people. By including the people as elements of the system, we are forced to treat the human as a 'design' consideration. This may seem strange, but remember that people have been around longer than machines, they do not change their basic characteristics at the same rate as computer chips, and they are crucial to the achievement of the purpose of most systems. It is also worth remembering that machines are usually designed to meet a 'purpose'; yet, 'purpose' is a purely human characteristic; machines in themselves have no purpose until they are put to use. What this means is that we need to include in the design team individuals who understand what people can and cannot do.

In order to analyse a system, we need to have an understanding of its requirements. While this is a concept clearly understood by all designers of systems, it is still difficult to arrive at a requirements description which both captures all aspects of the need and expresses realistic performance requirements. Part of this problem is understanding the process of procuring a complete system, and part is due to the difficulty of drawing an effective boundary between the system and the external world.

In an ideal world, we would be able to write a clear, unambiguous requirements document against which several suppliers could bid. In the real world, we often do not understand the full scope of the requirements until the day we scrap the system. We understand the requirements at that particular time because we have just written the requirements specification for the replacement system - which, incidentally, will be required to do different things from the system we have just scrapped.

In order to get a clear understanding of the requirements, we need to understand and give due attention to all the factors which influence the system. These factors can be grouped under three principal headings: Need, Technology and Commercial Factors (see Figure 7.1).

- 'Need' includes the functionality and performance requirements. It also includes such factors as availability, reliability, and maintainability targets.
- 'Technology' includes factors such as the availability of technology to meet the need, the maturity of that technology, and the ability to interconnect the various components.
- 'Commercial Factors' include price, cost of ownership, liability, and safety.

It follows that the requirements specification must be considered in the context of all these factors.

At this point we would seem to have done little that is different from 'good practice' in specifying a system. However, if we return to our original premise, we will find the critical difference to be that what we are aiming for here is a requirements description which includes human as well as machine components. This, to use jargon, may be referred to as a 'socio-technical' system.

For a socio-technical system, we can define the need in terms of goals (such as achievement of the safe control of aircraft within a specified airspace volume). We can define 'aircraft throughput' in terms of numbers per unit time or numbers per unit volume. We can define 'safe' in terms of minimum separations in height, distance and time. These definitions of goals of the system can be directly equated to the goals of the organization deploying the system, so we can achieve a clear statement of how the system meets or contributes to the overall business goals of the organization. Based on the goal description, we can define a set of functions which allow those goals to be achieved. We can then begin to model the system in terms of processes and information flows which support those functions.

If we consider systems used for fault-monitoring, such as those employed

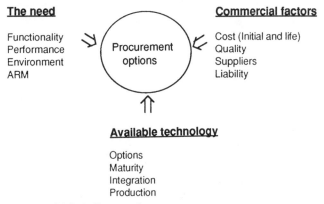

Figure 7.1: Factors which influence the system.

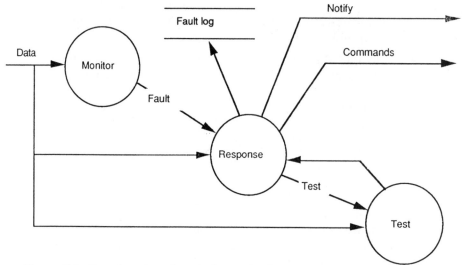

Figure 7.2: Core functions in a fault-monitoring system.

in the remote control of radar and navigation in support of air traffic control, then we can identify a number of core functions that have to take place (see Figure 7.2).

The first identifiable function is the Monitor function, which is concerned with receiving all input data regarding the state of the system. Some inputs will be direct data feeds, but others will be telephone enquiries and reports. The first step, then, is for the system to determine if a fault exists.

Once a fault is identified, the Response function can be initiated to diagnose the nature of the fault and to re-configure the system such that loss of service is obviated or minimized. In some cases there will be a need for repair actions to be initiated by remote agencies.

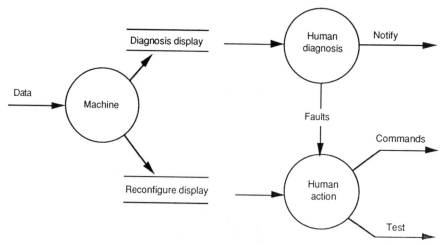

Figure 7.3: Functional partitioning between man and machine.

Table 7.1: Key attributes of men and machines

Men	Machines
Positive	*Positive*
High adaptability	Fast
Simple to task	Complex data handling
Capable of learning	Consistent
Able to make decisions	Reliable and available
Negative	*Negative*
Error-prone	Lack of 'common-sense'
Get bored	Limited in scope
Inconsistent	Persistent
Training required	

Once reconfiguration or repairs have been completed, tests will be carried out under the instruction and supervision of the Test function, prior to re-configured or repaired components or subsystems being re-incorporated into the operating configuration.

At this stage we still have not made any decisions about the partitioning between man and machine. Where we have concerns about safety, we carry out an initial hazard analysis to determine the levels of safety needed for the functions. In carrying out this analysis, we can consider alternative functional partitioning with the goal of minimizing the number of functions which need to operate at the highest level of safety.

Once the functional process partitioning has been achieved, we can consider the partitioning between man and machine for each process (for example, as in Figure 7.3). In this, we require an understanding of the relative merits of the men and machines for each activity - and their key attributes are summarized in Table 7.1.

Table 7.2: Human error probabilities (from [Kirwan 90])

Task	Failure probability
Simple, no stress	10^{-4}
Moderately complex, care needed	10^{-3}
Complex, unfamiliar, distractions	10^{-2}
Highly complex, stress	10^{-1}
Highly complex, rare, extreme stress	10^{0}

In addition, when we assign functions to the human component, we can group them so that they can be effectively carried out. Thus, where safety is an issue, we need to ensure that error-checking mechanisms are in place and that there are redundant paths: humans are very error-prone.

Table 7.2 shows the error rates which we can expect from humans in various situations. From these figures, it can be seen that, compared to machines, human reliability is low. Further, in many safety-critical systems with a high degree of automation, the human is only involved in conditions where errors are very likely - i.e. complex, unfamiliar tasks carried out in the presence of many distractions. If we are unlucky there are high or extreme levels of stress as well.

7.3   CONCLUSION

Where a machine carries out safety-critical processes, we need to ensure that it is designed to appropriate safety standards. This means careful design of functionality, with simple and checkable relations between processes. The new interim defence standard DEF STAN 00-55 [MOD 91], gives a rigorous approach to the design of such components.

If we are to ensure the integrity of a total system, we need the following:

- A clearly defined requirement;
- Clearly defined internal and external interfaces;
- An analysis from the integrity viewpoint.

If these criteria are not satisfied, we will have systems that are inherently unsafe. Nor can we avoid our responsibilities as designers by claiming that the machine is safe but that all safety-critical aspects are outside the machine components of the system. We must also design the human tasks, procedures, and interfaces so that the human component operates in a safe manner.

In summary, a system is only safe if all components (human and machine) interact in a safe manner. Leaving the safety interlocks to unaided humans inevitably leads to unsafe systems and is a major source of income for the legal profession.

7.4   REFERENCES

[Kirwan 90]   Kirwan B: "Human Reliability Assessment." In "Evaluation of Human Work", Edited by Wilson J and Corlett E N, Taylor & Francis, London, 1990.

[MOD 91] UK Ministry of Defence: "Interim Defence Standard 00-55, The Procurement of Safety-Critical Software in Defence Equipment". Issue 1, 5 April 1991.

8

A methodology for requirements management applied to safety requirements

John Dobson and Ros Strens

8.1 INTRODUCTION

Consider the following story, which concerns the AT&T network failure in New York on 17 September 1991:

> AT&T standard procedures require a power supervisor to assign a technician to inspect each power plant whenever the AT&T network automatically switches from the New York grid to its own electrical power supply. But on the occasion of this particular switch-over, the supervisor had taken all his technicians to a course on a new power alarm system, leaving the plant unsupervised. The switch-over blew a rectifier, an event which went unobserved for several hours, sending the communications switching centre to emergency batteries which quickly ran out of power, stalling all AT&T communications traffic in New York City, including safety-critical air traffic control information.

What seems to be important in this case is that the incident can be seen in terms not only of that aspect of safety related to 'no unobserved fault', but also that aspect related to 'no violation of duty of care' and that aspect related to 'no possibility of consequential failure'. Carefully defined use of terms could perhaps lead to these distinctions being made in terms of 'invulnerability', 'trust' and 'safety' respectively; but all these terms are already overloaded, and in any case we would probably informally use the term 'safety' indiscriminately to refer to some mixture of them all when we characterize the system (as a whole, including the human components) as being 'potentially unsafe', as it clearly was, since it could get into an unsupervised safety-critical state.

The rest of this chapter is structured as follows. Section 8.2 discusses issues of safety in a system with human components. Section 8.3 discusses obligations and responsibilities, the idea being that where there is a conflict of safety responsibilities, the system as a whole is potentially unsafe. Section 8.4 examines the context in which obligations are honoured and responsibilities discharged. Finally, Section 8.5 looks at the problem of determining safety requirements and indicates some implications for the design of a safety-critical system.

8.2   SAFETY IN A SOCIO-TECHNICAL SYSTEM

The first requirement that an organization will have of a technical system is that it has the functionality necessary to serve the organization's purposes. This defines the functional requirements on the system. Of equal importance, however, is the need for the system to support those functions in a way which matches the structure, objectives and characteristics of the organization - i.e. the organizational requirements. While the term 'non-functional' has sometimes been used to describe these requirements, this is a misleading term since it is the task of a methodology to allow such requirements to be expressed in a way which will enable them to be transformed into a form suitable for expression in a system specification. Thus, organizational requirements eventually become operationalized as functional requirements. A particularly important example of an organizational requirement is, of course, the set of safety requirements. In a safety-conscious organization, the requirement for safety not only influences the requirements on a technical system, but is pervasive throughout the whole organization and its human procedures, and therefore has to be treated as a requirement relevant not to just the technical system but to the whole socio-technical one.

The need to capture and deal with organizational requirements in the systems design process has long been recognized, and there are a number of methods now in existence to support the handling of such issues in IT systems design. These include forms of analysis which can detect and classify the range of organizational requirements within an organizational setting. One example is Checkland's Soft Systems Methodology [Checkland 1981] which provides methods for developing a 'rich picture' of organizational needs; it incorporates 'soft' and 'hard' requirements and shows their inter-dependencies. Other authors, notably Pava [Pava 1983] and Mumford [Mumford 1983] with the ETHICS methodology, have developed socio-technical system theory into analysis processes which show the requirements which the social system will lay upon any new technical system. The forms of task and user analysis developed, for example, within the ESPRIT HUFIT programme [Galer and Taylor 1989] are also capable of revealing the detailed requirements of users on usability and acceptability criteria.

In addition to analysis methods, there are many sources of design guidance to help design teams meet this kind of requirement. These are at their most developed with respect to the design of usable human-computer interfaces - see for example Schneiderman [Schneiderman 1986]. Methods also exist to support broader issues of acceptability and organizational match. Models or profiles have been developed, for example the model of the occasional discretionary user presented by Eason [Eason 1989].

However, in spite of the development of techniques to identify and incorporate organizational issues in the systems design process, there is very little evidence that they are widely used. A survey of design processes in use, undertaken by Harker [Harker 1987] as part of the Alvey programme, identified the following problems:

- The methods of analysing requirements did not formally collect information about organizational requirements, and even when these needs were recognized by designers, their methodologies did not provide ways of formalizing the requirements.
- In the design of technical solutions, there tended to be 'design drift' on organizational issues, as each designer made their own decisions as to what was important and how to treat it. The absence of a formal means of stating the requirement and offering support took this set of issues into the realm of opinion and guesswork.
- Finally, the methods of evaluation rarely incorporated any test against these criteria until the test of implementation, when it was usually too late for major redesign.

The conclusion to be drawn from this review is that it is imperative to bring organizational requirements into the mainstream of systems analysis and design. Since many of the analytical and design methods already exist, the most important need is to find a method of formalizing organizational requirements which will act as a focus for analytic and design efforts.

There are many prescriptive theories of organizations that could provide the basis for representation of organizations, for example Beer's cybernetic theory [Beer 1981]. However, it is not the aim of a design methodology to specify ideal organizational forms, but rather to enable system designers to build IT systems which match the critical features of a given organization. In order to achieve this, it is essential to be able to represent organizations as they actually exist or as the policy makers propose that they exist, rather than as they should exist according to some given theory. The approach adopted is to look for the most common denominator in organizations, i.e. the basic objects and the relationships between them.

Organizational theory emphasizes one feature of all enterprises: they operate by division of labour. The large tasks that are the 'primary tasks' [Rice 1958] of enterprises, e.g. manufacturing cars, are divided into smaller manageable tasks that are co-ordinated by control systems. These sub-tasks and their relationships give rise to information needs and information flows, and it is these which define the functionality requirements on an IT system to serve the organization. Consequently, traditional systems analysis techniques concentrate on capturing these aspects of organizational life.

However, division of labour is not only concerned with the division of tasks. In any organization consisting of more than one person, there will be a division of labour between members of staff, and normally this differentiation produces differing responsibilities. It is useful to describe this division as producing work roles which staff occupy. Each work role defines the responsibilities laid upon the role holder, the relationship with related roles (sometimes called the 'role set') and the expectations placed on the role by the role set.

The work role defines the task responsibilities of the role holder and therefore the functionality required of an information system to support the role holder. It also defines the rights and obligations of the role holders and therefore many features of expected role holder behaviour which give rise to organizational requirements; for example, we have expectations that a doctor will treat patient information as confidential. A work role analysis can therefore reveal many attributes that specify organisational requirements.

In the example cited in the introduction, for example, it is clear that the supervisor's responsibilities involved conflicting requirements (on this occasion): the responsibility to send a subordinate round to check the power plants conflicted with the responsibility for the training of subordinates. The misfortune arose from the fact that, in the event, in the presence of a conflict of responsibilities, the wrong decision was made. It would, of course, have been preferable to have identified this conflict earlier and to have given policy guidance on the resolution procedure to be adopted; it seems clear that this was overlooked. In the following section we shall describe a method of modelling responsibilities, which we are developing, that would enable such conflicts to be identified.

8.3   OBLIGATION AND RESPONSIBILITY

8.3.1 Types of Responsibility

Dictionary definitions of responsibility seem to agree on distinguishing two different meaning groups: (i) being accountable for something; (ii) being the primary cause for a result. The first meaning group has connotations of blame for a mismatch between the actual and a desired or expected state of account, without any implication of a direct causal connection between the responsible agent and the mismatch (the doctrine, now practised more in the breach than the observance, of 'ministerial responsibility'), whereas the second meaning group does have explicit connotations of causality. We shall therefore refer to these two distinct types of responsibility as *consequential* and *causal* responsibility, respectively. We must be clear about the sense in which we are using the term consequential here. It is being used to describe the type of responsibility where the agent is answerable to someone else: he is 'taking the consequences' for the state of affairs. This must not be confused with causal responsibility for the consequences of an action. For example, a child who throws a stone has causal responsibility for the action: he did it. Of far more significance is the fact that he is also causally responsible for the immediate consequences: he caused the window to get broken. The child can be blamed for breaking the window but it is the parent who has consequential responsibility: he is responsible to the rest of society for the actions of his children. We shall now examine these types of responsibility in more detail.

8.3.2 Consequential Responsibility

Our basic intuition is that one agent is responsible *to* another agent *for* something, and that this something can be described as a possible mismatch or non-conformance relation between an actual state of affairs and a desired, expected or feasible state of affairs. For example, an agent can be responsible for success (actual state of affairs better than expected) or failure (actual worse than expected) in some performance, or for the adequacy or inadequacy of a set of resources. The form of a consequential responsibility is therefore that it is a relation between a pair of agents and a mismatch relation, and it is important to note that all three elements are essential; in other words the actual responsibilities held cannot be looked at on their own but must always be considered within the responsibility relationship between the two agents. We shall refer to the two agents as the *responsibility principal* and the *responsibility holder*, where the *responsibility holder* is responsible to the *responsibility principal* for a *responsibility target*.

Both in reality and in terms of the model it is this relationship between the agencies that is important, and the question that we should be asking takes the form 'To whom are you responsible and in what respect?' Within an organization these responsibility relationships define the type of structural relationship between pairs of co-workers, thus forming an enduring framework for the basic 'socio' structure of the socio-technical system. In contrast a responsibility relationship between an external agent and an organization, where the relationship is essentially of the service type, is likely to be of a more transient nature, existing only for the duration of the specific contract. For example, a shipping company is responsible *to* a particular passenger *for* safety only while that passenger holds a ticket.

Associated with any responsibility is a set of obligations which must be discharged in order to fulfil that responsibility. At this point it is appropriate to make clear the distinction between responsibilities and obligations. Obligations, which are essentially constraints on the choice of action, are in effect the duties that must be performed to fulfil responsibilities. The distinction is apparent from the words we use: a responsibility is *for* something, whereas an obligation is *to do* (or *not do*) something. However, inseparable from a specific obligation is a responsibility for the discharge of that particular obligation. This responsibility is held by the holder of the obligation. If an agent chooses to pass an obligation to another agent, the new obligation holder then becomes responsible to the original obligation holder for discharging the obligation. Thus a new responsibility relationship is set up between them. In this way a whole chain of responsibility relationships can be established.

8.3.3 Causal Responsibility

The main distinction between consequential and causal responsibility is that whereas consequential responsibility is a three-way relationship between two agents and a state of affairs, the general form of a causal responsibility is a relation between a single agent and a state of affairs. In contrast to consequential responsibility, where the responsibility relationship between the two agents is paramount, causal responsibilities are driven by the target of the responsibility: the resource or activity. For example, we may ask 'Who is responsible, in a causal sense, for the appropriateness or adequacy of this resource?' or 'Who performed this action and is responsible for its outcome?' Causal responsibilities may be viewed as *operational* in nature since they come into existence only when an agent performs an action on a resource or as part of a process, and are held by that agent only. (Exceptionally, the initiator of an action may be deemed to have causal responsibility as much as the actual executor; for example, a supervisor may tell a subordinate to pull a lever.) Causal responsibilities are therefore of particular significance to considerations of safety and security and especially to the allocation of blame for an undesirable state of affairs.

8.3.4 An Example to Illustrate the Relationships between Consequential and Causal Responsibility

For our example we have chosen responsibility for safety in a shipping company. It is important to note the distinction between the responsibilities that agents hold *for* particular states of affairs such as 'profitability', 'safety',

'adequacy of service', etc., and the obligations that must be discharged to fulfil the responsibilities such as '*to* make a profit', '*to* take appropriate safety measures' and '*to* run a service'. These obligations are discharged ultimately by the performance of appropriate actions.

We first note that the directors in a shipping company have responsibility to the passengers (and possibly to the State) *for* the safety of passengers (Figure 8.1a). Obligations *to* take safety precautions, to maintain ships in a seaworthy state and suchlike arise from this responsibility. These obligations are passed to other employees such as ships' captains and, ultimately, to crew members who perform actions such as 'check lifeboats', 'ensure ship is not overloaded' and 'close hold doors on sailing' in order to discharge these obligations. Each time an obligation is transferred from one agent to another, new responsibility relationships associated with the obligation are created. For example, the directors are responsible to the passengers for safety in general, the captain is responsible to the directors for the safety of his ship (Figure 8.1b), and the crew members are responsible to the captain for the outcome of the actions which they take to discharge the obligations passed to them. In addition, a crew member acquires causal responsibility for his action and its outcome by virtue of performing that action. (In this example, the deckhand performs the action himself, so he has causal responsibility in addition to his consequential responsibility. However, if the action had been performed by another individual, that individual would be causally responsible.) A possible set of responsibility relationships for a single action is shown in Figure 8.1c.

An interesting case is the situation where the deckhand, who holds the obligation to close the hold doors, omits to perform the action. By virtue of holding this obligation, he holds the associated consequential responsibility for the outcome of the action, so that even although he has not performed the action he is still responsible for the ensuing state of affairs, and would be held negligent for not discharging his obligation.

8.4 MODELLING OF SAFETY-CRITICAL PROCEDURES

In the previous section, we showed how to model responsibilities for safety. However, requirements on a safety-critical system are not determined solely on the basis of analysing where responsibilities lie. A crucial part of many safety procedures is the context in which they occur; that is, the preventive measures often take place as part of a formal social protocol. We shall use the term 'conversation' to refer to such formal social exchanges.

There are a number of important entities and relations surrounding the idea of a conversation which we have explained elsewhere [Dobson 1990], and which are summarized in Figure 8.2.

There are three main types of entity in the language: Information or Resource Structures, Conversations, and Parties.

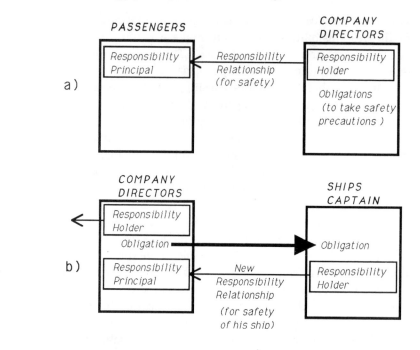

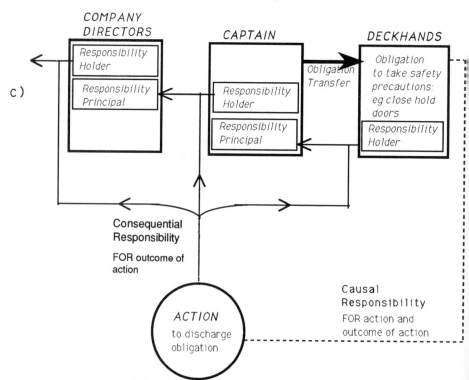

Figure 8.1: The responsibility relationships associated with an action.

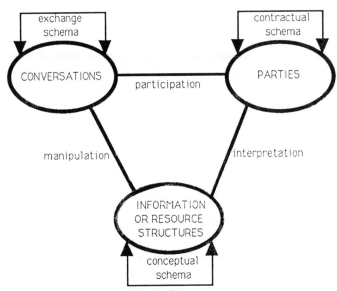

Figure 8.2: Basic entities and relations of a language for modelling conversations.

(i) **Information or Resource Structures**
In the case of information, these are conventional file or database structures. These structures therefore contain what is often referred to as 'data'. For convenience, we shall refer to this entity as 'information', though strictly speaking we are thinking of it in this context as a structured set of containers rather than as an interpretation of the contents of the containers. Other kinds of resource can similarly be related to each other, e.g. through relations such as 'part of' or 'requires'. 'Represents' is a typical relation binding an information structure to a resource.

(ii) **Conversations**
The role of conversations will be described later in this section.

(iii) **Parties**
These correspond to the agents in an enterprise model such as that described in our previous work [Dobson and McDermid 1989]. We use the word 'party' rather than 'agent' because we are here working in what is sometimes referred to as the information projection rather than the enterprise projection. (For an explanation of these terms, and their use as languages, see for example [ANSA 1989].)

Between these three types of entity there are six possible relations:

(i) **Information /resource - information/resource**
This is what is often referred to as the *conceptual schema*.

(ii) **Party - party**
The relation between parties is described in terms of the role relations between them, e.g. customer-supplier, client-server, colleague-colleague, etc. The set of these relations we call the contractual schema.

(iii) **Conversation - conversation**
Conversations can refer to each other, and one conversation can be dependent on another. The set of relations and dependencies between conversations we call the exchange schema.

(iv) **Party - information/resource**
Parties both access and interpret information. Rules can be expressed over which parties are allowed to access and interpret what information (as opposed to merely accessing it). For example, a secretary who reads a letter on behalf of a principal is certainly to be given access to the information; but in so far as the secretary is merely (so to speak) part of the access path, any interpretation by the secretary has no validity or authority as seen by the organization.

(v) **Party - conversation**
Parties participate in a conversation. Rules can be expressed over which parties can participate in which conversations, and with what powers and authorities.

(vi) **Conversation - information/resource**
Conversations manipulate information and information structures. (Manipulation includes the passive case of merely referring to information.) This means that information systems also participate in conversations, as when a secretary updates a database. This can be seen either as an abstract conversation between the secretary and a principal who later refers to the database, or as an abstract conversation between the secretary and the DBMS which would include such things as checks on the authority to access and update. Both views are, of course, equally valid; the relation between them is a relation between conversations and, hence, part of the exchange schema.

By examining the conversations that refer to each resource, we can determine the contexts of failure modes associated with it. In particular, by examining the conversations related to safety procedures, we can determine what resources each party needs to access, and in what circumstances, and so analyse the safety-critical failure modes. For example, in the case of the ship disaster, we might discover that a particular conversation, held prior to departure and referring to the hold doors, was a simplex (one-way) conversation ('Close the hold doors') with no positive acknowledgement ('Hold doors closed, Sir'). Such a conversation has a number of obvious safety-critical failure modes. Further analysis would also point out that this conversation gains its validity from the supervisor-subordinate relation between the captain and the deckhand (a passenger is under no obligation to close the hold doors even if ordered to do so by the captain, though it might be unwise to refuse or ignore the order), and that the conversation itself only makes sense in the context of a larger set of conversations concerned with preparing the ship for sea.

8.5 RESPONSIBILITIES AND CONVERSATIONS: A FRAMEWORK FOR SAFETY POLICIES

The development of supposedly safe socio-technical systems has not always been very successful, as many notorious disasters attest. Many of the problems, though, have been self-inflicted, sometimes by the policy authorities, but mainly by the technologists who have concentrated on modelling and analysing the technical aspects while ignoring the social ones. Technologists know how to analyse technical systems for technical failure; the problem is knowing how to analyse human systems for human failure, since the most critical safety failures have been those involving human error. By finding a different basis for models and methods of analysing requirements, we can provide an opportunity for better socio-technical systems designs.

As a starting point, safety should be modelled in terms of expected behaviour - or, more accurately, safety violations are modelled as deviations from expected behaviour. We are thus primarily concerned with modelling (un)expected behaviour in the human activity system as well as (un)expected mechanical behaviour in the technical system. But the important point is that, in the human activity system, safety procedures are not just concerned with performing appropriate safety-critical actions and preventive measures; they are also concerned with creating authorizations (the state of the ship has been checked as seaworthy, so it is authorized to leave port), honouring obligations (the master is obliged to remain on the bridge while the ship gets under way), and discharging responsibilities (the deckhand is responsible for closing the hold doors). Safety service specifications must therefore identify authorizations, obligations and responsibilities, and consequently reflect aspects of the organization (e.g. roles, authority structures, etc.) needed to articulate what constitutes expected behaviour. The technologists' failure is often in determining or understanding these organizational requirements.

There is a major difference between the processes of *capturing, eliciting* and *generating* requirements on a socio-technical system, and they require different kinds of models and support. Capturing requirements assumes that requirements are explicitly available, there for specifying; eliciting requirements is a matter of making explicit what is implicit; and generating requirements, which in our experience is the most common of these processes, cannot even assume that requirements are initially present, even implicitly.

The role of policy models (e.g. a model of a safety policy) in each of these processes, as applied to the requirements, is also correspondingly different. In the case of capturing requirements, requirements are mapped on to the model; in the case of eliciting requirements, the model is used to determine to what extent requirements can be mapped on to it; and in the case of generating requirements, the model is used to create an agenda for debate about what form the requirements might possibly take. This suggests that the kind of safety policy model that would be appropriate for any particular development or organizational system depends on the nature of the requirements process deployed during the development process. We shall therefore concentrate on the *process* of constructing a safety policy model, rather than on the model's attributes as a product or logical construct. This process has a generic form which will now be described.

First, use the conceptual model of responsibilities to construct a network of responsibilities and obligations, including the relevant actions and resources. This is needed to gain a clear picture of the authorization structures needed to bring this network into operation.

Starting from responsibilities is crucial, which is why this chapter has concentrated on showing how responsibilities and obligations might be modelled. Alternative starting points, such as activities or information (data) models far too frequently lead, in our experience, to conceptual models which, although they can be represented in a machine, somehow seem to act against organizational objectives and are widely perceived by their users as restrictive or even oppressive rather than supportive, particularly in situations - and there are always such situations - not foreseen by the designers.

Second, use the conceptual model of conversations to examine the conversations through which these obligations and responsibilities are established, invoked, and discharged. (See [Dobson 1992] for more details of this.)

The two-sided nature of a conversation model is crucial. It is all too easy to overlook the fact that all actions have a cause and an effect, that information is a medium of exchange, that responsibility is held *by* someone *to* someone. An adequate safety policy model must be able to represent fully this relational nature of its fundamental concepts.

Finally, avoid premature formalization.

In a sense, it is almost too easy to invent elegant new logical models of safety. It is also easier to *apply* a logical model *to* an organization's requirements than it is to *determine* the logical model *of* an organization's requirements. The hard part of modelling is to answer the following questions:

- What are the organization's objectives, its fundamental values, its criteria for evaluating its own failures? For example, a financial institution may prefer to insure against or recompense certain kinds of loss rather than prevent them, since its fundamental perspective is one of financial trade-offs.

- How can the answer to the above questions be conceptualized, i.e. what are the basic entities, attributes, and relations in terms of which the conceptual models will be constructed? For example, creating a logic and proving that an implementation is in conformance with it, is essentially a technique of fault prevention. However, an organization that is structured to deal with insurance and compensation is essentially an organization that values fault tolerance (forward error recovery), and any conceptual models that are formalized must be able to express concepts appropriate to an idealized fault-tolerant system; most logics fail this requirement. (See [Dobson and Randell 1986] for further discussion of the application of fault-tolerance to secure systems design.)

We have made a number of (unpublished) attempts to formalize our concepts of responsibility and obligations, and also of conversations. They still remain unpublished not only because the formalisms and logics were basically uninteresting and told us nothing we did not already know, but also because the attempt led us too far away from trying to understand the way the concepts worked *in the context of the organizations we were studying*. Forcing a problem to be expressed in terms of its solution may sometimes produce a good solution to the problem as stated, but not usually to the real (or whole) problem. That is why any conceptual model of safety must be largely based on a model of safety as part of a process in the human activity system, and not merely as a model of safety as an attribute of a technical system; and it is our belief that the concepts of responsibilities, obligations, and conversations are basic to the kind of process model required.

8.6 ACKNOWLEDGMENTS

This work has been undertaken as part of the ORDIT project supported by the CEC ESPRIT programme. It is a pleasure to acknowledge the contributions of our many colleagues on the project, and also of John McDermid.

8.7 REFERENCES

[ANSA 1989]   ANSA: "ANSA Reference Manual, Release 01.00." Architecture Project Management Ltd., Cambridge, 1989.

[Beer 1981]   Beer S: "The Brain of the Firm." J Wiley & Sons, 1981.

[Checkland 1981]   Checkland P: "Systems Thinking, Systems Practice." J. Wiley & Sons, 1981.

[Dobson 1990]   Dobson J E: "Conversation Structures as an Instrument of Security Policy." Database Security: Status and Prospects III, ed. D. L. Spooner and C. E. Landwehr, pp. 25-40, North-Holland, Amsterdam, 1990.

[Dobson 1992]   Dobson J E: "Information and Denial of Service." Database Security: Status and Prospects V, ed. C. E. Landwehr and S. Jajodia, Elsevier Science Publishers, Amsterdam, 1992 (in press).

[Dobson and McDermid 1989] Dobson J E and McDermid J A: "Security Models and Enterprise Models." Database Security: Status and Prospects II, ed. C. E. Landwehr, pp. 1-39, North-Holland, Amsterdam, 1989.

[Dobson and Randell 1986]   Dobson J E and Randell B: "Building Reliable Secure Systems out of Unreliable Insecure Components." Proc. Conf. on Security and Privacy, Oakland, IEEE, 1986.

[Eason 1989]   Eason K: "Information Technology and Organisational Change." Taylor and Francis, London, 1989.

[Galer and Taylor 1989]   Galer M D and Taylor B C: "Human Factors in Information Technology: ESPRIT Project 385 HUFIT." Contemporary Ergonomics 1989, ed. E. Megaw, Taylor and Francis, London, 1989.

[Harker 1987]   Harker S D P: "Classifying the Target for Human Factors Output." Alvey Annual Conference, UMIST, Manchester, 1987.

[Mumford 1983]   Mumford E: "Designing Human Systems." Manchester Business School Publications, Manchester, 1983.

[Pava 1983]   Pava C: "Managing New Office Technology: An Organisational Strategy." New York Free Press, New York, 1983.

[Rice 1958]   Rice A K: "Productivity and Social Organisation." Tavistock, London, 1958.

[Schneiderman 1986] Schneiderman B: "Designing the User Interface." Addison-Wesley, Wokingham, 1986.

PART THREE
EDUCATION AND TRAINING

9

Target qualities of safety professionals

Denis Jackson

9.1 INTRODUCTION

This chapter is not about training; rather, it is about the required personal qualities which should be developed by training. Nor are these qualities all of a technical nature.

The chapter covers the following issues:

- Why education and training are difficult issues at present;
- The many qualities likely to be required of safety-critical practitioners;
- The profiles of qualities likely to be required for various roles;
- The assessment and accreditation of courses;
- Expedient ways forward;
- The need for indoctrination of users and the general public.

9.2 EDUCATION AND TRAINING - DIFFICULT ISSUES

Past initiatives in the safety-critical sector have considered education and training without a clear idea of the true requirements of regulatory authorities, purchasers, suppliers, users and, especially, the needs of those who have to pay. To my mind, this 'cart before the horse' attitude may have resulted in nugatory effort being expended and may even have pre-judged issues and served to obscure requirements.

Safety-critical education and training also seems destined to run the gauntlet of a number of obstacles before the required qualities can be developed in practitioners. The obstacles seem to be:

(i)   That practitioners are individuals and have many existing and relevant qualities;
(ii)   That organizations are disparate and contain different sets of individuals;
(iii)   The difficulty and expense of gaining operational experience;
(iv)   Matching ideals to what is affordable;
(v)   Relations between supply, demand, and returns on investment;
(vi)   The complexity and obscurity of regulatory systems;
(vii)   The immaturity of most safety-critical standards;
(viii) Poor definition of safety awareness and professional ethics;
(ix)   The limited experience and vested interests of academia;
(x)   Poor management understanding of the high technologies involved, particular software management.

I admire the courage of those who attempt to design training schemes for safety-critical practitioners: however, I shall content myself with the task of attempting to clarify the requirements for such training.

9.3   SAFETY-CRITICAL ROLES

Examination of some established and draft safety-critical standards, such as those of IEC TC65A, Defence Standards 00-55/56, RTCA DO-178A, RIA 23, and IEEE standards, shows that there are many overlapping roles. In addition, there are some obvious tasks to be performed by unspecified but commonly accepted roles. Summarizing those roles into generic groups results in the following analysis:

(i)   Safety Regulation   8 roles
(ii)   Procurement   10 roles
(iii)   System assessment   8 roles
(iv)   Design and Proving   11 roles
(v)   Expert Consultants   2 roles

From the point of view of training, some of these roles are so similar that they can be addressed by the same training course, but there is still a need for a comparatively large number of courses. My tentative conclusion is that some ten one-week technical modules and eight semi-technical modules would be necessary. This is approximately in line with a conclusion of the CITI report [Youll 88] which was commissioned by the Ministry of Defence in respect of an early version of their Interim Defence Standard 00-55 [MOD 91a].

9.4 QUALITIES REQUIRED

I would summarize the desirable qualities as being:

(i)   Safety awareness;
(ii) Familiarity with user operations and their hazard analysis;
(iii) Familiarity with regulatory systems, standards, and codes of practice;
(iv) High-technology design and development;
(v)   System proving and auditor qualities;
(vi) Motivation and safety ethical behaviour.

Each of these qualities will be amplified under subsequent sub-headings.

9.4.1 Safety Awareness

The Ministry of Defence requires its tenderers for safety-critical systems to provide 'reasonable evidence that there is an awareness of safety throughout their organization' [MOD 91a (Clause 9a)]. Safety awareness is not defined, but it may be helpful for me to suggest that tenderers should offer some or all of the following types of evidence:

(i)   Management commitment to safety, e.g. through a policy statement;
(ii)   Recognition of the need for a disciplined workplace, such as would be found in an organization approved to a good quality standard;
(iii) Use of adequate design safety margins to allow for uncertainty;
(iv)   Recognition of threats to safety;
(v)   Recognition of vulnerabilities;
(vi)   Sensible priorities for limited resources;
(vii) Measures of the extent of safety awareness, e.g. whether it is confined to one or two individuals or a specialist department; or pervades the entire workforce and all departments;
(viii) Records of past experiences which stimulated fear, the imagination, and a healthy respect for threats.

9.4.2 Familiarity With User Operations

The training of users of safety-critical systems is nearly always expensive, and, were it not so, safety would be undervalued. To refresh or consolidate that training is also expensive, and even to acquire a superficial familiarity may take time and money.

Therefore, users sometimes find a second career in safety issues by exploiting their knowledge of user operations. However, it is only fair to point out that even very good operators do not always make good abstract thinkers and planners.

As regards the value of superficial familiarity, the charge that 'a little knowledge is a dangerous thing' may be valid, but it depends upon the individual concerned and upon his sense of ethics and of his personal limitations. The positive value of 'talking the language', and thus avoiding misunderstandings of needs and of specified requirements, may be sufficient justification for attempting some familiarity. Safety-critical practitioners should at least be motivated and willing to make the effort.

9.4.3 Hazard Analysis

The person who carries out a hazard analysis may have the technique prescribed by the relevant regulatory authority, or he may have to select his own method. Therefore he needs a good command of the methodology of hazard analysis.

A broad classification of the subjects of hazard analysis could be :

(i)   Operational systems, which may include
(ii)   Computer-based systems, including
(iii) Equipment and software, although the software by itself is incapable of being a hazard.

Examples of appropriate hazard analysis techniques include Fault Tree Analysis (FTA) for operational systems [MOD 41 (Part 4, Sect B), IEC 1025], Defence Standards 00-31 [MOD 87], 00-56 [MOD 91c] and RTCA DO-178A [RTCA 85] for computer-based aviation systems, and Defence Standard 00-41 [MOD 41] for hardware.

An important and often overlooked function of hazard analysis is the polarization of borderline hazards. Nobody minds expending effort on parts of a system which are clearly critical, but all too many hazards are borderline cases and the hazard analyst's efforts will be particularly appreciated if he can produce convincing arguments for polarizing such cases one way or the other.

Other benefits from hazard analysis include a complete and objective understanding of the operation, from which the analyst may be able to make constructive suggestions which will contribute to safety.

Thus the hazard analyst needs special qualities, including an ethical approach, as will be discussed later.

9.4.4 Familiarity With Regulatory Systems

The regulatory authority appropriate to a particular user operation is not always easy to identify, nor is the directive, system or procedures which should be followed. The regulatory system will usually invoke standards and hazard analysis techniques with which the safety-critical practitioner must become familiar.

Good knowledge of any regulatory system will be useful and will facilitate assimilation of new systems.

Particularly valuable is a good understanding of any flexibility which may be permissible in the safety case to be presented. Such flexibility should not be exploited to take short cuts which may jeopardize safety, but skilful interpretation can minimize the costs of assuring safety and complying with standards. It is noteworthy that some regulatory authorities, such as the Civil Aviation Authority [Sec. of State 86 (sub-paragraphs (a) i and ii)], have a directive to be economic in their regulatory systems, while others are assumed to be seeking safety almost regardless of the realities of costs.

9.4.5 Standards/Codes of Practice

Safety 'standards' are seldom standards but, more usually, codes of practice requiring or permitting some interpretation. They are often 'moving targets', in that they are judged against changing political, economic, cultural and professional attitudes.

Professionals must have a good understanding of relevant standards, but, unfortunately, standards tend to be dull reading, and no little dedication is necessary if they are to be assimilated.

Unfortunately also:

(i)   Standards-making is a ponderous process and lags behind technology;
(ii) '....the most competent people are not always involved' [ACARD 86 (Para 5.26)].

9.4.6 High-Technology Design and Development

In modern systems, complex logic, including software, is often inescapable. Moreover, software generally has a poor record of reliability. When it is safety-critical, some safety-critical practitioners may have to be expert in software development practices.

Additional requirements are for advanced techniques of:

(i)   Requirements specification;
(ii)   Hazard analysis;
(iii) Configuration management;
(iv)   System proving, possibly involving the use of Formal Methods.

Unfortunately, senior managers are often weak on the management of complex software, especially for safety-critical applications. This is particularly unfortunate as, in the opinion of the author, compromize decisions have to be made in order to manage complexity. By the 'management of complexity', I mean the voluntary limitation of complex design features in order to minimize vulnerable features or facilitate the proving of safety-critical logic. Modern software packages, in particular, contain many features which are superfluous to a particular application and could therefore be a source of unreliability. This has to be offset against the advantages of 'off the shelf' (OTS) software, which may claim above-average reliability and trustedness because of its maturity.

Another managerial decision concerns investment in education and training, and such decisions require good understanding of the development processes involved, possibly on an international scale, and of the likely technical and financial returns from investment.

9.4.7 System Proving

System proving is one of the most technically demanding aspects of safety-critical work, and one which stimulates a continuing demand for education and training. The techniques of system proving may be laid down by a regulatory authority and supported by standards, but the system-prover is usually left to select his own tools. Needless to say, this requires a good general command of what tools are available and their respective strengths and weaknesses. Training in specific tools is one obvious recurring training need.

Testing is a fundamental source of confidence in a system and is likely to be required by purchasers, suppliers and regulatory authorities alike. The balance between normal system testing, overseen by QA authorities, and more rigorous system proving, needs to be agreed between the many interested parties at an early stage of a project because it will affect needs for education and training. Testing strategies agreed in this way need to recognize the practices and cultures already existing within the organizations concerned: new techniques may be 'better', but their adoption may be counter-productive in terms of safety and cost.

Safety-critical practitioners also need to keep abreast of the developing topic of reliability and safety metrics, which may beneficially be applied to complete systems, rather than to selected critical sub-sets, if the necessary tools are available.

There is a tendency for some practitioners to concentrate on the mechanistic proving of reliability in terms of the integrity of system outputs and the expectation of their continued availability. However, Reliability and Safety are not synonymous, since the latter depends upon, for example, relatively ill-defined human factors which must therefore be considered in hazard analyses.

9.4.8 Formal Methods

Much has been said and written about Formal (i.e. mathematical) Methods of specification, refinement and system proving, and confused ideas abound. In so far as education and training are affected, it should be pointed out that there are at least 50 formal notations and variations, but little method associated with them. Some are much more popular than others, but only three are standardized or near to being standardized. Therefore, it is hard for any organisation, be it a supplier, purchaser, regulatory authority, or consultancy, to know where best to invest in training.

Once an organization has some commitment to a particular Formal Notation or Method, specialized training is likely to be needed by some part of the workforce. With the present low level of safety-critical work recognized generally, few organisations could justify more than, say, 1 per cent of their workforce to be so trained; the notable exceptions being in the avionic and nuclear industries. Even so, it should be possible to distinguish between those individuals who need to be creative designers and manipulators of formal expressions and those who need only to have the ability to interpret the meanings of such expressions.

Despite the undoubted rigour of Formal Methods, and the heavy backing by MOD Defence Standard 00-55 [MOD 91a and 91b] and by the Defence Research Agency, industry has practical doubts. In this respect, the following questions are pertinent:

(i)   Can Formal Methods be applied on the scale likely to be required?
(ii)   Can we afford to abandon techniques which have been adequate in the past?
(iii) Can a safety benefit be guaranteed?

Such reservations need to be resolved before much investment can be committed to education and training.

There is a tendency for consumers and providers to think in terms of training, but the acquisition of real skills with Formal Methods may depend on an adequate educational background in formal mathematics. Such a background was once the province of a select few, mostly academics, but under the current educational system, the necessary foundations are being laid even in schools, and many graduates now qualify with an understanding of Formal Methods. Thus, while the longer-term future of Formal Methods education and training seems to be assured, there remains the short-term problem of supplementing the knowledge of key practitioners in the existing workforce.

9.4.9 Auditor Qualities

Some roles of safety-critical practitioners require that the work of others be audited or that the systems by which they work be assessed. The qualities required of auditors should include most, if not all, of the following:

(i)   Adequate knowledge and experience of the managerial and technical aspects of the proposed audit, including the methods, tools, and

procedures in use;
(ii)   The determination to find necessary objective evidence;
(iii)   The experience and tact to facilitate its discovery;
(iv)   Judgement of the completeness or incompleteness of the evidence;
(v)   Sound judgement of the acceptability of the evidence;
(vi)   Objective and constructive reporting.

Qualification criteria for quality auditors are being developed as an International Standard. However, there is a major ethical difference between quality and safety auditors: Quality Assurance must be economic, and a sample check is easily justified, but safety requires more exhaustive auditing, even in today's climate of stringent economy and fixed-price contracting.

Strangely, the only mention of training in Defence Standard 00-55 concerns the training of Independent Safety Auditors [MOD 91b (Clause 16.1.2)]. Few of the above qualities are mentioned, but it is suggested that Chartered Engineer status and a minimum of five years' experience of safety-critical software implementation would be appropriate experience.

9.4.10 Motivation

It is important that management motivates its staff who are engaged in safety-critical systems work, even though their precise activities are not judged to be safety-critical. Clear lines of demarcation cannot be drawn, and safety-critical activities must not be jeopardized by lack of motivation in supporting staff.

It is suggested that, in the context of safety, motivation means:

(i)   Taking an interest in safety;
(ii)   Taking pride in achieving safety;
(iii)   Fear of failing to achieve safety;
(iv)   A determination to update knowledge;
(v)   A conviction of good career prospects in safety-critical and reliable systems.

Regarding the updating of knowledge, the safe and reliable systems field is likely to be evolving rapidly for the foreseeable future, so that training courses are unlikely to be kept completely up-to-date. Therefore, the true professional will be self-motivated to maintain his understanding of current thinking, preferably on an international scale.

Demotivating factors include:

(i)   Safety-critical work is spread very thinly over the existing purchasers, suppliers, regulatory authorities, etc., so that few of those organizations have much opportunity to develop true professionalism;
(ii)   Suppliers' and users' liabilities under European Community and UK legislation are very extensive and may be unavoidable, with little

compensating return for the risk and the investment of money and valuable human effort;

(iii) Organizations and individuals may be judged culpable in criminal and civil actions;

(iv) Those actions could be heard not only in UK courts but also in foreign courts under foreign legislation;

(v) It may be difficult to insure safety-critical practitioners against such claims, and they may not have the comfort of an indemnity from their employers;

(vi) Staff may be attracted by other sectors of industry requiring high reliability systems but primarily motivated by factors other than safety, for example, security, economics, and the need to comply with the law.

9.4.11 Safety Ethical Behaviour

Safety ethical behaviour is currently ill-defined, but it covers the duty of corporate bodies and individuals towards the public, the environment, the employer, and colleagues. Issues of loyalties, priorities, conflicts of interest, and incompatible requirements inevitably arise and should ideally have been anticipated and planned in a promulgated code of practice.

There is a great need for such codes of practice, and some are emerging in a hierarchy which, in its ideal form, would resemble the following order of preference:

International
European
National
Professional Bodies
    (examples of which are:
    Engineering Council [EC 91];
    IEE Bye-law 42;
    RAeS Bye-law 4)
Sector
Local Corporate
Departmental
Project

The professional institutions have always taken a lead in defining professional ethics, including those relating to safety, but The Engineering Council has specifically addressed safety and environmental risk issues in its *Embryo Code of Practice* [EC 91]. The latter identifies ten desirable non-technical practices to be followed, and it continues with a statement of the promotional actions required by companies, individuals, professional bodies, educationalists, Government and The Engineering Council itself.

Doubtless, the professional bodies affiliated to the Council will amplify their Bye-Laws and Codes of Practice accordingly.

The status of Chartered Engineers is interesting in that some professional bodies **require** them to observe **all** the Rules, whilst other grades of members may only be required to observe **some** of the rules.

Codes of Practice should include remedial procedures for resolving ethical problems.

9.5   ROLE PROFILES

There are many different roles in the safety-critical field, and different authorities frequently use the same role-name for different functions. Perhaps the best example of this is the role of 'project manager', which varies considerably according to whether it represents a system supplier, a system purchaser, or the organizer of a large programme. One is forced to invent a large number of different mixtures of qualities for the role of project manager in different circumstances. In practice the roles differ in the extent to which some qualities are not essential.

From the point of view of training, the extent to which a quality must be developed influences the content, duration and affordability of a course. But the measurement of the effectiveness of training is a problem: there are few metrics of the extent of development of an individual's qualities. It is largely a matter of subjective judgement by peers. In Figure 9.1, I present my personal assessment of the qualities required by two kinds of project manager, with the extent of each quality needed being indicated by the

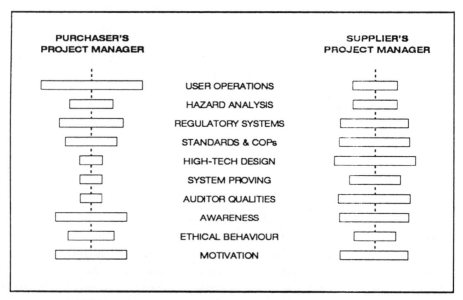

Figure 9.1: Role profiles.

width of its bar.

The roles of a purchaser's and a supplier's project manager are compared. Both need to have similarly developed qualities of awareness, ethical behaviour and motivation, although it is likely that these will be applied in different ways. The supplier's project manager will be a technician who has risen through the ranks and has a good command of modern system-design and proving techniques, whereas the purchaser's representative is unlikely to be so qualified and has no need to be. Both roles find common ground in their need to understand the regulatory system through which their system will be certified as fit for service, but the supplier will probably need deeper knowledge of mandatory and desirable standards. The purchaser's project manager should be quite an authority on the operational environment of the system and its likely use: his opposite number may have less operational knowledge and experience, but to have little or none would bring into question the competence of the supplier.

9.6 AN EXPEDIENT WAY FORWARD

If a large number of safety-critical practitioners were to be required tomorrow, it would be logical to harness the disparate expertise of existing practitioners to the best effect. I suggest that the top priority should be given to 'crash courses' designed to standardize each individual's approach to his designated role. Longer term actions would then seek to bring his technical competence up to the required standard.

There are several existing schemes which might be applied to safety-

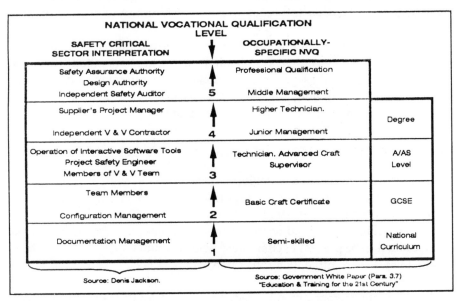

Figure 9.2: Safety-critical national vocational qualifications.

critical training, one of which is the Government's White Paper 'Education and Training for the 21st Century' [Dept. of Ed. 91]. I would like to make three points about this document.

(i)   At first sight, the White Paper seems to cater mainly for the 16 to 19 year old age group, but this is no bad thing if the future of the safety-critical industry is to be assured;

(ii)   On closer inspection, it can be seen that provision has been made for adult education, and that a comprehensive range of National Vocational Qualifications (NVQs) are envisaged (see Para 3.7);

(iii)   The NVQs need to be interpreted for the safety-critical area, and if our community takes this initiative and the Government fulfils its apparent intentions, we have a vehicle for future training. Figure 9.2 suggests a possible interpretation of NVQs for the safety-critical sector.

9.7   COURSE ACCREDITATION

Once courses are in place, there comes a need for monitoring, accreditation, improvement, and updating of each course. This involves comparison of the training requirement, as represented by the qualities outlined in this paper and the training syllabi eventually developed, and the results actually achieved. The White Paper [Dept. of Ed. 91] refers to this as Quality Assurance and sees it as the responsibility of colleges, examining bodies, Councils, and external assessors. The main sources of this quality assurance expertise were named as Her Majesty's Inspectorate and the LEA advisers, but I suggest that the safety-critical community is so specialized that it would be well advised to prepare itself for a monitoring and accrediting role.

The qualification of a practitioner needs to be recognized by some form of certificate, which implies examinations and arguments about their real significance. I favour 'essay' type questions as likely to reveal a candidate's command of a searching topic. As regards the standing of a particular certificate, the marketplace will be the ultimate judge.

9.8   INDOCTRINATION OF USERS AND THE GENERAL PUBLIC

Although this may seem a novel form of training, and somewhat tangential to the main topic of training safety-critical practitioners, it seems to be a necessary complement for three reasons.

Firstly, there is the need to stimulate safety-consciousness, which cannot be assumed to be present even in those who encounter specific risks in their daily lives. For example, vigorous safety campaigns have been mounted in the aviation sectors, including confidential incident reporting schemes where human factors are involved, and have reduced already low risk levels to even lower achieved levels; and this despite the increasing complexity of modern operational systems.

Secondly, it seems only right to inform users and the general public of the risks which they may face, and of the underlying threats and inherent system vulnerabilities. The Air Transport and railway industries, despite their superb safety records, are understandably reluctant to alarm their travelling publics. Similarly, the Nuclear industries assume that the public will over-react to their relatively intangible risks. However, there could be compensating benefits for providing such information, in that the industries would be better able, in the event of litigation, to invoke the legal defence of *volentia non fit injuria* ('to the willing is done no injury'). That defence might be valid if it could be shown that an injured party was both understanding of the risks involved and voluntarily accepting of them.

Thirdly, the youthful public, and their parents, need to be convinced that there is a worthwhile career in safety-critical systems: otherwise, recruitment will suffer, and the existing situation of an ageing and increasingly expensive workforce will not be alleviated.

9.9   CONCLUSION

I am painfully aware that this chapter does not constitute a detailed training requirement, but I hope that it will form a well-rounded basis, including some less-obvious features, from which training professionals can develop usable requirements and training schemes. However, the latter will need much discussion if they are to be acceptable to regulatory authorities, users, purchasers, suppliers, and the third parties likely to be involved.

9.10   REFERENCES

[ACARD 86]   UK Cabinet Office: "Software: A Vital Key to UK Competitiveness." Advisory Council for Applied Research and Development (ACARD) Report, HMSO, 1986.

[Dept. of Ed. 91]   UK Department of Education and Welsh Office: "Education and Training for the 21st Century." Cmmd 1536, HMSO, August 1991.

[EC 91]   THE Engineering Council: "Engineers and Risk Issues". An embryo Code of Practice issued for comment, 1991.

[IEC 1025]   International Electrotechnical Commission: "Fault Tree Analysis."   IEC 1025.

[MOD 41]   UK Ministry of Defence: "Defence Standard 00-41, MoD Practices and Procedures for Reliability and Maintainability." (Issued in 6 parts).

[MOD 87]   UK Ministry of Defence: "Interim Defence Standard 00-31, The Development of Safety-Critical Software for Airborne Systems." Issue 1, 3 July 1987.

[MOD 91a]   UK Ministry of Defence: "Interim Defence Standard 00-55, The Procurement of Safety-Critical Software in Defence Equipment - Part 1: Requirements."   Issue 1, 5 April 1991.

[MOD 91b]   Idem: "Part 2: Guidance."   Issue 1, 5 April 1991.

[MOD 91c]   UK Ministry of Defence: "Interim Defence Standard 00-56, Hazard Analysis and Safety Classification of the Computer and Programmable Electronic System Elements of Defence Equipment."   Issue 1, 5 April 1991.

[RTCA 85]   US RTCA: "Software Considerations in Airborne Systems and Equipment Certification."   Doc. RTCA/DO-178A, 22 March 1985.

[Sec. of State 86]   UK Secretary of State for Transport: "Civil Aviation Authority: Chairman's Objectives."   Letter to the Chairman, CAA, 24 July 1986.

[Youll 88]   Youll D P and Simms P G: "Study of the Training and Education Needed in Support of Def Stan 00-55." Cranfield Information Technology Institute Ltd., 16 September 1988.

10

Organization of industrial training

David Thewlis

10.1 INTRODUCTION

The purpose of this chapter is to discuss some of the factors which affect decisions within companies on when and whether to train their staff. The chapter is more general than safety-critical computing; it also applies to other kinds of training. In it I shall touch on three questions. First, decisions on what training should be given; second, the organizational factors which encourage or discourage training activities; and, finally, the type of training which works in an organization whose main objective is undertaking projects. It is this type of organization which ought to supply most of the customers for training in safety-critical computing.

10.2 WHY TRAIN ENGINEERS?

It is necessary to have a licence to practise many professions or trades. Estate agents, travel agents, even publicans and tobacconists have to have a licence in order to practise their trades. In each case there is a body empowered to grant licences, there are specific conditions which must be satisfied before a licence can be granted, and there exists a mechanism for withdrawing the licence should the conditions become unsatisfied.

In the cases of airline pilots, medical doctors, lawyers, and teachers, a necessary requirement is that the individual should undertake an appropriately accredited training course and pass the examination at the end. An appropriately accredited training course is one which teaches a specified curriculum with suitable controls on the quality of the teachers and teaching. For these professions, decisions about training become simple: the accredited courses are taken and the appropriate exams passed. The effort required to take the course and pass the exam, together with the responsibility of holding the licence, welds the people who have acquired the licence into a group, proud of themselves and their profession. Enough people come forward to man the committees which ensure that the curriculum remains up to date. There is peer pressure to maintain standards.

Doctors, lawyers, accountants and such professionals are recognized as having respectability and authority. People have been sent to jail for impersonating a doctor. Has anyone been sent to jail for impersonating an engineer? A recent letter in the *IEE News* concerned acceptable signatories to verify identity. The approved list was Public Notary, Justice of the Peace (JP), medical practitioner, accountant and lawyer. Engineer was not mentioned. Perhaps engineers think of themselves as forming a profession, but does anyone else? For most branches of engineering, there is no concept of a licence to practise.

Anyone can be an engineer. The control exercised by the engineering institutions over who can join their institution is not strong compared to that exercised by accountants, lawyers and doctors over who can practise their professions. And lack of membership of an engineering institution is no bar to practising as an engineer and being called an engineer.

The question of whether engineering can be considered a profession comparable to medicine or school teaching is not the purpose of this chapter. But the looseness of the definition of an engineer is a problem: if we do not know what an engineer is, how can we determine what such an individual should know? How do we convince an accountant to spend money on teaching them whatever it is we need them to know?

For safety-critical engineering, the situation is not consistent across different engineering disciplines. Some types of mining and civil engineering works have to be signed off by a 'responsible person'; and 'responsible person' has a legal definition: it results, in effect, in a licence to practice. It is unlikely, but not illegal, that the senior person responsible for the design of a power station should not be a member of a recognized engineering institution. But for safety-critical software it is both possible and likely that the software engineers have no recognized engineering qualification.

This is disquieting for many reasons. In the context of this chapter, the lack of the requirement for a licence to practise safety-critical software engineering has an impact on the decisions which companies make about training.

The issue of what should be taught is taken up in other chapters in this book - in particular, Chapters 11 and 13. Much of this may be ineffective unless the status and licence issues are tackled simultaneously.

10.3 ORGANIZATIONAL FACTORS

In order to understand the organizational factors which affect decisions about training, it is useful to consider training from the point of view of four parts of an organization: higher management, the trainee's immediate manager, the trainee, and the training department.

Higher management is interested in training. It wants a well trained work force. Some members of higher management may sit on government committees to advise on how UK Ltd gets a better trained work force. It runs a 'people company'. It really does believe that the company's strength is its people.

But the trouble with higher management is that it is interested in everything. Whether training is regarded negatively, as just an overhead, or positively, as an investment in the future, it has to compete for resources against all other possible investments in the future. It has been shown above that a lack of training in safety-critical computing does not disbar a company from having safety-critical computing as part of its business. When funds are tight, or an organization is over-stretched, training can be cancelled or postponed. Management is eager to commit itself to the end - having a well trained work force; but not so eager to provide the means - funds and making people available.

The key individual in the training process is the trainee's manager. Potentially he gains from having one of his people trained: the individual may, eventually, be more useful to him. The gain, however, is problematical, and in the future. The loss is certain and immediate. There is direct delay: while the training course runs, the work the trainee would have done has to be postponed or done by someone else. There is indirect delay: the absence of the trainee can cause other people's work to be disrupted. And there is a re-integration problem: the trainee has to learn what has happened while he was away and re-establish himself as part of the team.

Although funding will always be a problem, the three factors, direct delay, indirect delay and re-integration are more significant. Though the cost of the training course and possibly the individual's time may well be funded; higher management won't cover consequential loss and is reluctant to accept 'training' as an excuse for lateness of the project. Any training plan which fails to take account of these three factors will fail.

The individual being trained must be eager to learn the new skills and capable of learning them. That much is obvious. Without the desire and the capability, the training effort will be nugatory. It is equally important that the trainee make use of the skills immediately upon, or very soon after, his return. Both the company and the trainee gain from this, as it reinforces the training.

The trainee will feel to be a more valuable employee as a result of the training, and this needs some recognition which is not necessarily financial.

Just carrying on from where he was before the training course, as though he had been on holiday, will not do. If the training is not used and not recognized the trainee becomes dissatisfied and is likely to leave the company. Thus, in the less well-run parts of a company, managers will refuse to have their people trained lest it cause people to leave and join their competitors.

The training manager has the awesome responsibility of ensuring that the company achieves and retains a sufficiently well trained work force in spite of the difficulties outlined above. Like any other manager, he will acquire a budget, devise a strategy, and make a plan. The key to success is in knowing the factors which tend to stop training taking place and the factors which may cause it to be of little value. The tactics are to get the company's management committed to the strategy, then to the plan, and then to the implementation of the plan.

Once management are committed, effort is necessary to ensure that they remain committed. All too often a manager agrees in February to release someone for training in September; then finds out in August that releasing that individual next month is going to be rather difficult; then tries to wriggle out of the commitment. The strategy and tactics used by the training manger will depend on the structure of the organization he is serving and its way of working.

The organization of a company and the way in which it works are, in part, determined by what the company is intended to do. In turn, they affect what organization for training is likely to work and what isn't. Here are two contrasting examples.

Figure 10.1 shows part of the management structure of a power station. The objective of the organization is to keep the power station operating.

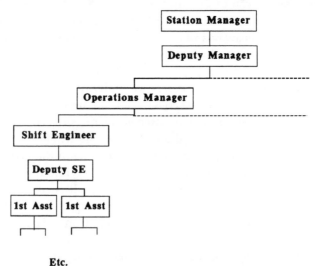

Etc.

Figure 10.1: Everyone has a defined position in a permanent structure.

For the purpose of this chapter, its two major characteristics are stability and the existence of a number of posts with similar job descriptions. The job descriptions are stable, but the personnel must inevitably change: they get promoted, they leave, or they die.

In such a structure, many aspects of staff management can be planned. The jobs can be analysed and the training courses devised and delivered to program. The factors which tend to inhibit training activity can be avoided by careful planning. Delays need not occur, because the trainee can be replaced by an equivalent individual. Re-integration, even after a long absence, is a small problem, as the work situation will not have changed by much. Use of the training should not be a problem, and nor should recognition of the individual's new skill, as the training can be planned to precede a change of role or to contribute to an individual's readiness for promotion.

The structure of a company whose revenue is earned by undertaking projects is shown in Figure 10.2. It is necessarily different from that appropriate for a power station. Its main characteristic is fluidity. Each new project enforces some reorganization, and the evolution of a project forces changes in role if not changes in title. In this environment, planning is a hit-and-miss affair.

In project work, there is no equivalent individual who can replace the trainee: so delays occur. The project moves on while the trainee is being trained, so the trainee requires some time on his return to become acquainted with what has happened. Often the training is not put to use immediately because the project timescales or requirements have changed within the timescale of planning and booking the training course. And recognition by increase of status or change of role can be achieved only within the

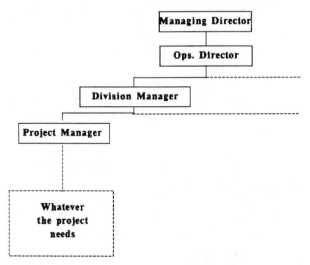

Figure 10.2: Below Division Manager, no one has a permanent role.

constraints of the project.

These are difficulties, not impossibilities. The difficulties become less when everyone concerned with the process understands them and agrees to work round them. Even so, it may be that, on safety-critical computing courses, the proportion of regulators and users is higher than it should be when compared with the proportion of system builders - because system builders have greater difficulties in organizing training than regulators or users.

10.4 ORGANIZATION OF TRAINING

The final part of this chapter deals with how the designers of training courses should organize these courses so that people working for project-oriented organizations can take advantage of them. Various appreciation courses, courses on particular topics, etc., have been proposed as part of what is required in safety-critical engineering training. However, the consensus seems to be that the heart of the matter should be an MSc-level course which could eventually become a requirement for those in senior positions in either building or procuring safety-critical computer systems. It is assumed that the trainees would be engineers with eight or more years' experience.   The detailed curriculum is not the topic of this chapter; organization is.

There are two organizational issues. One is structure and timing, the other is relating the training to the trainee's normal work.

Companies are reluctant to fund full-time MSc courses. The re-integration problem is too severe; it is rarely solved: so many trainees leave the company within three months of finishing the course. A two- or three-year part-time MSc is better: the trainee remains in touch with the company, so the re-integration problem is minimal. But a part-time MSc is a severe commitment. The trainee's total work load is much greater than for either normal work or a full-time MSc, so a company cannot *send* someone on a part time MSc. The usual mechanism is that an individual persuades his company to give time off to attend the course and to pay the fees.

For part-time MScs the initiative has to come from the potential trainee, not the company. Therefore, such courses cannot form the major part of an organization's plans to ensure that it has enough suitably learned safety-critical computing people. A better option is a modular MSc, using distance learning where possible. This has the flexibility to be fitted around project work. Often, a number of people from the same organization can do a module together, and completed modules are of value in themselves before the trainee has finished the full set.

In the fullness of time, when the licensing issues have been sorted out, the acquisition of a few modules could lead to the qualification necessary for a partial licence, restricting the level or type of work the individual would be licensed to do. A part of the course needs to be directly related to the trainee's normal work. Usually this is a project and is best done at the trainee's normal place of work. Finding suitable projects is not easy, but it is essential. The students need the project to relate their academic work to the real world. The teachers need the projects to ensure that the academic content taught by them is of value in the real world.

10.5 SUMMARY

The three points which I wish to conclude this chapter are:

- The licensing issue needs as much attention as devising what should be taught;
- The hidden costs of training - indirect delay and re-integration of the trainee - cause   more difficulties than the obvious costs of the course fee and the individual's time;
- Training has to be organized in modules so that the trainee does not lose touch with his parent organization.

11

The IEE draft policy on educational requirements for safety-critical systems engineers

Andrew McGettrick

11.1 INTRODUCTION

The Safety Critical Systems Committee of the Institution of Electrical Engineers (IEE) has created a Working Party to address the general problem of training and education in this area. A first report has been produced and has the status of a discussion document; it reflects the initial thinking about the stance the IEE should take on this important matter.

In essence the report concludes that:

- All professional engineers should read a professional brief, which has been prepared by the IEE;
- All professional engineers working in the area should undertake a core of training modules which address the issues of the responsibilities and competencies required of all involved in the area;
- Specialist modules can be offered by Higher Education Institutions and it is appropriate to think of these being offered at Masters level.

In addition it is recommended that accreditation committees within IEE should encourage attention to safety issues at an appropriate level.

This chapter presents the findings of the report, and offers insight into the thinking behind its recommendations.

Before embarking on a discussion of the policy of the Institution of

Electrical Engineers (IEE) in the area of safety-critical systems, it is appropriate to place in perspective some of the relevant activities of the Institution.

11.2 ACTIVITIES IN SAFETY-CRITICAL SYSTEMS

Within the Institution there is a Safety Critical Systems Committee (chaired by Dr Phil Bennett) which reports directly to the Public Affairs Board. This Committee spawned several subgroups or working groups to address areas of particular concern.   One of those was set up to address questions of education and training as they relate to safety-critical systems.   The work reported here is an overview of a report produced by this group [IEE 92a]. It must be said that this is an initial report on a continuing activity and the report should be viewed as a discussion document; its preface invites views on the contents, the intention being to learn from these reactions and to modify the report in the light of subsequent discussions.

The members of the working group were: Ron Bell (UK Health and Safety Executive), Bob Malcolm (Malcolm Associates Ltd), Andrew McGettrick (Chairman, University of Strathclyde), and Clive Ross (NEI Parsons).

In addition, mention must be made of the important feedback and continued support from the IEE's Safety Critical Systems Committee and of the support supplied by an enthusiastic Consultative Group composed of parties interested in developments in safety-critical systems.

11.3 IEE VIEW OF SAFETY-CRITICAL SYSTEMS

Central to the IEE position on safety-critical systems is the recognition that safety is a **systems** issue.   In considering safety, it is essential to view the entire system, not one particular aspect of it; often it is the interaction and complementarity of subsystems which are vital.

The fundamental nature of the topic needs to be recognized by all aspiring engineers. Accordingly it is recommended that 'the safety culture' should be included in all undergraduate courses. The consequence of this observation is that accreditation committees should ask questions of course teams with the intention of raising awareness of the topic.

Since IEE members are involved with electronic devices and/or computers - and the IEE must respond to the needs of its members - the main concern of the IEE in the area of safety-critical systems is in the design, construction and maintenance of systems involving these devices. The relevant educational and training requirements must then relate to those who build such systems and are responsible for such activity; in particular the needs of project leaders and managers must not be ignored.

It is relevant to recognize that the use of software in safety-critical systems introduces a new set of concerns.   The potential benefits include a greater degree of flexibility, increased functionality, greater ease of maintenance, the possibility for increased safety, and reduced costs. However the potential is not always realized.   In addition, the characteristics of software produce considerable scope for error, principally due to the limitations of testing and the complex nature of software (and associated errors).

In considering the software of safety-critical systems, it is important to stress the systems context and the systems view.   There is little benefit to an overall system in proving the correctness of a piece of Ada code, for example, if that code is then translated by an unreliable compiler, is otherwise processed by bug-ridden software tools, or allowed to run on unreliable hardware.   There emerges a need for provably correct software, provably correct compilers, provably correct operating systems, provably correct hardware, and management procedures which ensure the necessary adherence to the rigorous requirements of safety.   These stipulations lead in turn to a need for formal languages, formal definition of these languages, and so on.

Recognizing the potential role of formal methods in the development of safety-critical systems, the Safety Critical Systems Committee of the Institution set up a working party with the explicit aim of placing formal methods in perspective.   This report has been published [IEE 91].

11.4 DEVELOPING COURSES - SOME CONSIDERATIONS

It is just not realistic to think in terms of developing a course which covers all aspects of safety-critical systems.   There are a number of factors which suggest this view:

(i)   Courses need to be broadly based, covering such matters as the legal frame-work, the technical framework, and standards, as well as theory and practice;

(ii)   In one course it is not sensible to try to cover all the technical material related to safety - software engineering, chemical engineering, medical topics, and so on;

(iii)   The very necessity to compartmentalize and address a relatively narrow technical area itself holds dangers; often interfaces are where potential hazards reside.

Having mentioned these considerations, it does seem desirable and important that all well-conceived courses should share a common set of considerations.   This range of topics is referred to as the **core** - and will be outlined in more detail in Section 11.5 below.

11.5 THE IEE DRAFT STRATEGY

In formulating their draft strategy, the IEE Working Party was very conscious of two requirements. In the first place, it was necessary specifically to address the needs of the members of the IEE. Additionally, however, it was necessary not to appear to exclude other participants from involvement in safety-critical systems activities. In effect then, it was not only necessary to provide a strategy for professional engineers, but also a context within which that strategy should operate.

There are three main strands to the draft policy:

(i)   All members of the IEE should receive a 'professional brief' on Safety-Critical Systems. This would draw to their attention relevant issues of which they as professionals should be aware. In addition it would recommend appropriate courses of action to those who were involved in some way in the area.

(ii) All (professional engineers) involved in safety-critical systems should undertake a **core** of training modules.

(iii) All involved in the design and construction of safety-critical systems should embark on additional modules which should be pitched at Masters level.

The Professional Brief is available [IEE 92b]); the Core is described in Section 11.5 of this paper; and, in Section 11.6, comments are made about the nature of the modules to be offered at Masters level.

An important observation is that, beyond the core, a spectrum of specialist activity is envisaged, leading to Masters qualifications of differing kinds. A range of professional bodies would have a legitimate interest in these. Note also that there is provision for offering these core modules at a basic or advanced level.

11.6 THE CORE

The central role of the Core within the IEE draft policy has already been referred to. Its purpose is to produce, for all participants, a responsible and well-balanced attitude to safety matters as well as to simplify the roles, requirements and responsibilities of all professional engineers (and those for whom they are responsible) working in the area of safety-critical systems.

The basic content of the Core is captured within four fundamental modules:

(i)   Legal Issues in Safety Critical Systems;
(ii) Case Studies in Safety Critical Systems;
(iii) Safety Engineering;
(iv) Systems Engineering.

These are each seen to be 4 - 5 days in duration and organized in such a way that there is appropriate industrial involvement; this can appear in the case studies and also in the planning and presentation of the modules. It is recommended that successful completion of these modules should lead to an award.

The details of the various modules are included in the IEE report [IEE 92a], together with comments on the nature of the modules and the learning outcomes. For completeness, a synopsis of each module is presented below.

11.6.1   LEGAL ISSUES IN SAFETY-CRITICAL SYSTEMS

The intended audience includes those responsible for the management and implementation of safety-critical systems and the aim is to provide an overview of the legal issues as they apply to this area.

The recommended syllabus includes such matters as:

*   Criminal liability;
*   Civil liability;
*   Safety audit:
    -    Actuarial aspects;
    -    Standards;
    -    Management of disasters;
    -    Future directions in forming an appropriate legal framework.

11.6.2   Case Studies in Safety-Critical Systems

The purpose of this module is to provide experience of realistic case studies and the intention is to include, for a range of disaster situations, the background, the design, the standards employed, and the lessons learned. The roles and responsibilities of the different players in each case should be examined and emphasized.

The recommended syllabus includes illustrations from many sectors of industry and draws attention to such matters as appropriate aspects of design, human factors, and the infrastructure from which the disaster arose. The lessons learned form an important aspect of the module.

11.6.3   Safety Engineering

This module is intended to provide the background to the evaluation of safety within a system, and to show how the evaluation is carried out and applied.

The recommended detailed syllabus covers:

*   The system context;

- The safety life-cycle model;
- Hazard analysis and risk management;
- Safety validation and accreditation procedures;
- Management issues.

11.6.4   Systems Engineering

This module addresses best practice associated with the specification, design, construction and maintenance of systems.

The recommended syllabus includes such topics as:

- The definition of a system;
- The system's life-cycle;
- The concept of a process;
- Systems specification;
- Design and maintenance.

In addition there is an overview of a range of technologies, with a consideration of appropriate trade-offs and a discussion of system management issues.

11.7 RECOMMENDATIONS REGARDING MASTERS COURSES

As mentioned earlier it is unrealistic to think in terms of a Masters course which covers all aspects of safety-critical systems. Masters courses can and should be designed to address particular aspects of the topic, but it is necessary to be selective, at least in terms of the technical area addressed. Ultimately, such courses will be judged for quality, using mechanisms which include traditional criteria such as technical excellence. But, given the nature of safety-critical systems, it would be natural to expect such courses (for practicing engineers) to exhibit certain criteria:

- They should provide a balance between theory and practice;
- Participants should be exposed to relevant standards;
- Modular, credit-based courses are attractive to industry;
- Industrial involvement is needed in the design of the overall course, in the design of individual modules, and in providing access to genuine case studies;
- They must provide, in successful participants, the well-found confidence needed to practise in this area;
- Projects of an appropriately technical nature should be included;
- They must be well resourced.

An additional set of comments can also be made. There are transferable skills which ought to be emphasized - these include effective communication skills, an ability to work in a team, and, generally, skills which increase personal effectiveness.

As a final observation, these comments begin to suggest that such courses (which aspire to produce technical people who can practise in the area of safety-critical systems) ought to undergo some form of public scrutiny with the aim of providing guidance to industry. Some form of 'accreditation' beckons.

11.8 REFERENCES

[IEE 91]   Institution of Electrical Engineers: "Formal Methods in Perspective." IEE PAB Report No. 9, published by and available from the IEE, Savoy Place, London, 1991.

[IEE 92a] Institution of Electrical Engineers: "Draft Policy on Education and Training Requirements." IEE PAB Report No. 12, published by and available from IEE, Savoy Place, London, 1992.

[IEE 92b] Institution of Electrical Engineers: "Professional Brief on Safety Critical Systems." IEE, Savoy Place, London, 1992.

12

Technology transfer through the teaching company scheme

Ed Robson

12.1 INTRODUCTION

There is no doubt that since the middle of this century the number of people throughout the world who are engaged in fundamental research activity within university departments and other centres of research has increased enormously. The consequent technological advances are providing a wide range of opportunity, not only for the manufacture of new products and for the improvement of manufacturing processes, but also for making significant improvements to the delivery of social, medical, financial and other services. Furthermore, the rate of change of technology shows no signs of diminishing, so it is reasonable to expect that opportunities for additional improvements will remain a permanent feature of industrialized society well into the twenty-first century.

In these circumstances, if industrial, commercial, social and other organizations are to thrive, it is imperative that they successfully embrace the outputs emanating from research. They need to ensure that they have the capacity, not only to identify and assess, in a professional way, any opportunities for improvement that become available, but also to manage any organizational changes required to take maximum advantage of them. In other words, it is extremely important that effective means are available for the successful transfer of technology (in its broadest sense) to take place from research establishments to organizations that can derive benefits from it; and that there is an adequate availability of staff able to act effectively as 'agents of change'.

The Teaching Company Scheme (TCS) is probably the best arrangement yet devised to satisfy these requirements. The purpose of TCS is to stimulate and support the creation of partnerships (programmes) between Higher Educational Institutions (HEI) and industrial and business organizations in order that technology transfer will be accomplished, and that bright young graduates will receive training and properly supervised experience that will fit them to become high quality 'agents of change'.

Although collaboration between universities on the one hand and business organizations on the other is more prevalent now than it was, say, 15 years ago, there is still a recognized need to broaden and deepen the relationships between the two sectors so that there will be a quicker and more effective commercial exploitation of the results of scientific and technological investigation.

12.2 THE TEACHING COMPANY SCHEME

The declared aim of the Teaching Company Scheme is to strengthen the competitiveness and wealth creation ability of the UK by:

(i)   Facilitating the transfer of technology and knowledge, and encouraging industrial investment in innovation and development;
(ii)   Providing industry-based training and development of graduates, which is supervised jointly by academic and industrial staff and which leads to accelerated career progression in UK industry;
(iii)   Establishing, between industry and academia, collaborations which will enhance the intellectual capital of industry and the relevance of teaching and research in academia.

The scheme is currently sponsored by two research councils, the Science and Engineering Research Council (SERC) and the Economic and Social Research Council (ESRC), and four government ministries, the Department of Trade and Industry (DTI), the Ministry of Agriculture, Fisheries and Food (MAFF), the Department of Employment (DoE) and the Department of Economic Development in Northern Ireland (DED(NI)). These provide finances (currently about £12M per annum), which are then augmented by the participating industrial organizations, to fund TCS programmes. They also support a Teaching Company Directorate which manages the scheme.

Each programme aims to carry out one or more projects defined to be central to the long-term strategy of the industrial partner and requiring, for its successful prosecution, a significant input of knowledge and expertise from the academic partner. Such projects are undertaken, with the joint supervision of staff from both the industrial and academic partners, by bright young graduates, called associates, each of whom is recruited for a two year period.

Thus, a project team is established, and the project is initially determined to be within the compass of such a team working for two years. As for any project, the definition and direction of projects have continually to be monitored and, over time, they may need to be adjusted by the Local Management Committee established to run the programme concerned. A simple diagramatic representative of a Teaching Company programme is given in.

In addition to pursuing the particulars of a project, all associates spend about 10 per cent of their associateship undertaking training which is agreed by their Local Management Committee and which is intended to equip them for successful future careers in British industry.

12.3 SUCCESS OF TCS

Since its modest beginnings in 1975 (when the target was to establish only a handful of programmes), the Scheme has grown and prospered. It has involved departments from just about every university and polytechnic in the United Kingdom and it currently supports nearly four hundred programmes, with the participation of companies of all sizes, ranging from large multinational firms to those employing only a handful of staff. The one thousandth programme was approved in early 1992.

The success of the scheme is acknowledged by the vast majority of industrial and academic staff who have participated. Indeed, in a recent review of the scheme [SERC 91], about 90 per cent of academic and industrial participants said that they would like to undertake a second programme after the completion of the first, and a very high percentage of participants rated the schemes as 'very beneficial'.

Over two and a half thousand young men and women have taken advantage of the scheme and, at the end of their projects, a high proportion were readily given employment by the industrial partners of their programmes. Most have made rapid progress to important posts in industry where they continue to develop and apply the knowledge and skills acquired during their Teaching Company experience. Indeed, some are now in positions from which they have initiated Teaching Company programmes in which their own companies are participating. It has been reported [SERC 91] that Teaching Company associates achieve, on average, 20 per cent higher salaries than graduates of a similar age who have entered industrial careers by alternative routes. This suggests that the scheme is providing the associates with significantly enhanced career development.

Further testimony to the success of TCS is provided by the large number of lasting partnerships between industry and academia that have remained in place after the conclusion of the Teaching Company programmes themselves. In addition, many academic staff have gained extensive understanding of modern industrial practices and of the real requirements of industry through their involvement in TCS. This has helped to improve the quality and relevance of their teaching, with the result that potential future recruits into industry are deriving the benefit of being better equipped for a career in industry.

12.4 SCOPE OF THE SCHEME

Initially TCS was directed at batch manufacturing, and this is the area in which training has been given to most past associates. However, not long ago the remit of the Scheme was broadened to include process engineering and the service sector. More recently still, construction, food processing, biochemicals and pharmaceuticals have also been added. In line with this, academic involvement has also been increased. Whereas, in the early stages of the Scheme, there was a predominance of manufacturing engineering, there is now the wide range of disciplines necessary to support the participating industrial sectors mentioned above. Examples are information technology, management, and science subjects including chemistry and biotechnology.

The number of live programmes to date is 380, and the details of the industrial and academic participants are given below.

(i)   The industrial sectors can be broken down as follows:

Manufacturing	72%
Information	8%
Service	5%
Civil Engineering	6%
Agriculture/Food	2%
Other	7%

(ii)   Company sizes are as follows:

Small (up to 50 staff)	20%
Medium (50 - 500 staff)	30%
Large (> 500 staff)	50%

(iii)   Academic disciplines are broken down as follows:

Engineering	62%
Science	5%

Information	11%
Management	17%
Other	5%

It is worth noting that a number of programmes are directed towards solving environmental problems and, as such, have been identified for support from the Clean Technology unit of the SERC.

12.5 CONCLUDING REMARKS

Over a significant period of time, and in a considerable number of programmes, the Teaching Company Scheme has proved its worth. Its advantages to all participants - industrial and academic partners, associates, and its sponsors - have been demonstrated. Some of these benefits are summarized below.

(i)   Advantages to companies

● Strategic projects undertaken;
● Links with academics created;
● Two year support from associates who may later be taken into employment.

(ii)   Advantages to academics

● Professional development through increased involvement with industry;
● Application of academic research;
● Post-graduate training experience;
● Financial overheads paid.

(iii)   Advantages to associates

● Invaluable industrial experience, leading to enhanced career development;
● Qualifications and/or professional recognition.

(iv)   Advantages to sponsors

● Improved performance of industry and academia.

Now that the Scheme has proved itself, and collected data has shown it to be a success, it is hoped to extend its scope so that the results from an even wider range of research activities may more rapidly and effectively be applied to practical issues and problems, not only in the industrial sector, but also in various service organizations. The objective of this is that TCS should enlarge its contribution to improving the performance of British industry and to increasing the quality of service provided in other areas of national life.

It is particularly important that those involved in the design and implementation of safety-critical systems should exploit the new techniques and technologies emanating from research and development in software engineering and other relevant fields. The TCS provides a successful mechanism which could make a significant contribution to this.

12.6 REFERENCE

[SERC 91]   Science and Engineering Research Council: "Review of the Teaching Company Scheme." Report of the Panel, Chaired by Professor B E F Fender, SERC, 1991.

13

An industry view of training requirements for safety-critical systems professionals

Jim Thomas

13.1 BACKGROUND

Today's computer systems engineers are likely to find that the demands for their skills will change markedly over their careers. They will also continue to be trained and retrained to extend their skill-sets, with such training being provided by their employers in industry.

In general, industry invests in training to meet some requirement (such as a contractual or statutory demand), to gain a business advantage, or to improve and develop its staff. However, the costs for such training must be recovered, either directly, in the selling price of some product, or indirectly, by productivity improvements.

Training must also fit in with other activities and, in particular, with project work. Hence, the probability of staff being sent on extended courses is low, not only because of the cost, but also because of the loss of continuity incurred on projects.

13.2 SAFETY-CRITICAL TRAINING REQUIREMENTS

In the area of safety-critical systems, it is usual for training to be expected to meet one or more of the following requirements: legal, contractual, business, or social. At present, there is no legal requirement to train staff especially for safety-critical systems work, nor to have staff licensed or registered for such work. Similarly, there are no contractual requirements in most cases.

Further, even if we believe that training would help to produce safer systems, the training ought to include some case studies, drawn from practical experience and presented by active practitioners. But even though such case studies can help give staff some of the essential benefits of real-life experience, they are not sufficient, and some practical work with more experienced colleagues is needed. This applies to most areas of training for work with computers, but it is even more important in the area of safety-critical systems, where a major consideration is to provide protection against the unexpected.

13.3 COMPETENCES

From this approach of learning by experience comes the model of 'Competences' to be gained during the work process.

Both the British Computer Society (BCS) and the Information Technology Industry Training Organisation (ITITO - formerly the Computing Services Industry Training Council (COSIT)) have been working at defining training schemes for the computing industries. These schemes, the Professional Development Scheme (PDS) from the BCS, and the Industry Standard Development Programme (ISDP) from ITITO, both have a hierarchy of competences covering the skills needed for the various roles in the computer industry.

13.4 INDUSTRY STANDARD DEVELOPMENT PROGRAMME

The ISDP hierarchy of competences is based on a project lifecycle model, and it defines technical and business competences. Its first level is shown in Figure 13.1. Technical competences are those associated with the systems

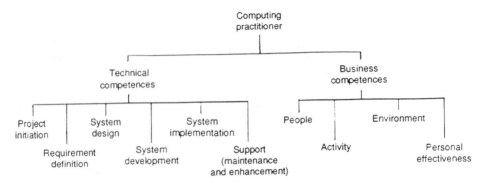

Figure 13.1: ISDP lifecycle hierarchy.

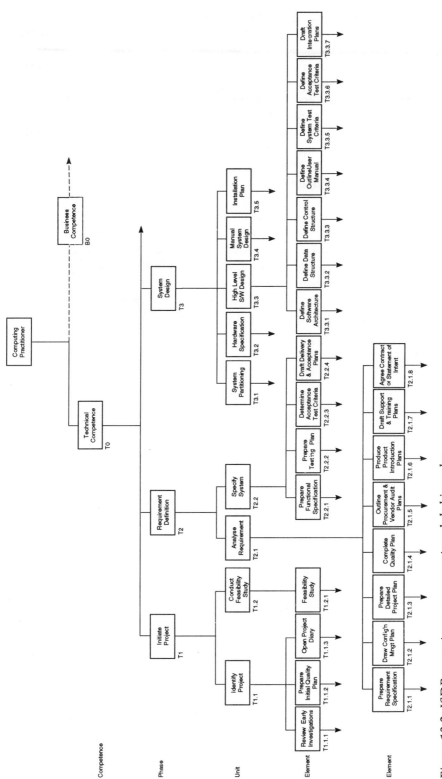

Figure 13.2: ISDP competence assessment module hierarchy.

engineering processes of a typical project lifecycle model. Business competences are those associated with managing projects, staff, customers, and oneself.

At the lowest level of detailed decomposition, each activity is expressed in a precise and stylized fashion. This format is the preferred style of the National Council for Vocational Qualifications (NCVQ) from whom both the BCS and the ITITO are seeking accreditation of their programmes.

An example of the breakdown into modules of part of the technical competence section of the model is shown in Figure 13.2 which presents the given phase of the lifecycle at the top level, then the breakdown into the units of that phase and, finally, the decomposition into the elements of each unit.

The competence statements are intended to be sufficiently objective and precise to describe the activities in such a manner that participants can be assessed to be performing tasks to set standards. Each element of competence specifies in detail its performance criteria and, together, they specify the overall standards of performance of the programme. The various competence elements are designed to be used in an appraisal review. An example of the statement for one of the units is detailed in Figure 13.3.

COMPETENCE:	Technical (T0)
PHASE:	System Design (T3)
UNIT:	High Level Software Design (T3.3)
ELEMENT:	Define Software Architecture (T3.3.1)
DESCRIPTION:	The participant must be able to select and validate software architecture policies, including choice of programming methods and tools (such as programming languages, compilers, program generators, database management packages). The participant must be able to define in outline the software components and their relationship and justify the architecture according to functional requirements, development constraints, and hardware constraints (such as memory size, distributed processors).

CONDITION	ACTIVITY	CRITERIA
Hardware Specification Requirement Specification Development Constraints	Design Software Architecture	Identifies all software components
		Identifies use of bought-in and supplied components
Existing Software Component Specifications		Identifies and describes relationships between components
		Relates software components to hardware components

Figure 13.3: A competence statement.

The scheme works by participants being allocated, by the employer, training and tasks which are mapped onto the hierarchies of competences. Each participant is allocated an ISDP Supervisor whose function is to monitor the progressive training and development of the staff entrusted to their care and to perform the quality assurance role with respect to the work experience and training recorded in the participants' log books. Every six months each participant has a performance review and appraisal.

The sequences of training and work experience activities completed by different participants are as varied as the computer industry itself. One of the advantages of the ISDP concept is the flexibility it exhibits in providing a very wide range of possible paths from registration to certification.

13.5 SAFETY-CRITICAL COMPETENCES

13.5.1 CSA Safety-Critical Systems Group

Within the Computing Services Association (CSA), the Safety Critical Systems Group was formed in 1989 to monitor developments in the area of safe software and to advise the CSA Council and its member companies on matters related to safety-critical systems. The group set out to investigate different subjects and produce advice on them, and, to do so, it set up three appropriate working parties:

(i) The Legal and Commercial Working Party;
(ii) The Standards Working Party;
(iii) The Training Working Party.

Of interest here is the CSA Safety Critical Systems Training Working Party, which considered the requirements for and approaches to developing competent engineers for safety-critical systems work. In particular, it determined to analyse the situation prior to there being requirements imposed by legislation.

13.5.2 Training Model

The working party studied the problem. It took the ISDP scheme and looked at extending it to include competences required for safety-critical systems. It concluded that this could be done either by adding new units in each phase specifically targeted at safety-critical systems or by introducing additional elements within each unit to address the required additional competences. It would also be possible for some elements to be extended in themselves to introduce additional items addressing safety-critical issues.

It was decided that the addition of elements, with appropriate element extensions, was the preferable route, since:

(i) A general background in all areas of computing is essential before working on safety-critical systems;

(ii)   Safety-critical skills are only an extension of normal skills in most areas;

(iii) New units would make safety-critical skills special instead of just extensions.

Staff gaining competences would record these in their personal log book to enable future assessment for participation in projects. These records would also be used as evidence towards any future accreditation process leading to registered or licensed status.

13.6 PROJECT TEAMS

In setting up a project, it is necessary to identify the skills and competences required to implement the target system, and any sizeable project needs a team to provide the effort. Figure 13.4 illustrates how the skills and competences are met by a team to ensure that all the requirements are covered; the matrix identifies the skills of each team member against those required for the project as a whole. This applies to any type of project, but is essential with safety-critical systems. It is not possible to train every team member to cover all the skill areas required - this could lead to the danger of each being a 'Jack of all Trades, Master of None'.

Additionally, only a few team members need to be specialised in safety-critical systems, the remainder needing only to have an awareness of the issues involved. The creation of a project team would require the selection

	ANO1	ANO2	ANO3	ANO4	ANO5	ANO6	ANO7	etc	
Project Mgt.	X								
Requirement Anlys	X	X							
System Design		X	X						
S/w Design		X	X						
S/w Testing			X						
S/w Integration			X						
System Integration			X						
System Testing		X							
Safety Eng.				X					
Safety Assmnt					X				
V and V						X			
etc									

Project Skill Requirements vs Staff

Figure 13.4: Project team skills matrix.

of the necessary competences from the records of each possible staff member.

13.7 BENEFITS

This approach has the benefits that all staff do not have to become specialised in safety-critical systems and that they can be used on other projects when there is less demand for safety-critical work. However, all staff should be aware of the issues associated with safety-critical systems.

Under the scheme, all training would be recorded in the member of staff's log book. Then, while working on a project, the trainee would be supervised and the work assessed regularly.

It is likely that in ten years (say) the approaches taken now for safety-critical systems will have become commonplace in a much wider area of computer system development and test. Given this, it is preferable that the techniques are integrated now into the training lifecycle and not provided as 'special' topics.

13.8 SUMMARY

The issues regarding training for safety-critical systems are:

(i)   Appropriate training is not yet defined;
(ii)   The required skills continue to change;
(iii) Training by classroom courses is not enough;
(iv)   There is a need to learn by experience as well as by tuition;
(v)   It is not cost-effective for industry to send staff on extended courses;
(vi)   Projects suffer when staff are away on training;
(vii) Staff have also to be competent in non-safety-critical work.

One approach to reconciling these issues is to implement the ISDP training scheme and to develop staff competences to meet the requirements of projects.

13.9 NEXT ACTIONS

A programme of work to extend the competence model to include safety-critical aspects needs to be undertaken so that staff can then develop their skills and competences in a planned manner. Included in staff development, there is a need for qualifications to be derived in conjunction with the competences.

One option would be for the scheme to be extended to include various safety-critical roles specifically in the career model. Another option would be for the roles (or as many as necessary) to be extended to include specific skills and competences needed to take on the various safety-critical tasks.

As with all approaches to developing staff for safety-critical systems work, the above plan is for the development of staff from their entry into the computer industry. For staff already in the industry, approaches for accrediting them need to be agreed and will probably involve some form of peer evaluation.

Besides developing the skills needed for specialist staff, it is necessary to make all staff on safety-critical projects aware of the issues involved. One of the first courses to be developed should therefore be on the awareness of safety-critical issues for all staff on such projects.

13.10 CONCLUSIONS

The preferred approach to developing staff for work on safety-critical systems is to follow a competence-based experience model. This approach will enable project teams to be set up to implement such systems.

In training its staff, business seeks to gain an advantage so as to attract further work, but it also needs to perform that work in a low-risk manner. As the key responsibility for any safety-critical system rests with the company, it would be prudent for each company to ensure that its procedures address the issues of training and experience in this field.

In order to lower the risks of working in this area, it is prudent that all staff should have some formal training in relevant topics, but it is even more important that they should have a period of working with more experienced colleagues in on-the-job training.

14

Safety-critical software professionals in the BCS industry career structure

Mike Falla

The British Computer Society publishes an Industry Structure Model (ISM) which provides a set of performance standards covering most areas of work in the field of Information Systems Engineering. The ISM is designed to provide guidelines to define the training needs, career development structures, and experience requirements for those who wish to become professionally qualified within the industry.

At many points, the ISM refers to the need for special attention to be paid to safety matters, and the BCS felt that an appendix should be provided indicating the specific attributes, knowledge, and competence regarded as important for those engaged in the development, maintenance or management of safety-related software. Some initial ideas were put together in the form of a 'brainstorm' paper by Prof John McDermid and the late Alan Taylor, and I was contracted to draft a text, to consult expert opinion, and to produce an appendix to the ISM in line with this advice.

14.1 THE INDUSTRY STRUCTURE MODEL

The ISM is constructed as a matrix. In one dimension it is divided into fourteen career streams, as shown in the list below.

- Information Systems Policy and Management
- Information Systems Development
- Information Systems Service Delivery
- Information Systems Technical Specialisms
- Information Systems Quality Audit (Third Party)
- Information Systems Research

- General Consultancy
- Hybrid management
- Information Systems Procurement and Contracting
- Information Systems Sales and Marketing
- Information Systems Education and Training
- Information Systems Specialist School Teaching
- Information Systems Audit
- Technical Authorship

Many of these streams are divided into substreams. Thus, for example, the 'Information Systems Development' Stream, is divided into eight substreams, including 'Development Management', 'Programming', 'Software Engineering', and so on. The second dimension of the matrix is divided into 'levels' corresponding to different stages in career development, ranging from unskilled entry (Level 0) to senior manager or director (Level 9). Each stream or substream thus consists of a number of cells, over a range of levels. Each cell describes a job function in terms of the recommended academic background, the experience and level of skill required at entry, typical tasks carried out, personal attributes expected, and the training and development required for individuals at a particular level within the (sub)stream.

Thus, for example, the Software Engineering substream at Level 4 ('Fully Skilled Practitioner') requires the individual's education at entry to be 'preferably to degree level ...' (but with alternatives) and either at least two years' satisfactory performance at Level Three in any development substream or a minimum of four years' experience at Level Three in any other stream which includes significant amounts of software development.

It specifies particular skills and attributes required, such as 'must be conversant with quality-control techniques and be able to select and apply them appropriately at all stages of the life cycle', and it describes the training required as including 'deeper training as necessary in: oral and written presentation skills, project leadership, estimating techniques'.

14.2 PURPOSE AND STRUCTURE OF THE APPENDIX

As noted above, the purpose of the Appendix is 'to give guidance on the attributes, knowledge and competencies regarded as of specific importance for those engaged in the development, maintenance or management of safety related software'. The target audience, as I saw it, is made up of personnel, training, and general managers - that is, people who are not expert in the subject - together with individuals working in, or wishing to enter, the field. A further constraint on the Appendix was a size limit of about ten to twelve pages.

Clearly, within these constraints there is no way in which one could or should attempt to present a handbook on safety-related software. The objective therefore was to identify the areas which are relevant from the point of view of staff development and training, and to indicate the importance of the subject and the need for serious consideration at all levels of management. The emphasis throughout is on the knowledge and capabilities required of individuals rather than on technical issues, techniques, or tools.The Appendix notes:

> This Appendix ... can provide guidance only: it remains the responsibility of employers and managers to satisfy themselves of the knowledgeability and competence of their staff in relation to any specific safety related work which they may be required to undertake.

Although safety is referred to from several streams within the ISM, four principal roles were identified in relation to safety-related software: practitioners, managers, assessors and purchasers. Four separate sections, however, would have involved considerable overlap, so I drafted one text with guidance for the reader as to which sections were relevant to each role.

Discussion of the role of 'Assessor' led to the realization that the career path of Software Safety Specialist should be recognized. This recognition has been given by adding a new substream to the ISM within the development stream.

The role of 'Purchaser' was included (despite someone asking caustically 'since when do you have to be qualified to purchase things?') because it was felt that, in practice, a safety-related software system (or even complete information-processing system) will be used, and can only be judged safe or otherwise in the context of some wider system which is the direct responsibility of the purchaser.

14.3 CONTENTS OF THE APPENDIX

Whereas the full Appendix cannot be presented here, and interested readers should refer to the document itself, the contents list is given for information and to assist readers to follow this chapter.

1 INTRODUCTION
 1.1 Safety Related Software
 1.2 Structure of this Appendix

2 EXPERIENCE AND QUALIFICATIONS
 2.1 General
 2.2 Training
 2.3 Experience

3 KNOWLEDGE AND COMPETENCE
 3.1 Knowledge and competence required for different roles
 3.2 Characteristics of risk and safety
 3.3 The regulatory framework

14.4 KEY ISSUES

Most of the Appendix proved non-contentious, although respondents were helpful in improving the wording throughout. Some issues, however, did provoke debate.

14.4.1   Software Versus Systems

A fundamental issue was whether the Appendix should be concerned with software or with systems. Clearly software has to be set in a systems context, but it was felt that software issues were worth addressing in their own right in the context of the ISM and that seeking also to address the wide variety of hardware and general systems issues would be too ambitious. This position is described by the following paragraph from the Appendix:

> Software can affect safety only in the context of a wider system which it is used to control, to monitor, or to design or construct. Safety is thus a property of the complete system. Although the guidance given in this Appendix is concerned with software, the reader should remain aware that all such knowledge and competencies should be set in the context of the complete system, including computing and other hardware and any people who form part of that system.

It did, however, seem important to include topics such as 'The systems approach to safety' and 'Human interface for safety'.

14.4.2   Safety Versus Correctness

Several respondents emphasized that safety and correctness are not the same thing. A safe system may contain incorrect software, a 'correct' system may not be safe. This distinction is perhaps blurred by the somewhat confusing uses, within the field, of terms such as 'reliable', 'dependable', and so on. It seemed useful to include the following paragraph:

> The non-specialist reader may find it helpful to note that the knowledge and competencies described in this Appendix can be divided into two broad areas: (a) those specific to the achievement and validation of safety, and (b) those targeted at achieving and validating as near as possible fault-free design and production. Many systems which have no, or low, safety requirements may need to be developed with the same degree of care as safety related systems in order to achieve other objectives such as high availability, reliability or security.

14.4.3   References

The standards situation is evolving and quite complex, so it did not seem wise to try and include a definitive reference list. On the other hand, it seemed desirable to include a few key standards in order to establish the point that standards exist (although as yet insufficient) and need to be taken account of. Some standards are therefore referenced, although some respondents argued that the Appendix should list either all the relevant standards or none.

Similar reasoning applied to the inclusion of references to books and papers. A few were included as a way into the wider literature and to indicate that such a literature exists.

14.4.4   Education and Training

The topic on which there was the most dissent was that of educational requirements. The first draft suggested that 'all personnel engaged on safety related work will be expected to be of graduate status or to possess equivalent intellectual capabilities'. Some respondents thought this essential, advocating, indeed, a requirement for CEng status at senior levels. Others argued that much work undertaken by juniors required care and application rather than academic brilliance and that graduates were positively unsuited for this.

The final text tries to draw the best from both these schools of thought with the following paragraph:

> Each cell definition within the body of the ISM describes the recommended academic background for the cell. Where graduate status is preferred at levels 3 (i.e. 'Trained Practitioner') and above for general software, education to degree level or equivalent is strongly recommended for safety related work. At senior levels, CEng status is particularly appropriate.

However, there no doubt remain some who would like to see graduate and/or CEng status as a firm requirement for all except the most junior roles.

Given the objectives of the Appendix, it would have been very desirable to be able to point personnel and training managers, and individual practitioners, at recommended training curriculums. Unfortunately, at the time of writing, no such curriculum was available (although contact was made with the IEE working party drawing up a draft curriculum). It did, however, seem necessary to emphasize that training is not just a cosmetic feature provided for the benefit of staff morale, but a necessary part of the 'tooling up', responsibility for which lies with management. The following paragraphs were therefore included:

> At present it is not possible to prescribe specific training or qualifications. This is partly because the necessary courses and qualifications do not exist, and partly because such requirements would need interpretation for particular industries. A working party has produced a draft curriculum for training in this area, and this is available as a chapter in Software in Safety-Related Systems. [Wichmann 92]

> Where, however, personnel are required to work with a particular technique, method or tool, it is the responsibility of management to ensure that adequate training has been provided. Adequacy implies that the person undergoing training is able to apply the knowledge gained confidently and with precision, and that he or she understands the applicability and limits of what has been learned.

14.4.5   Experience

The ISM specifies the minimum number of years of experience required for entry to a given level within a stream. Clearly, for work on safety-related software, a proportion of that experience should have been gained on safety-related or other high-integrity software. The first draft proposed a firm figure of 50 per cent, but some respondents thought this too inflexible and that, if it were applied, it would be likely to lead to staff shortages. The Appendix therefore states that, for safety-related work:

> Typically, at least half of the experience necessary for entry to each subsequent Level of the ISM will have been gained through appropriate work on safety-related or other suitable high-integrity software.

14.4.6   Personal Qualities

Several respondents emphasized the need for certain personal qualities and suggested strengthening the wording in the initial draft. The Appendix therefore says:

> All personnel must possess a mature reliability, with a positive attitude, and a commitment to safety as an overriding goal of their

work. They should be able to communicate effectively and work co-operatively within a team. More senior staff must increasingly display balanced and mature judgement.

The section on individual professional responsibilities states that:

(each individual) will be expected to be aware of his or her personal responsibility and liability for the application of the best available methods and tools, and the best care and attention, to all safety related work

and that:

(he or she) should take all reasonable steps to make their own managers and other relevant authorities aware of risks which he or she identifies, and make anyone overruling or neglecting their professional advice aware of the consequent risks, ensuring that there is a written record, kept in a safe place, of their disagreement.

This last statement is in line with the advice in the IEE's draft Professional Brief on Safety Related Systems.

Attitudes form one part of a safety culture. If I were drafting the Appendix now, I would, I think, structure parts of it more clearly around this concept. Culture, however, is a complex and wide-ranging issue. While it is easy, for example, to express the criterion that a manager must be able to 'plan and schedule work in conformity with quality and safety plans and with due regard to overall plans and budgets', it does not remove the problem for the manager of balancing confidence in safety against inevitable commercial pressures.

14.4.7   Technical Issues

On the technical side, the Appendix seeks, in sections on 'Technical and lifecycle management' and 'Software techniques and tools', to give non-specialist managers a feel for the range of topics about which their staff should be knowledgeable and competent. These sections quote a number of tools and techniques, but it is emphasized that this is done purely by way of example to clarify the text and to act as pointers for the reader. These examples proved surprisingly non-contentious.

It is perhaps worth mentioning, particularly in the context of the Safety-Critical Systems Club, one comment on the 'Technical and lifecycle management' section which observed that it was cast purely in terms of the traditional lifecycle and third generation languages. This did strike me as being by far the majority case, particularly among the target audience, but the Appendix now recognizes emerging technology by noting that:

In those (currently infrequent) cases where other approaches are used, the criteria should be adapted appropriately.

14.5 THE CONSULTATION PROCESS

The initial 'Brainstorm' paper had been circulated for comment to 14 experts in the field of safety-related software, but with no response. In order to elicit a response from busy people, it seemed best to put together a draft which could act as a focus for comment: clearly it is far easier to comment on a specific proposed text than to respond to a description of what the text would be like.

My first draft was based on the 'brainstorm' paper and on material kindly supplied by Barry Daniels and Lindsay Jones (of NCC) and others. This help was particularly welcome because my own background is in software engineering, project management and staff management rather than specifically in the field of safety-related software. (An old joke has it that a consultant is someone who borrows your watch to tell you the time. I saw my task here as borrowing many people's watches in order to get a consensus on the time!)

This first draft was circulated to 30 people, of whom 21 responded. I am extremely grateful to these people for taking the time and trouble to read the draft and to respond. It is a tribute, I think, to the importance which they attach to staff development for safety-related software.

After an editorial meeting with Brian Wichmann of NPL and Denise Him of the BCS, a second draft was circulated to everyone who had responded to the first draft and to a further 9 people. This second round produced 9 responses (not only from the 'new' 9). Changes from the previous draft were highlighted, so it is reasonable to assume that most of those who did not respond to this second round had at least glanced at the changes and seen nothing to worry them. Overall, responses were received from 27 experts out of a total of 42 consulted.

14.6 CONCLUSIONS

The consultation process worked well, probably, as remarked above, because of the importance which the experts who were consulted attach to the subject.

My belief is that it has been possible to produce a text which broadly reflects the consensus of the people consulted and to which none of them would take too strong an exception.

I am aware that many people would like the BCS, the IEE, or *someone* to be more prescriptive as to the training and skills requirements of those who work in the field of safety-related software. The role of the ISM, however, is to set a framework of awareness and to act as a reference model for employers. Responsibility for the knowledge and competence of its staff lies with the supplier of the software, as a component of the supplier's responsibility for his product. The purpose of the Appendix is to give guidance in this area and, hopefully, to act as a stimulus to management and a lever for individuals.

14.7 ACKNOWLEDGMENTS

I would like to thank all those who commented on the drafts. I would also particularly like to thank for their help, in addition to those mentioned by name above, Brian Jepson of BAe and David Whitfield of NII.

The Industry Structure Model is published by the British Computer Society, P.O. Box 1454, Station Road, Swindon, SN1 1TG. Release 2, including the Appendix on Safety-related Software, is now available.

14.8 REFERENCE

[Wichmann 92] Wichmann B A (Ed.): "Software in Safety-Related Systems." John Wiley & Sons, 1992.

PART FOUR
LESSONS FROM THE MEDICAL SECTOR

15

Safety of medical robots

Brian Davies

15.1 INTRODUCTION

Unlike industrial robots, medical robots do not have clear safety guidelines. The health and safety requirements for industrial robots suggest that they should not operate in contact with people, but should be isolated in a cell with safety interlocks, for example on the doors, to prevent the robot functioning while people are in the cell. The only exception to this is that the robot may be programmed by a skilled operator in the cell. During programming the robot can only move under reduced speed conditions while the operator keeps out of reach of the moving arm. If medical robots were to operate under the same requirements as industrial robots, they clearly would be very limited in their capability and application.

Medical robots, like domestic robots, are a new application in which, to be fully effective, they must operate in contact with people. Such a concept represents a new departure for robots, and appropriate safety procedures have yet to be defined that would allow them to carry out their functions with adequate safety margins. On the other hand, such safety margins should not require the robots to be so complex and high in cost that they are priced out of the market. The questions of how adequate the safety must be and how safe is 'safe' are matters that need to be discussed by the community at large.

It is generally recognized that even where safety is of over-riding importance, for example, in the space shuttle, there is no such thing as 100 per cent safety, and errors in software and failures of hardware do occur, in spite of replication of systems and the very high costs which ensue. What is needed is a recognition that the benefits to be obtained from medical robots are such that a small amount of risk is inherent in their use, and a confidence that this is justifiable and acceptable. This is not to say that unsafe or unsound medical robot systems should be utilized. Every reasonable effort should be made to ensure that the system is as safe as it possibly can be. Having done this, it is likely that some risk, no matter how small, will still be present.

However, in the field of medical robotics, there is almost never a case where failure to function will result in a life-damaging situation. Provided that the medical robot is designed to fail in a safe manner and come to a controlled halt so that it can be removed and the procedure completed manually, no danger to life should ensue. This is unlike the case of, say, a military aircraft, which could not be flown manually if the computer control system failed. In the event of failure, medical robots can generally be removed and the procedure completed manually without any risk to the patient, and this is preferable to having a very long mean time between failures (MTBF), which is a less important criterion.

Justification for the use of medical robots is not easy to quantify. In the early days of the motor car, it was considered necessary for a man to walk in front with a red flag. It is accepted nowadays that motor cars bring sufficient benefits for their unconstrained use (even when being driven at high speed along motorways) to be considered acceptable, and for the number of injuries and deaths which occur annually to be considered justifiable. If a medical robot allows a life-saving operation to be performed, such as when a surgery robot is used for brain tumour removal (a process which could not be carried out as accurately manually), then one could argue that, provided all reasonable safety measures have been taken so that failure of the system is rare, the overall use of the robot is justified. Because its use would save lives which would otherwise be lost, the use of expensive safety measures would also be easy to justify.

However, such arguments do not generally apply to the majority of robot surgery applications or to those of manipulators in the rehabilitation field. Here the robots are generally functioning as a replacement for human activity, simply because they are more accurate, are faster, or do not require the continuing attendance of a person. The benefits that accrue are therefore generally less easy to quantify and are concerned with cost saving or convenience. Since these benefits are not life-critical, the safety measures needed, and to what extent they can be justified in terms of complexity and cost, are less clear. What is needed is for the medical community to make recommendations of a level of safety which is acceptable, with the various implications discussed so that users, helpers, relatives, and the public at large, can come to a consensus on what is an agreed standard.

If such a consensus is not achieved, the development of medical robots (and domestic robots) will continue to be slow. Companies are understandably reluctant to develop new products when the required levels of safety and the attendant legal issues are not clear. It appears that in the UK and, to some extent, in the rest of Europe, it is an adequate defence, in the event of an accident resulting from equipment failure, for the equipment to have been designed and manufactured to 'best current practice'. However, since standards of best current practice have yet to be laid down, the issues are still not clear and would have to be tested in law before they can be clarified.

The situation in the USA, which is a potentially large and lucrative market is even less clear, since design to best practice is not considered to be an adequate defence in the event of an accident. The American practice of charging legal fees only when a court case has been successful makes the likelihood of being sued in the USA even greater. Such concerns about the uncertainties of how safe products should be, and about the legal implications, have limited the development of medical robots.

15.2 SURGEON ASSISTANT ROBOTS

One approach to the safety of surgeon assistant robots has been to suggest that their safety levels should be better than those achieved by conventional surgery. At first sight, this is an attractive proposition because the robot would be safer than the traditional surgeon. However, in practice this concept would give rise to considerable difficulties. Firstly, the exact safety record of traditional surgery, in specific applications, is very difficult to obtain. Secondly, statistical estimates of robot surgery safety would not be acceptable. It would be necessary for the robot to perform a number of operations to a degree of safety greater than that expected of a human surgeon. However, if a failure did occur earlier than a given predicted time, which is statistically possible, it would be difficult to argue a case in a court of law on the basis of statistics. No matter when a robot failure occurred, if this resulted in an accident, it is unlikely that the damaged parties would waive their rights to sue the robot supplier simply on the basis of statistical probability.

A further aspect to this problem is that, when surgeons use simple tools and an error occurs, it is seldom that those tools and the manufacturers are blamed. It is often accepted that surgery is a risky business and unless the surgeon has been negligent, no court case results. However, when the surgeon uses a relatively autonomous piece of equipment, such as a robot assistant, it is difficult to see how the surgeon will be totally liable. It is for this reason that the author believes it is essential, when using robot assistant surgeons, to involve the surgeon wherever possible to confirm decisions throughout the surgical procedure. On the basis of the information displayed by the sensor systems and the human-computer interface (HCI), it would then be the surgeon's judgement whether to proceed with the operation.

One successful approach to these difficulties has been undertaken by a group in Grenoble for head surgery [Lavallee 89]. Here a six-axis robot has been used to carry a jig or fixture close to the head of a patient. When the fixture is at the correct position and orientation, a series of cutting instruments are clipped to the jig and used by the surgeon manually. Thus the robot is reduced to a preliminary role as a positioning jig and not for direct intervention. The safety of the robot is further assured by introducing a very large reduction gear ratio to each of the motor output drives. This means that in the event that something goes wrong with the robot, there is plenty of time to hit the emergency 'off' button, because the robot is moving so slowly.

Another approach has been suggested in which a standard robot uses high-level software to monitor the motions of the operational robot. This may have problems, because the monitoring is at a high level and not at the hardware servo level and, hence, it may be slow to act. It is possible to imagine a scenario in which the servo is moving in a straight line when failure causes it to try to take off at high speed in the same direction. The inertia of the system may cause the robot arm to travel some distance before the fault is detected by the high-level monitor and the brakes can bring the arm to a halt. It could be argued that only hardware monitoring at the servo level will give the necessary speed of response to avoid damage in critical instances, even though the robot is restricted to the role of carrying a jig or fixture.

Some redundancy in sensors and software systems is also desirable for reliability. Dual sensors, one on each servo motor and one on each output drive, could act as checks that the drive output system is not slipping and that encoder integrity is being maintained. Dual software systems running on separate transputers in parallel are another means of checking for errors. Additionally, all software codes must be assured. While dependable computing systems have made great strides, complex software still cannot be guaranteed to be totally safe.

One answer to these computing problems could be to have two software systems running simultaneously on two different pieces of hardware. For further integrity, the software would need to have been independently generated by separate groups using completely different language systems. The two systems would need to be run in parallel and to come to the same conclusion before an action could be taken. The cost and complexity of such a system would be likely to prohibit its use from all but the most life-critical robot surgeon assistance.

A solution adopted at Imperial College has been to design a special-purpose robot for a particular surgical procedure to operate within a localized region. Associated with this concept is that of a mechanical constraint which physically prevents motion outside a limited area. This approach was arrived at because it was felt that anthropomorphic robots capable of reaching a large volume space (the very feature which makes them attractive to industry) could, in the event of failure, fly off in any direction, causing damage to patients, surgeons and other participants.

A further implication of this approach is that, where possible, axes should be moved sequentially, one at a time rather than in parallel, to minimize the volume of space which can be swept out by an unforeseen motion. This implies that complex shapes resulting from the interaction of many axes of motion may need to be approximated by a series of simple shapes, resulting from a sequence of single-axis motions. In addition to the usual sensor-based software limits on motion, mechanical stops may need to be positioned for each programmed size of cut, physically to restrict the range of motion to a safe and acceptable limit should anything unforeseen occur.

This concept of a special-purpose robot with mechanical constraint has been developed at Imperial College Robotics Centre, for the design of a surgeon assistant for prostatectomies [Davies 91a], [Davies 91b].

15.3 A ROBOTIC SYSTEM FOR PROSTATECTOMIES

A special-purpose frame has been designed for transurethral resection of the prostate. The frame carries a standard resectoscope and is driven by rare-earth permanent magnet motors with integral optical position encoders. The control system is monitored by a PC for which software has been written to allow the surgeon to specify the size of the prostrate and its shape at different cross sections. Using information obtained from a prior ultrasound inspection, automatic curve-fitting routines define the combined motion of the motors. This produces the required curved trajectory of the cutter, and also a sequence of single-axis motions which approximate the required shape.

Safety checks are incorporated throughout the software to ensure that at no time can the motor/encoder system be asked to move the cutter outside the predefined limits of the prostrate. In addition, a physical clamp system attached to the arch drive ensures that even if the motor should attempt to move the cutter outside of the predetermined conical shape, it would be physically prevented from doing so and the motor controller would cut out. The system is under the continuous control of the surgeon who can observe the procedure on a monitor via a camera attached to the endoscope. The motions can be interrupted at any time, incorporating inherently safe techniques for shutdown, and the procedure then completed manually. In this way a special-purpose robotized device has been constructed which is inherently safe.

The system has been applied clinically on four patients to partially resect the prostrate, with the process being completed manually by the surgeon. This represents a 'world first' in using a robot system directly to remove quantities of tissue from a live patient. Further improvements in the prior imaging procedures are being undertaken to ensure a completely automated prostatectomy.

Many of the safety implications of robotic surgery are being avoided by the use of computer-assisted surgery. A typical example is that at Aachen where ear, nose and throat surgery is being carried out [Adams 89]. Here a passive arm is used to carry tools. Each joint on the passive arm is instrumented and can be locked using electromagnetic brakes. Prior to the operation, an NMRI scan of the head is used to provide three-dimensional coordinates of targets to a computer database, with reference to a chosen datum object.

In the operating theatre, the passive arm is referenced to the same datum object, so that motions of the arm can be referenced to the images in the computer database. A display screen can then track the position of the tools on the end of the arm, with respect to the head target area. Since the surgeon is holding the tool and moves it directly to provide its power, he is in control of the process and relies on the computer system for tracking information. Thus the possible malfunction of robot arm servo systems is removed from the activity. The accuracy of the arm pointing system and the associated database can be checked beforehand, thus minimizing possible problem areas; and safety is increased by reducing the function of the robot to that of advising the surgeon rather than carrying out operations for him.

15.4 MEDICAL ROBOTS IN REHABILITATION

The use of medical robots in assisting the disabled is becoming more common-place. Potential locations for the manipulator range from no contact to full contact with the user. The former case emulates the industrial situation, so that the medical manipulator is part of a workstation with an envelope of reach which is always out of contact with the user; thus, potential safety problems are largely avoided. In this case, the robot can only place items on to a receptacle, for example a rotary table, from which the user has access to them. Unfortunately, although this is potentially a very safe solution, it is also most limited in its benefits to the user. Also, it is necessary to fence off the manipulator arm from both helpers and the public.

The next safe concept is one in which only the extreme reach of the extended manipulator arm comes near the user. This is often used as a workstation configuration in which the arm is used as a feeding aid, presenting food at its full reach for the user to move the head, for example to eat from a spoon. Although this a fairly safe solution, it is seldom possible to fix the user location rigidly. Thus, if, say, the user slumps down in a wheelchair, he could be within the envelope of arm motions. Similarly, long tools held in the gripper could also strike the user.

An alternative solution would be to make the arm have very low force and speed, not just limited by software or, say, force control, but by the intrinsic capabilities of the arm. This has some merit because the disabled user is usually content with a slow motion, as long as there is not a long delay before an observable motion starts. However, the low force usually implies that the arm must be capable of lifting the heaviest design load at the longest reach. Thus, when the arm is in a bent configuration with a light load, it will still be capable of exerting a significant force. Also, even if the arm is so lightly powered that it can be pushed away with the chin, the resulting force capability could still damage the eye if the gripper were carrying a sharp object.

A further possible configuration is to place the arm totally within reach of the user, for example on the arm of a wheelchair. This has the merit that it can be of considerable benefit to the user, particularly if the arm can also reach to the floor and to a high shelf. However, it can potentially reach (and hence damage) not only the user, but helpers and passers-by. This can be partially guarded against by designating 'no-go' areas for the patient, operating at slowest speed when the arm configuration is, say, near the head, and totally preventing motion where the arm could strike the head. This, however, has the problem mentioned earlier that it is very difficult to so constrain the user that the no-go areas are constant with reference to the chair.

While this objection could be overcome with additional sensing which could adapt the no-go areas to suit the user's current posture, this implies considerable extra cost and does nothing for the public passing by, who may adopt any position and breach the no-go concepts. For them, much more sensing would be needed to warn of an impending collision and stop the arm. All such emergency procedures would require elaborate safety status checks before the arm would be re-initialized. It can be seen that as further systems are added to take care of potentially unsafe situations, the complexity and cost rise until the system becomes unlikely to be used. At some level of complexity, it is likely that we must all accept that medical manipulators are potentially hazardous devices and that reasonable care is needed when they are used.

The medical manipulator becomes more of a hazard when part of a complex control system, for example a powered wheelchair with powered adjustable seat position and an environmental controller. The integrated control system needs to take account not only of the individual devices, but also of the potentially unsafe outcomes of a combination of the device activities or capabilities, for example attempting to pass through a doorway at speed while the arm is extended, or trying to turn the chair abruptly while the arm is carrying a load at full reach.

Many of the problems of this type of system have come to light in a

European 'TIDE' project concerned with medical mobile manipulator systems, in which the author is concerned with safety issues [Davies 92]. Whilst this TIDE project has been primarily concerned with the specification of an international bus structure for a collection of sub-systems (powered wheelchairs, manipulators and environmental controllers), it has also highlighted particular problems for medical manipulators in this role. For the wheelchair and other systems, a 'dead man's switch' (DMS) has been recommended. With this, for any prime mover to continue to act, a switch has to be positively held in an 'on' position. The moment that the DMS is released, power is removed from the local prime mover power relays. However, such a severe stop would be disadvantageous for the smooth control of a manipulator, so, instead, it is proposed for this device to have a DMS linked to a zero velocity command, fed into the normal control system.

This concept is further supplemented by a speed cut-off, at the prime movers themselves, if the zero velocity control command fails to act within a certain time. Safety integrity is further enhanced by the use of safety monitoring, both of the central control functions and at the sub-system power module levels. The safety monitors would remove power from different areas, depending on the fault, and report back to the central display unit. In addition to the continuous action of holding a DMS closed, there is also a need for a large red button, prominently displayed, as a final emergency 'off' switch.

Probably the most unpredictable environmental configuration is when the manipulator arm is placed on a free-roving mobile robot. The whole system is then so complex that a simple but safe HCI is difficult to achieve. Also, the arm can be carried by its mobile platform into many different configurations, out of sight of the user, who then has to be reliant on the partial view obtained from camera systems attached both to the mobile platform and to the manipulator arm. The use of 'islands of safety', implemented, for example, by light curtains, may become necessary.

15.5 CONCLUSIONS

From the above discussion, it can be seen that the greatest potential for benefit tends to come from medical robot systems which put the user and public at the most risk. While it is possible to guard these systems with additional software and sensing, this has the penalty of increased complexity and cost.

The integrity and fail-safe nature of software and hardware (including sensors) has to be rigorously considered, with an evaluation of the additional potential to be gained from formal methods of software development, duplication of software and hardware, and the use of such analytical techniques as Failure Mode and Effect Analysis and Fault Tree Analysis.

These may well require the presence of separate positive, continuously acting, dead man's switches and 'Kill Lines' to provide a hardware stop independent of the software and computer-based control system. All of this will usually need the addition of a large red button for turning everything off in an emergency.

It is hoped that this chapter has helped to illustrate some of the safety problems inherent in medical robot systems, together with a range of possible solutions. A further range of discussions with all groups, experts, users and the public, will be necessary before a consensus can emerge on what is good practice and how safe is 'safe' for medical robotic systems.

15.6 REFERENCES

[Adams 89]   Adams J, Gilsbach J, Krybus K, Ebrecht D and Mosges R: "CAS - A Navigation Support for Surgery." IEEE Eng. in Medicine & Biology Soc. 11 Int. Conf., 1989.

[Davies 91a]   Davies B L, Hibberd R D, Ng W S, Timony A, and Wickham J E A: "A Surgeon Robot for Prostatectomies." Proc. 5th I.C.A.R. Pisa, Italy: IEEE. U.S.A., June 1991.

[Davies 91b]   Davies B L, Hibberd R D, Ng W S, Timoney A and Wickham J E A: "Development of a Surgeon Robot for Prostatectomies." J. Eng. in Medicine. Proc. H. of IMechE. Vol 205. M.E.P. ltd., July 1991.

[Davies 92]   Davies B L: "Safety of Robots in Medicine." Proc. of IMechE Seminar on Safety of High Technology Devices in Medicine. IMechE, London, June 1992.

[Lavallee 89]   Lavallee S: "A New System for Computer Assisted Neuro-Surgery." IEEE Eng. in Medicine & Biology Soc. 11th Int. Conf. pp 926 - 927, 1989.

16

Engineering safety into expert systems

John Fox

The problems of developing sound and safe expert systems are discussed, with particular reference to medicine. The concepts, notations, methods, results and technologies which have emerged from the study of mathematical logic as a computational paradigm offer many benefits for improving the quality of expert systems. Logic programming offers a better discipline for design, specification and implementation than *ad hoc* development methodologies. When logic programming is combined with software engineering methods, such as a software development lifecycle, the probability of routinely developing large-scale yet efficient and sound applications will be increased. However, although soundness is a necessary property of any technology it is not sufficient for assuring safety. Traditional methods for improved software safety are discussed, and a number of candidate approaches to improving the safety of medical expert systems are identified. The possibility of introducing an appropriately extended lifecycle, and the potential benefits of a formal theory of safety are discussed.

16.1 INTRODUCTION

Expert systems are computer systems that give advice in areas where human expertise would normally be required. Although the idea of using computers to advise on specialist decision making has been discussed for many years, it only achieved prominence with the introduction of 'knowledge based' techniques from the field of Artificial Intelligence (AI). Knowledge based systems emphasized:

- Symbolic computation, as distinct from traditional numerical methods, with symbolic data structures used explicitly to represent the specialized knowledge of human experts;
- Declarative representations of knowledge (encoding what needs to be done while leaving to the computer the question of which algorithms to use);
- Domain-specific heuristics, or rules of thumb, for problem-solving, rather than formalized information-processing techniques;
- Strict separation of the knowledge base from the shell program that applies the knowledge in a particular situation;
- Shell design based on one or more generalized tasks, such as diagnosis, event monitoring, planning, or design tasks.

Many early expert systems were developed for advising on medical decisions, such as the diagnosis of diseases, selection of tests, and treatment planning. Medicine has in fact provided one of the most important stimuli to the development of expert system technology. So far, however, the practical penetration of expert systems into clinical use seems to have been much less than into commercial and industrial environments. The reasons for this relative lack of success are many and varied. However, it seems likely that the special sensitivities that surround medical decision making have played an important part in delaying the adoption of expert systems. It is often said of course that doctors are conservative and unwilling to accept new ideas. They can certainly be difficult to persuade of the value of novel technologies, but the medical profession is constantly being offered new technologies, and, given the serious consequences of adopting unproven methods, its standards of acceptance are rather high. From this point of view, one of the great weaknesses of expert systems technology has been the relatively *ad hoc* nature of applications development. The idea of using 'rules of thumb' is hardly likely to inspire confidence in doctors or patients, and the lack of a strong theoretical foundation for expert system development compares unfavourably with other branches of engineering. It is not surprising if doctors, and their patients, prefer to stick with professional human 'judgement' rather than adopt a technology which, for many, implies a surrendering of responsibility to a machine, particularly one that is poorly understood.

The routine adoption of expert systems into clinical practice will require many obstacles to be overcome. From the point of view of safety engineering, however, medicine offers an interesting challenge generally. Medicine can play a role that it has often played before - to present problems which stimulate innovative technical solutions, which are useful well beyond the borders of medicine. This chapter is therefore concerned with ways in which we might address the challenge of making medical expert systems sound and safe, by introducing more formal design and development techniques. The particular approaches proposed here are based on techniques from mathematical logic.

16.2 LOGIC ENGINEERING

Logic programming can be defined as the development of software using the concepts, formalisms, methods, results and technologies which have emerged from the study of mathematical logic as a computational paradigm. Following Kowalski's seminal book on the use of logic for problem-solving [Kowalski 79] and Colmerauer's development of Prolog as a practical language [Colmerauer 83], logic programming has proved itself to be a powerful, flexible and practical basis for developing sophisticated software, with the special feature that its mathematical foundations are uniquely well understood. Knowledge-based and expert systems have been an important area for the application of logic programming. The Oxford System of Medicine (OSM), a large-scale medical decision support system which will be discussed extensively in this chapter, has drawn heavily on ideas from logic programming [Fox 90].

Although logic programming has many strengths and has become widely accepted in computer science, it has been slow to gain general acceptance in knowledge engineering. Perhaps this is because the logic programming community has, to date, put less emphasis on practical engineering needs than on demonstrations of technical elegance and versatility. Techniques which are commonplace in software engineering are still relatively weak in logic programming. The importance of experience in software engineering is increasingly recognized by researchers in knowledge-based systems, and there is growing emphasis on the use of systematic methods for design, verification and validation [Lydiard 92]. In particular, the use of systematic methodologies for developing software systems, such as 'lifecycle models' (e.g. the waterfall and spiral models), are being introduced. Lifecycle models offer improved project planning, resource requirements estimation, better project control and documentation, improved quality management, and the ability to carry out quality and cost audits [Wilson 89].

The best known development methodology in Europe is the KADS methodology [KA 92]. KADS is aimed at providing general tools and techniques to support design, specification, knowledge acquisition, knowledge reusability, verification, etc., within a well-defined lifecycle.

The paradigm of logic programming is not in any way incompatible with lifecycle approaches. On the contrary, it can contribute substantially to many of the principle phases of a lifecycle. Logic engineering is the practice of logic programming, within a systematic lifecycle methodology. Taken together, KADS and the OSM span much of the logic engineering approach to developing knowledge-based systems, with logic-based techniques contributing to many phases of the lifecycle, including design, prototyping, software specification, implementation and installation.

16.2.1   Conceptual Design

Experience has shown that the use of purely 'symbol-level' techniques in expert systems needs to be guided by a 'knowledge-level' understanding of the applications. What this means is that, as in other kinds of engineering, designers need an understanding of the functions of the components of the system as well as their form. In expert systems, this implies that we develop an understanding of what the different kinds of knowledge in a knowledge base are good for and why, and not just a range of technologies to choose from.

This requirement is reflected in the KADS and OSM approaches. Both recommend that knowledge bases should be organized into distinct components to reflect their different functions. In KADS, distinctions are made between 'task', 'inference' and 'domain' knowledge layers (there is also a strategic layer, but this seems to be used infrequently). There are three broad classes of task: analysis tasks (e.g. involving various kinds of diagnoses and prediction procedures), synthesis tasks (e.g. various forms of design and planning), and modification tasks (e.g. for repair and control). For each task there is intended to be a generic, reusable tool, a standard component that can be instantiated with a variety of domain knowledge (e.g. medicine) and different inference techniques.

KADS provides help in designing applications by means of a standard model for structuring the knowledge base and by providing reusable task and inference methods.

The OSM is less general than KADS since it has a single generic task model, which focuses on decision making under uncertainty. This is similar to KADS' analysis tasks, but more emphasis is placed on developing a formal theory and design schema for decision making. This aims to be more comprehensive, flexible and appropriate for knowledge-based expert systems than classical mathematical decision theory or the *ad hoc* methods of early expert systems [FoxK 92]. Also like in KADS, knowledge is layered in the OSM. The first layer can be viewed as knowledge about decision making in general, and the second is knowledge about specific kinds of decision (like diagnosis, treatment selection and test-selection decisions). The third layer encodes knowledge of medicine (about diseases, symptoms, drugs, etc.), and the final layer records knowledge about specific patients (see Figure 16.1).

There is an increasing emphasis on knowledge-based systems which exploit 'deep' knowledge as well as shallow empirical knowledge embodied in rules of thumb. This is commonly intended to mean that the knowledge embodies some sort of causal theory, but there are many other kinds of deep knowledge if we allow other sorts of formal theories into the knowledge base, including knowledge of time, space, processes, events, tasks, actions, etc. There is growing interest in the systematic development of natural 'ontologies' around which to organize bodies of knowledge [Lenat 90] and we therefore require knowledge about how and when these different types of knowledge should be used. Logic offers an effective medium for

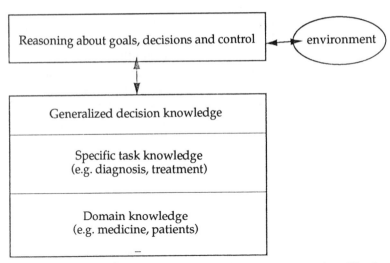

Figure 16.1: Schematic organization of a symbolic decision procedure like that used by the Oxford System of Medicine.

developing and formalising ontological theories, as demonstrated by the countless specialized forms of logic in the literature. Davis [Davis 90] provides an overview of logics which have been developed to capture the 'common-sense' meaning of a variety of ontological concepts. Many of these logics, of time, space, events, mass, action, causality, change, belief, etc., are now in a rather mature state.

The common motivation of KADS and the OSM is that designers should be offered not just a set of implementation technologies but a higher-level language of tasks, theories, logics, etc., in which to conceive and design applications, and well-understood theories to under-pin their construction.

16.2.2   Prototyping

A feature of KBS development has been that full-scale implementation of applications is often preceded by the construction of a prototype. In some cases the principles involved in the design of the application may be unproven, or the idea of AI and knowledge-based systems may arouse scepticism among one's colleagues (a declining but still common experience in medical informatics). For any one of a number of reasons, there may be an understandable reticence to commit substantial resources to the development of a novel technology, and development of a convincing prototype may smooth the path.

It has also been argued that the natural method of developing AI systems is the 'RUDE' (run, understand, debug, edit) cycle, which permits requirements to be flexibly altered as empirical investigation leads to better understanding of the application. While one could not accept this as a sufficient method for developing high-quality KBSs there may well be a role for this sort of iterative prototyping in the early phases of a project.

The logic language Prolog has been frequently used as a 'rapid prototyping' tool. It has a number of features which make it appropriate for this purpose:

(i)   What not how. A pure Prolog program is a declarative description of the relationships which hold in the application domain, but since such programs also have a procedural reading (i.e. the program provides all the information necessary for a Prolog interpreter to derive all implied relationships), the programmer is freed from writing code to control execution. There is no guarantee that the execution will be as efficient as a program written for a specific purpose, but efficiency is not a primary concern in prototyping.

(ii)   Succinctness and expressiveness. Prolog programs are constructed directly from clauses which encode rules and facts. These naturally express some of the basic constructs of knowledge-based systems and can easily be extended to express other computational metaphors without compromising the formal semantics and soundness of the underlying computational model (e.g. ideas like those of objects and inheritance [McCabe 92]). Prolog's declarativeness and powerful pattern matching and variable unification capabilities lead to programs that are shorter (frequently much shorter) than equivalent programs written in conventional languages.

(iii) A built-in database. Most, if not all, knowledge-based and expert systems require database facilities (for storing and retrieving data or knowledge, blackboard structures, etc.). A Prolog program can be viewed as a relational database extended to include deduction [Grant 90], from which facts can be retrieved directly by pattern matching or realized by executing proofs over the database. Since the programmer is freed from designing and implementing DBMS functions, the construction of prototypes is substantially simplified.

(iv)   Interchangeability of facts and rules. Complex applications frequently require external utilities (such as simulation or planning utilities, or even external devices like sensors or instruments). The construction and interfacing of such utilities can require considerably more effort than the main procedure whose behaviour we want to demonstrate. In the full program, the utilities would be incapsulated in a set of first-order rules or in external procedure calls. Whatever the implementation, we can view any procedure as equivalent to some (possibly infinite) database of the results generated by the procedure, without altering the semantics of the overall program. The prototyping effort can be reduced by including a few facts from this 'database' to represent results that the utility would produce. When required, the full utility may be substituted for the facts without other program changes.

(v)   Meta-level expressiveness. One of the most powerful properties of the first-order predicate calculus is its ability to express other logics. This carries over into logic programming languages in their ability succinctly to express, and hence implement, specialized procedures. For example, Prolog is based on a purely logical view of computation which does not naturally model time-evolving processes. However, it is straightforward to implement mechanisms with very different properties from those of Prolog. We have made extensive use of this in a language which combines the deductive power of Prolog with the flexibility of event-triggered execution [Hajnal 89]. This has been used for prototyping mechanisms for simulation, planning, sensor monitoring, and so forth. Non-classical inference, execution optimization techniques, and natural language dialogue systems are among the many other functions whose implementation is simplified by the meta-level expressiveness of logic programming languages. Formal models for meta-logical reasoning are now being actively investigated [Abramson 89].

16.2.3   Logic and Formal Specification.

The emphasis on methods based on logic is partly because of benefits in designing and implementing knowledge systems, but there is another matter that I believe to be of long-term importance for medical information technology. This concerns the way in which we expect to assure the integrity of new clinical technologies.

Wyatt and Spiegelhalter have reviewed evaluation methods used in knowledge-based system development. A comparison of these methods with standard methods for evaluating medical techniques, such as clinical trials of new drugs [Wyatt 90] showed that testing methods need to be substantially improved. Empirical testing of expert systems certainly needs improvement, but this cannot be our only methodological goal. I would draw a different analogy, with mature engineering disciplines. Many branches of engineering have moved beyond purely empirical testing (such as test-flying aircraft prototypes) because they have established strong design theories (e.g. for stress analysis for predicting properties of the airframe, laminar flow models for predicting turbulence and aerodynamic behaviour). The consequence is that designers can confidently predict failure modes, performance boundary conditions, and so forth, before the systems are implemented. The formulation of a comprehensive design theory, which guides the design process and provides a basis for predicting the behaviour of specific application systems, seems to be an important objective for expert systems research.

A promising approach to formalization may be to use well-defined specification languages and verification procedures. Van Harmelen and Balder [VanH 92] summarize the advantages of using formal languages for describing the structure and/or behaviour of software systems as:

• The removal of ambiguity;

- The facilitation of communication and discussion;
- The ability to derive properties of the design in the absence of an implementation.

Logic offers an expressive language for capturing different kinds of knowledge in different functional layers. Not only is the predicate calculus (and the logic programming language Prolog) sufficiently expressive to capture the different types of knowledge, it can also serve the role of a specification language for formalizing layers as (reusable) domain theories, task theories, and so on.

Two different specification tasks need to be undertaken for the classical expert system architecture; one for the 'shell' and one for the knowledge base. These specifications may be rather different and may require different tools, though logic can contribute substantially at both levels.

At the level of the inference engine, for example, the use of careful specification techniques can reveal a lack of soundness in a design. Some time ago, I programmed a truth maintenance mechanism for use in a prototype expert system. A colleague, Paul Krause, examined the properties of this mechanism and showed that under certain circumstances the TMS was unsound and could lead to pathological reasoning. A modified truth maintenance system was specified, using a formal specification language [KBHF 91] and the consistency and effectiveness of the specification was formally proved [KBHC 91].

The use of formal techniques for specifying knowledge bases is not so straightforward, since domain knowledge may be poorly defined and incomplete. However, recent proposals for formal specification languages which are specifically adapted for knowledge-base design seem promising [VanL 92]. One such language has been developed within KADS. This language $(ML)^2$ provides constructs for viewing knowledge bases as organized collections of logical 'theories', for communication between theories and for describing meta-level operations on theories [VanH 92].

Theories in a logic consist of a set of formal terms (sentences) which are to be interpreted according to the inference rules of the logic. A theory in FOL consists of a set of facts and implication rules to be interpreted according to the rules of the propositional calculus extended with quantifiers. Theories in $(ML)^2$ are essentially equivalent to theories in FOL, together with meta-information about the kinds of objects that the theory mentions. Loosely speaking, each task, inference technique or body of domain knowledge can be specified as a theory in $(ML)^2$. The formalism provides a language in which such theories can be specified in a modular, and hopefully reusable, way.

A theory in $(ML)^2$ consists of a signature which defines a language plus a set of axioms expressed in that language. The general structure is presented below (this is not a formal presentation so I have slightly simplified the syntax):

```
theory <name>
      import <set of theory names>
      signature classes <class hierarchy>
             constants <set of constants and their classes>
             functions <set of class —> class mappings>
             predicates <set of predicates and arguments>
      variables <set of symbols and their classes>
      axioms <set of facts and rules>
end-theory
```

A knowledge base consists of a collection of theories and sub-theories. Theory definitions can assume (import) the definitions of other theories. This clarifies the structure of the knowledge base and avoids repetition if a sub-theory is reused. The signature of a theory defines the syntax to be used in expressing axioms of the theory and a collection of integrity constraints on them; the facts and rules of a traditional knowledge base (or Prolog program) would form the axioms of a theory in $(ML)^2$. If axioms include first-order rules (i.e. rules including variables), the classes of values the variables can have is also specified.

A concrete example of $(ML)^2$ being used to define a simple layered structure similar to that of the OSM is given in Figure 16.2. The three theories express a fragment of knowledge dealing with the diagnosis of disease from qualitative knowledge of the causal relationships between symptoms and signs and diseases. The diagnosis procedure is a simplification and specialization of a more general symbolic decision procedure [Huang 92]. The definition assumes (imports) a medical layer (here just a set of causal facts) and a patient record (a set of findings).

Specification techniques for knowledge engineering need not be restricted to classical logic. Krause *et al* [KBHC 91] made use of modal logic in specifying their revised truth maintenance system; van Harmelen and Balder [VanH 92] proposed the use of quantified dynamic logic for specifying complex procedures and tasks (an extension of FOL which permits the expression of programming concepts like sequences of operations on states, iteration, etc.), and the diagnosis procedure in Figure 16.2 assumes that 'arguments' are constructed using LA, a logic of 'argumentation' described in [FoxKA 92].

Van Harmelen and Balder remark that 'if knowledge engineering wants to live up to its name and is to become a proper engineering activity, a similar development of the field towards a formal treatment of the models it is concerned with must take place'. Formal specification languages are intended to enable software engineers to produce a mathematical model of the software they wish to build before committing themselves to coding it. As well as providing an unambiguous statement of the program's intended behaviour, the specification may be subject to mathematical proofs and analyses of its properties, helping to avoid potentially disastrous errors. This is not to say that formal specification is a panacea, for formal

theory diagnosis-procedure
    import medical-knowledge patient-record
    signature
        classes
            findings(symptoms signs)
            diseases arguments numbers signs(+ - ++ --)
        predicates
            argument: findings x diseases x sign
            causes: diseases x findings
            finding: findings
            candidate: diseases
            best: diseases
        functions: merit: arguments $\longrightarrow$ numbers
    variables F,F1,F2:findings D1,D2:diseases M1,M2:numbers
    axioms
        finding(F) $\wedge$ causes(D,F) $\rightarrow$ argument(F,D,+)
        argument(F1,D,+) $\wedge$ not(argument(F2,D,--)) $\rightarrow$ candidate(D)
        candidate(D1) $\wedge$ merit(D1)=M1 $\wedge$
            not(candidate(D2) $\wedge$ merit(D2)=M2 $\wedge$ M2>M1) $\rightarrow$ best(D1)
end-theory

theory medical-knowledge
    signature
        classes (symptoms (weight-loss pain(severe-pain mild-pain...))
            diseases(gastric-cancer peptic-ulcer))
        predicates
            causes:diseases x symptoms
    axioms
        causes(peptic-ulcer,severe-pain)
        causes(peptic-ulcer,weight-loss)
        causes(gastric-cancer,weight-loss)
end-theory

theory patient-record
    signature
        classes (personal-details symptoms)
        predicates finding: symptoms
        constants weight-loss, severe-pain:symptoms
    axioms
        finding(weight-loss)
        finding(severe-pain)
end-theory

Figure 16.2: An example of a layered knowledge-base specified in (ML)² notation.

specification is difficult on large-scale applications and there are certain technical restrictions on its use, but it offers a promising discipline. Tools for simplifying the use of specification methods are under active development.

16.2.4   Implementation.

Implementation of an efficient application raises issues that are not addressed by prototyping and specification techniques. Indeed, a successful prototype has often fostered a false sense of security about the ability to deliver a practical application. For some applications, such as simple diagnosis systems, full implementation may require only refinements of the original prototype. Frequently, however, the prototype may only incorporate part of the functionality and/or knowledge of the intended system, its function being solely to establish, or demonstrate to others in an organization, that the application is viable in principle. Unfortunately, it has frequently been found that developing a prototype expert system into a practical delivery system proves more problematic than expected; the pilot application does not 'scale up'.

Scaling up may raise problems for ensuring the integrity of the knowledge base or achieving acceptable efficiency when the application is reasoning over a large knowledge base. These are both significant challenges to the Oxford System of Medicine. The OSM is concerned with general practice and primary care, and general practitioners have to deal with a wide range of tasks and a very large body of general medical knowledge. (We estimate that to cover a substantial proportion of general medicine the OSM knowledge base could require a domain theory equivalent to around 10M facts.)

(a)   Integrity.

An important goal of the KADS and OSM projects is the development of knowledge acquisition tools which include verification facilities. The $(ML)^2$ formalization provides a basis for some automated verification. The TheME editor makes use of the syntax information in the signature of an $(ML)^2$ theory to check that knowledge updates are consistent with the signature and to guide extensions to the knowledge base [Balder 92]. Checking the content of axiom sets requires different techniques. There is now a considerable literature on checking of knowledge bases for coherence and consistency [Charles 91] and for identifying anomalies in the domain knowledge, where logic provides a clear set of semantics for anomalies [Preece 92]. 'Second-generation' knowledge-based systems, in which emphasis is placed on the use of models in the knowledge base (such as causal models for diagnostic systems), can also benefit from logical verification procedures [Guibert 91], as can reasoning about the integrity of temporal information [Cardoso 92]. Taking a different but similarly motivated approach, the OSMOTIC editor uses a generalized model of medical concepts and their interrelationships to detect model violations and to suggest repairs to the OSM domain layer [Glowinski 91].

(b) Efficiency.

AI tools have acquired a (rather exaggerated) reputation for inefficiency, but use of very general representations and meta-level programming techniques does tend to entail heavy computational costs, and this may be unacceptable for large applications. However, recent work has led to a number of techniques for improving efficiency without ignoring the security of the logic programming model. Inefficiency of logic programs is commonly due to re-computation resulting from unnecessary backtracking during searches. Partial evaluation is an optimization technique whereby unnecessary computation is avoided by compiling a very general Prolog program into a more specific and more efficient one [Hogger 90]. Meta-level or 'piggy back' interpreters can be used to exploit specific control knowledge by dynamically re-ordering goals during execution of Prolog programs [Owen 88]. In constraint logic programming, efficient constraint-solving algorithms are substituted for classical backtracking searches [VanH 91]. Commercial systems are becoming available that combine efficient database management techniques with the power of FOL, facilities for integrity constraint checking, fast run-time constraint solving, and the ability to run on parallel machine architectures. This combination of capabilities is likely to have considerable implications for our ability to deliver complex, yet efficient and sound applications.

16.2.5   Installation

Introducing novel software into established work settings commonly demands tolerance and flexibility from users, imposes changes to work practices, and causes organizational disruption. Adopting a formal methodology for software design and development does not solve these problems, but there are indirect benefits from carefully articulated design: the opportunity of staff to try out (and participate in the development of) prototypes, and enhanced quality and reliability of delivered software. However, the principal challenge to the software designer, particularly in a medical context, is to achieve the trust of those affected by the new techniques. Demonstrations of effectiveness, using proven clinical evaluation techniques, will foster trust, and good design facilitates convincing evaluation, but even these are insufficient. The most stringent empirical testing cannot prevent the occurrence of unanticipated events or side-effects of use and consequent disasters. Proving that software satisfies the formal requirements and complies with the software specification cannot help much, since the requirements and specification may be at fault.

Given the controversies that still surround the use of AI, the crucial question is, Can we make expert systems provably safe in some sense? Traditional safety engineering techniques for electromechanical systems have proved to be capable of reducing risk of failure to extremely low levels. Unfortunately, software raises new and severe problems, and decision support systems exacerbate these problems. The fundamental difficulty is that safety engineering has been primarily concerned with component failure, whereas decision support software may operate perfectly and yet have unacceptable down-stream consequences. In the next section I review some of these difficulties in more detail, and explore some possible directions for development.

16.3 THE SAFETY OF DECISION SUPPORT SYSTEMS

Much medical software is 'safety-critical', meaning that errors in operation or use can lead to death or injury (and legal liability). To pick just one example, problems with the over-/under-dosing of patients receiving radiotherapy have been caused by software design errors [THERAC 87].

Decision support systems can behave unsafely in a number of ways. The software may fail to:

- Detect a hazardous situation (e.g. a possible disease);
- Recommend an appropriate action (e.g. an effective treatment);
- Predict a hazardous side-effect of some recommended action (e.g. a potential drug inter-action);
- Recommend an action to prevent a latent hazard turning into a disaster (e.g. post a veto on using drugs which could interact with a prescribed drug).

The increasing use of AI techniques in decision support and other systems, particularly in the context of autonomous systems, has attracted significant concern. The THERAC problems arose in the context of conventional software, for which there is not only vast experience but also many techniques for assuring software quality. Since our understanding of the behaviour and consequences of using expert systems is limited, we cannot be complacent about their use in safety-critical applications. As one author succinctly puts it, one of the problems with software design and development is that we have been overly concerned with what a system shall do, and insufficiently concerned with what it shall not do. It is hardly surprising, therefore, that there have been calls for restrictions on the deployment of unsupervised or autonomous systems in safety-critical applications [Boden 89] and for keeping a human operator 'in the loop' in medical applications [Mellor 92].

Even if we restrict our attention to advisory systems (under the supervision of professional clinical staff) there are still reasons for concern. We have discussed how formal design and development techniques can help to ensure soundness and, hence, quality of software. Soundness is a necessary condition for safety, but unfortunately it is not a sufficient condition. Soundness is a technical property which ensures that a program complies with a formal specification, but it does not ensure that the original specification is correct or that the consequences or side-effects of using the software are only those that are intended by the designers and users.

Classical safety engineering developed within aerospace, process control, power, and other industries, involving complex electromechanical systems. It has been extraordinarily successful. If established safety engineering methods are adopted, designers can be confident of achieving extremely high reliability levels. Requirements for system failure rates of the order of 10^{-9} over years of operation are not untypical [Redmill 92]. Perhaps we should look at engineering practices in such domains for techniques we can use in expert systems?

16.3.1   Traditional Strategies for Minimising Disasters

Safety engineering has been traditionally concerned with 'faults' and 'hazards'. A fault is a failure to behave according to the intentions of the designers (for which the specification is a partial indication) and a hazard is a situation which might lead to a total or partial failure having death or injury as a consequence. Faults do not necessarily lead to hazards, and hazards do not necessarily lead to disasters (e.g. near misses of aircraft), but potential errors need to be understood and prevented. Traditional safety engineering therefore involves two main kinds of activity:

- Analysing faults and the hazards they give rise to;
- Incorporating techniques for minimizing the likelihood of faults and for preventing hazards from turning into disasters.

The need to design quality into software from the beginning of the development lifecycle is now generally accepted. An analogous view can be taken of software safety: 'The goal of system safety is to design an acceptable safety level into the system before actual production or operation....' [Leveson 86]. The adoption of lifecycle methodologies has helped to improve the quality of conventional software and promises to do the same for knowledge-based systems. Figure 16.3 suggests an approach in which a safety lifecycle is executed in parallel with the quality lifecycle. The remainder of this section considers the activities composing this lifecycle, considering the relevance of established safety techniques and ways in which they might be enhanced to address the special challenges of expert systems.

(a)   Hazard Analysis

Before formulating a safety strategy for a proposed system, it is necessary to establish a clear picture of the circumstances that may lead to hazards.

Among the techniques traditionally used are fault likelihood estimation and hazard analysis.

When designing any new equipment, it is normal to use standard components wherever possible. For safety-critical systems, this may have the great advantage that historical failure data are available for such components. Failure data provide a basis for estimating the likelihood of operational faults (and collections of faults) and hence to predict the expected reliability of the total system.

As we have discussed, there is now considerable effort being expended to develop reusable software components in software engineering and, increasingly, in knowledge engineering as well. However, in the context of safety, the analogy with standard physical components does not take us

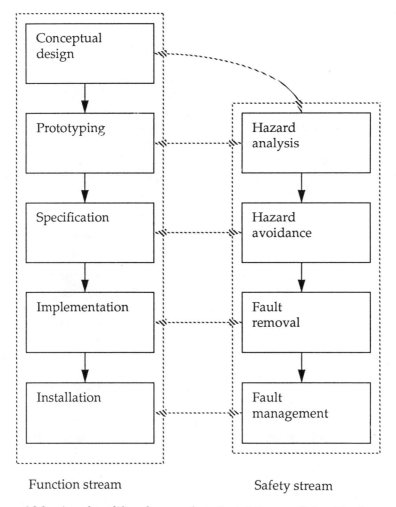

Figure 16.3: A safety lifecycle may be adopted in parallel with the normal development lifecycle.

very far. It does not make much sense to collect historical data to assess the 'reliability' of software components. Ideas like 'mean time between failure' which are so informative about electromechanical systems are not applicable to software. Software does not fail for the same sorts of reasons as physical devices (e.g. wear and tear). If a fault is manifested, we call this a bug and fix it, so it should not happen again in that form. Indeed it is not currently feasible to arrive at a meaningful estimate of the likelihood of a software component 'failing' at all [Leveson 86, Parnas 90, Abbott 90].

Another procedure for analysing likely sources of hazard involves the systematic exploration of those faults that could conceivably arise during system operation, possible interactions between faults, and interactions between faults and environmental events. These methods are part of 'hazard analysis and risk assessment', and frequently involve building a model of all the causal dependencies in the proposed system, its failure modes, etc.

Hazard analysis is naturally helped by a systematic approach, but in the end its effectiveness depends on the imagination and assiduousness of the design team. With software, the problems seem to be much worse because of the abstract nature of software processes, the ease with which systems can be made very complicated and the awesome potential of software to manifest unexpected interactions. Hazard analysis can be considerably helped by constructing prototypes and/or simulating the use of the software to reveal faults, software errors, and so on. However, it is difficult to provide realistic test conditions, and there is no guarantee that the prototype or simulation is accurate or complete.

In short, there are no techniques which can guarantee that all possible faults and hazards are exhaustively identified for any but the most trivial software, nor techniques for reliably estimating the relative likelihood of hazardous situations. Strategies for preventing and minimizing the consequences of hazards must, in some way, take this into account.

(b)   Hazard Avoidance

The engineering ideal is to be able to design a system so well that problems simply cannot occur. Formal specification, refinement, and verification of software can substantially improve the integrity of a program, as can the use of formally verified standard components, such as knowledge bases and specialized theorem provers. However, there are severe limitations on the capability of formal design techniques completely to prevent hazardous situations arising. It is well known that current formal design methods are time-consuming, difficult to use, and practical only for relatively modest applications. Even if we reserve formal techniques only for the safety-critical elements of a system, we have seen that the soundness guaranteed by the techniques can only be as good as the specifier's ability to anticipate the conditions and possible hazards that can hold at the time of use.

These problems are difficult enough for 'closed systems' - in which the designer can be confident, at least in principle, of knowing all the parameters which may affect system performance and of being able to design the software to respond to abnormal states or trends. Unfortunately, all systems are to a greater or lesser extent 'open'; they operate in an environment which cannot be exhaustively monitored and in which unpredictable events will occur. Furthermore, reliance on specification and verification methods assumes that the operational environment will not compromise the correct execution of software. In fact, software errors can be caused by transient faults causing data loss or corruption, user errors, interfacing problems with external systems (such as databases and instruments), incompatibilities between software versions, and so on. The clinical environment is a prime example of an open environment in which the carefully formulated recommendations of an expert system may be quickly compromised by unforeseen interactions and side-effects.

(c)   Fault Removal

Hazards, and consequent disasters, cannot be totally avoided even with the best intentions and best design practices. Inadequate design foresight, including specification errors, has been found to be the greatest source of software safety problems [Ericson 81, Griggs 81]. The use of formal specification techniques has not removed the need for rigorous testing and debugging of conventional software [Parnas 90]; the adoption of analogous techniques in AI systems is similarly unlikely to remove the need for empirical testing.

The need for rigorous clinical trials of new medical technologies is generally accepted. However, Wyatt and Spiegelhalter have raised serious doubts about testing in practice: 'only about 10 per cent of the many medical knowledge-based systems that have been described over the years have been tested in laboratory conditions, while even fewer have been exposed to clinical trials. This may be because systems were built to investigate certain tools or techniques, or because of lack of resources, or it may be because of confusion about what to test, and how to test it.' [Wyatt 90].

Even if the best available methods for empirical evaluation of the performance of an expert system are employed prior to installation, this will not remove all residual sources of difficulty. Even if we follow the best practice for clinical trials, we will not fully address the safety issue. 'Live testing of computer responses to catastrophic situations is ... difficult in the absence of catastrophes.' Conventional systems have provided reliable service over long periods only to fail disastrously (for the patient) in unanticipated conditions of operation or use (e.g. the THERAC example) and there seems to be no reason to think that current decision support systems will be any different. More techniques are clearly needed; one possible strategy is to build some sort of fault tolerance into the design.

(d) Fault Tolerance

If it is not possible to avoid all errors, perhaps it is possible to manage them when they occur. A proven technique with mechanical and electronic systems is to build fault tolerance into systems. The classic fault tolerance technique involves redundancy, in various forms. For example, mechanical systems may be replicated so that if one fails others are likely to remain operational.

Analogous techniques have been explored for software design. Simple duplication of software is of course unlikely to be effective, since identical programs will have identical error behaviour. However, so-called 'N-version' techniques, in which a number of different versions of the software are run simultaneously have been discussed (e.g. [Abbott 90]). Assuming that the different versions have different failure modes, supervisory software can resolve conflicts by letting the different programs 'vote' and act on the majority conclusion. This idea might be applied to knowledge-based systems. For example, in diagnosis one might compare the conclusions from applying statistical reasoning with those from deterministic causal simulation, and with reasoning from 'textbook' cases, with a meta-level component resolving any conflicts that arise. Unfortunately we cannot be complacent that introducing redundancy into knowledge-based systems will necessarily substantially reduce the likelihood of problems. Knight and Leveson were unable to find independence of failure behaviour between independently produced versions of software [Knight 86], and there is as yet little evidence that different reasoning techniques have distinct error characteristics.

This is illustrated by a study of medical expert systems which compared the performance of two very different methods in diagnosing abdominal

(a)	F	Ch	DU	GU	Ca
F	5		4	1	
Ch	1	7		1	1
DU			8	2	
GU	1		1	6	2
Ca	1			1	8

(b)	F	Ch	DU	GU	Ca
F	4		2...	1...	
Ch	1	6	1		2
DU	1		9	2	
GU	1		1	6	2
Ca				2	8

Figure 16.4 (a) and (b): Similarity of diagnosis patterns of rule-based and statistical diagnosis methods [Fox 80]. The objective diagnosis is on the vertical axis and the computer diagnosis on the horizontal. Dots in (b) indicate that there was a tied assignment.

pain. Fifty patients who were known to fall into one of five clinical categories (non-organic or Functional disease, Cholecystitis, Duodenal Ulcer, Gastric Ulcer, and Cancer) were classified from clinical symptoms and signs into these categories using (a) a Bayesian calculation of probability and (b) a set of logical rules. As Figure 16.4 shows, the error patterns produced by the two apparently different techniques were almost identical [Fox 80].

16.3.2   Towards a Formal Safety Theory

From the foregoing, one might conclude that using a basket of safety methods (hazard analysis, formal specification and verification, rigorous empirical testing, fault tolerant design) will significantly decrease the likelihood of hazards and disasters. However, there is at least one weakness common to all these methods. They rely on the design team being able to make long-range predictions about all the clinical circumstances that may hold when the system is in use. This is unrealistic, if only because of the countless interactions that can occur.

The problem is well illustrated by the OSM. It is conceivable (just) that all hazards that could arise in specialist clinical management could be anticipated, but in general practice it is common that patients suffer from multiple, independent problems, with concurrent treatments in progress. Indeed different specialist clinics may be taking primary responsibility for managing certain conditions. The scope for unforeseeable interactions is vast.

To address this problem, provision might be made for developing a dynamic safety strategy to complement the static techniques described. Here the expert system would be assigned a task of reasoning about safety issues in parallel with its principle tasks of diagnosis, test and treatment selection, etc. An interesting illustration of this idea in a non-medical domain is suggestive. The 'safety bag expert system' [Klein 91] was developed for managing routeing of rolling stock through a rail network. Simply planning the shortest or some other least-cost route through the network is clearly hazardous. For example, a section of the route may have other wagons on it, or certain points (switches) might be set such that another train could enter the section. The safety bag expert system has a dual channel design in which one program proposes viable routes through tracks and points while a second system monitors the proposed routes for potential hazards. The latter system is a rule-based system in which the rules' conditions embody knowledge of safety regulations, and their actions are to veto (or commit) proposed routes. Examples of rules for vetoing and committing proposed rail routes used in the safety bag expert system are:

IF there is a route element of shunting route
AND the new route is a train route
AND the start signal of the shunting route is not contained in the new

route
THEN the route is not admissible

IF there is a request to perform the global locking check
AND all switches in the route are in correct position
AND all switches in the route are interlocked
AND all switches in the route are flank protected
AND the status of the route is admissible
THEN commit the request and change the status to locked.

The two main hazard points for expert systems are:

(i)   Failure to maintain continuous data surveillance and anticipation of the effects of proposed actions;
(ii) Failure to take or recommend appropriate action in the light of these assessments.

For surveillance, an established technique is to introduce 'watchdogs', such as rules for detecting the simultaneous prescription of incompatible medications. Current watchdog techniques use purely shallow reasoning; research into deeper surveillance techniques is required. For example, we need general techniques for detecting possible hazards resulting from a clinical action taken for one purpose compromising some other completely independent clinical objective. Dynamic hazard analysis might also include a process of forward projection of clinical recommendations to establish whether there are unacceptable 'possible worlds' which could result from a recommendation being followed. Candidate techniques for possibilistic projection are qualitative simulation [Dvorak 89], model-based prediction [Uckun 92], and reasoning methods employing possibilistic logics [Dubois 88].

We also need to explore new ways of deciding how to act in hazardous situations. The safety bag expert system approached this in terms of rules for vetoing routes through the rail network, where the rules embody safety regulations. A simple veto is something of a blunderbuss; it may be desirable to have reasonable assurance that an expert system will fail safe (if use of a drug is contraindicated then the user must be told), but we may also be willing to accept that it 'fails soft'; if reasoning methods yield contradictory diagnoses, then a management plan that covers both possibilities is required (the generic antibiotic is an instance of this).

The rules in the safety bag represent application-specific safety conditions. Generalizing this idea, one might consider extending the inference methods and theories of a clinical decision support system to include an abstract safety theory which sets out in general terms what is permitted and what is not. An illustrative domain-independent 'safety theory' specified in $(ML)^2$ style is given below.

```
theory safety
     import application-theory
     signature
          classes states(safe unsafe) actions authorities
     functions
          simulate: actions x states —> states
     predicates
          unsafe: unsafe
          permitted: actions
          obligatory: actions
          proposed: actions x states
          possible: actions x states
          authorized: authorities x actions
     variables Act:actions State,New:states Auth:authorities
     axioms
          simulate(Act,State) = New
                    -> possible(Act,New)
          proposed(Act) ^ not(possible(Act,New) ^ unsafe(New))
                    -> permitted(Act)
          proposed(Act) ^ possible(Act,New) ^ unsafe(New)
                    -> obligatory(authorize(Act))
          obligatory(authorize(Act)) ^ authorized(Auth,Act)
                    -> permitted(Act)
end-theory
```

The basic idea behind the theory is that if an action is proposed and the system cannot project a possible hazard arising from the action, then it is permitted to take that action, but, if there is a possible hazardous consequence, then approval by an empowered authority is obligatory. The specification assumes that possibilistic projection is carried out by a simulation function. This function, as well as the details of safe/unsafe states, actions and authorities, would be specified in an imported application-theory. The signature places constraints on the definitions of the classes, functions and predicates in the application theory that can instantiate the general safety regulations. Mathematical logic and AI offer some appropriate tools for formalizing the regulations in such theories, such as deontic logic, and the modal logic of permission and obligation.

Ideally, we would like this theory to be a reusable component, providing a general structure which can be used to guide and verify the construction of application-specific knowledge bases for dynamic hazard management. Naturally this is speculative, but it is really only an elaboration of established approaches to improving safety in conventional software, in which software layers, specialized for event and trend monitoring and for effecting panic operations, are integrated into the design.

16.4 CONCLUSIONS

Almost two decades' experience of building expert systems has shown that strong methodologies are needed to ensure high quality systems. I have tried to make the case that the concepts, notations, results, techniques, and technologies of logic programming, combined with software engineering methods, offers a potent discipline. Not only have logicians arrived at a deep understanding of logical formalisms during the long history of their development, but contemporary work in AI has yielded powerful and practical tools that embody their results. From such observations I have tried to demonstrate the potential of a systematic logic engineering approach to the design and implementation of verifiably sound expert systems.

However, if we are to achieve trust in any medical technology, it is not enough to prove soundness. We must also demonstrate, so far as is possible, that the technology is safe. Alongside the pursuit of rigorous development techniques, therefore, we also need to invest effort in investigating general safety principles, together with formalisms and practical design techniques which incorporate them. Some techniques may prove to be straightforward extensions of existing safety engineering methods, such as a safety lifecycle, but AI techniques also suggest novel ways of interpreting traditional ideas and the possibility of developing a 'dynamic safety strategy' as well.

16.5 ACKNOWLEDGEMENTS

I am grateful to Peter Hammond, Frank van Harmelen, Jun Huang, Isaac Khabaza, Paul Krause and Felix Redmill for many comments that have helped to improve this chapter.

16.6 REFERENCES

[Abbott 90]   Abbott R J: "Resourceful Systems for Fault Tolerance, Reliability, and Safety." ACM Computing Surveys, 22(1), pp 35-68, 1990.

[Abramson 90] Abramson H and Rogers M H (Eds): "Meta-Programming in Logic Programming." MIT Press, Cambridge, Mass., 1990.

[Balder 92]   Balder J and Akkerman H: "TheME: an Environment for Building Formal KADS-II Models of Expertise." Technical Report KADS-II/T1.2/TR/ECN/007/1.0, Netherlands Energy Research Foundation, 1992.

[Boden 89]   Boden M (Chair): "Benefits and Risks of Knowledge-Based Systems." Report of Council for Science and Society, Oxford: Oxford University Press, 1989.

[Cardoso 92]   Cardoso A and Costa E: "Consistency Checking Along

Time." Applied Artificial Intelligence, 6 (2), pp 207-248, 1992.

[Charles 91]   Charles E and Dubois O: "MELODIA: Logical Methods for Checking Knowledge Bases." Chapter 7 in Ayel M and Laurent J-P (Eds): Validation, Verification and Test of Knowledge Based Systems, John Wiley, 1991.

[Colmerauer 83]   Colmerauer A: "Prolog in 10 Figures." Proc. Eighth International Joint Conference on Artificial Intelligence, pp 487-499, Los Altos: Kaufman, 1983.

[Davis 90]   Davis E: "Representations of Commonsense Knowledge." Morgan Kaufman Publishers, San Mateo, 1990.

[Dubois 88]   Dubois D and Prade H: "Possibility Theory - An Approach to Computerised Processing of Uncertainty." Plenum Press New York, 1988.

[Dvorak 89]   Dvorak D L and Kuipers B: "Model-Based Monitoring of Dynamic Systems." Proc. 11th International Joint Conference on Artificial Intelligence, Detroit, pp 1238-1243, Morgan Kaufman Publishers, San Mateo, 1989.

[Ericson 81]   Ericson C A: "Software and System Safety." Proc. 5th Int. System Safety Conf, Vol 1, Part 1, System Safety Society, Newport Beach, 1981.

[Fox 80]   Fox J, Barber D C and Bardhan K D: "Alternatives to Bayes: A Quantitative Comparison with Rule-Based Diagnosis." Methods of Information in Medicine, 19(4), pp 210-215, 1980.

[Fox 90]   Fox J, Gordon C, Glowinski A J and O'Neil M: "Logic Engineering for Knowledge Engineering: the Oxford System of Medicine." Artificial Intelligence in Medicine, 2, pp 323-339, 1990.

[FoxK 92]   Fox J and Krause P J: "Qualitative Frameworks for Decision Support: Lessons from Medicine." Knowledge Engineering Review, 7:1, pp 19-33, 1992.

[FoxKA 92]   Fox J, Krause P J and Ambler S: "Arguments, Contradictions and Practical Reasoning." Proc. European Conference on Artificial Intelligence, Chichester: John Wiley, pp 623-626, 1992.

[Glowinski 91] Glowinski A J, Coiera E and O'Neil M: "The Role of Domain Models in Maintaining Consistency of Large Medical Knowledge Bases." In Proc. AIME'91, Lecture Notes in Medical Informatics, Berlin,

Springer Verlag, 1991.

[Grant 90] Grant J and Minker J: "Deductive Database Theories." Knowledge Engineering Review, 4(4), pp 267-304, 1990.

[Griggs 81]   Griggs J G: "A Method of Software Safety Analysis." Proc. 5th Int. System Safety Conf, Vol 1, part 1, System Safety Society: Newport Beach, 1981.

[Guibert 91]   Guibert V, Beauvieux A and Haziza M: "Consistency, Soundness and Completeness of a Diagnostic System." Chapter 8 in Ayel M and Laurent J-P (Eds): Validation, Verification and Test of Knowledge Based Systems, John Wiley, 1991.

[Hajnal 89]   Hajnal SJ, Fox J and Krause P J: "Sceptic User Manual." Advanced Computation Laboratory Technical Report, Imperial Cancer Research Fund, London, 1989.

[Hogger 90]   Hogger C J: "Essentials of Logic Programming." Oxford University Press, 1990.

[Huang 92]   Huang J, Fox J, Gordon C and Smale A: "Symbolic Decision Support in General Practice, Oncology and Shared Care." Technical Report, Advanced Computation Laboratory, Imperial Cancer Research Fund, Lincoln's Inn Fields, London, UK, 1992.

[KA 92]   Knowledge Acquisition, Academic Press London. Special issue on KADS, Vol 4, 1992.

[KBHC 91]   Krause P J, Byers P J, Hajnal S J and Cozens J: "The Formal Specification of a Data-base Extension Management System." Technical Report, Advanced Computation Laboratory, Imperial Cancer Research Fund, London, 1991.

[KBHF 91]Krause P J, Byers P, Hajnal SJ and Fox J: "The Use of Object-Oriented Process Specification for the Validation and Verification of Decision Support Systems." Chapter 6 in Ayel M and Laurent J-P (Eds): Validation, Verification and Test of Knowledge Based Systems, John Wiley, 1991.

[Klein 91]   Klein P: "The Safety-Bag Expert System in the Electronic Railway Interlocking System Elektra." Expert Systems with Applications, Vol 3, pp 499-406, 1991.

[Knight 86]   Knight J C and Leveson N G: "An Empirical Study of Failure Probabilities in Multi-version Software". In Proc. 16th Intenational Symposium on Fault-Tolerant Computing, New York, IEEE, pp 165-170,

1986.

[Kowalski 79]   Kowalski R: "Logic for Problem Solving." North-Holland, 1979.

[Lenat 90]   Lenat D B and Guha R V: "Building Large Knowledge-based Systems: Representation and Inference in the Cyc Project." Addison-Wesley, Reading, Mass., 1990.

[Leveson 86]   Leveson N G: "Software Safety: What, What and How." Computing Surveys, Vol 18 (2), pp 125-163, June 1986.

[Lydiard 92]   Lydiard T: "Review of Current Practice and Research Initiatives for the Verification and Validation of Knowledge Based Systems." Knowledge Engineering Review, 7, (2), 1992.

[McCabe 92]   McCabe F: "Logic and Objects." Prentice-Hall, London, 1992.

[Mellor 92]   Mellor P: "Software Systems for Safety in Medicine." Technical Report, Centre for Software Reliability, City University, London, UK, 1992.

[Owen 88] Owen S G: "The Development of Explicit Interpreters and Transforms to Control Reasoning about Protein Topology." Technical Report HP-ISC-TM-88-015, Hewlett-Packard Laboratories, Bristol, UK, 1988.

[Parnas 90]   Parnas D L, van Schouwen J and Shu Po Kwan: "Evaluation of Safety Critical Software." Communications of the ACM, 33(6), pp 636-648, 1990.

[Preece 92]   Preece A D, Shinghal R and Batarekh A: "Principles and Practice in Verifying Rule-based Systems." Knowledge Engineering Review, Vol 7, 2, 1992.

[Redmill 92]   Redmill F: "Computers in Safety-Critical Applications." Computing and Control Engineering Journal, pp 178-182, July 1992.

[THERAC 87]   "Software Bugs, A Matter of Life and Liability." Datamation, 15th May 1987.

[VanH 91] Van Hentenryck P: "Constraint Logic Programming." Knowledge Engineering Review, 6 (3), pp 151-194, 1991.

[VanH 92] Van Harmelen F and Balder J: "(ML)2: A Formal Language for

KADS Models of Expertise." Knowledge Acquisition 4, pp 127-161, 1992.

[VanL 92]   Van Langevelde I and Treur J (Eds): "Formal Specification Methods for Complex Reasoning Systems." Proc. ECAI'92, Vienna, 1992.

[Wilson 89]   Wilson M, Duce D and Simpson D: "Life-cycles in Software and Knowledge Engineering: A Comparative Review." Knowledge Engineering Review, 4 (3), pp 189-204, 1989.

[Wyatt 90] Wyatt J and Spiegelhalter D: "Evaluating Medical Expert Systems: What to Test and How?" Medical Informatics, 15(3), pp 205-217, 1990.

17

Safety-critical system monitoring using default-trained neural networks

Nigel Dodd

The term 'default training' denotes a technique used for training artificial neural networks where there are no examples of one or more of the classes which the network is required to identify. In this chapter, the theory behind default training is discussed and several applications of the technique are described.

17.1 INTRODUCTION

Alarm-state detection is a form of novelty detection for which there have been a number of proposed algorithms. Kohonen [Kohonen 88] describes a linear system which becomes 'habituated' to the input vectors of its training set. The training set $S = \{x_1, x_2, \ldots, x_m\}$ is taken to span a subspace L of R^n. Novel input x can be decomposed into the sum of $\hat{x} \in L$ and $\tilde{x} \notin L$ and iterative training of the network causes it to output only the novel component, or *residual*, $\tilde{x}$ to any input x. By contrast, Grossberg's ART [Gail 88] uses non-linear mappings between input and output. A *vigilance* factor determines whether a new centre is created for classifying a new input, or whether an existing centre is moved closer to the mapping of the input. A third algorithm makes use of the multi-layer perceptron (MLP) as an encoder [McClelland 86]. The MLP is trained to reproduce outputs identical to its inputs for the training set. A novel input will not be faithfully reproduced, and so the distance between an input and the output of the network gives some indication of the novelty of the input.

The work reported here uses a fourth approach in which the unobtainable alarm class is emulated by pseudo-random vectors with specific distribution. A neural network in the form of a multi-layer perceptron is trained both on real inputs coming from sensors, and synthesized alarm vectors.

17.2 NEURAL NETWORKS

A neural network consists of a number of simple processors, or *neurons*, linked together as in Figure 17.1. The neurons combine their inputs and subsequently produce an output which is passed to other neurons. The links between neurons contain *weights* which control the amplitude of the signal passing through. In addition, each neuron has an associated *bias*, which is effectively a connection to a neuron which is always in the *on-*, or 1-, state. It is the weights and biases that embody the information required to classify the input signals, just as in the biological brain it is the links

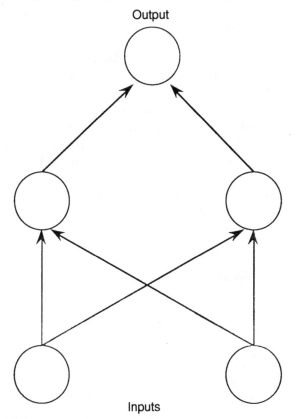

Figure 17.1: A simple multi-layer perceptron.

between the neurons that determine function. In the training stage, the weights and biases are iteratively improved by applying input and output pairs to the network.

A common use of neural networks is for *classification* of input patterns into one of a number of output classes. It will be shown later that, under certain fairly general conditions, a neural network can perform as a probabilistic classifier, i.e. outputting a *probability* of an input pattern belonging to one of the output classes. One way of viewing the operation of the Neural Network is as *interpolation* in a space defined by its parameters.

The training patterns are the representative examples of classes. After training, previously unseen patterns are classified according to an interpolation between the training examples. The number of neurons in the network determines the complexity of the space in which interpolation is carried out. In this way, with enough neurons, a division of feature-space by arbitrarily complex boundaries can be made, assimilating the fine distinguishing features of the input patterns. Alternatively, by providing only a few neurons, the network is forced to generalize and the outliers in its training set will be effectively ignored.

17.3 DEFAULT CLASSIFICATION

If no example of one class of output is available, inputs corresponding to this class must be inferred by default. For example, if a particular system is being monitored for some dangerous condition, and if that dangerous condition cannot be produced at will to train the network explicitly, then the only examples available for training will be consistent with the healthy, non-dangerous state of the system. Training a network only on one class of inputs, with no counter-examples, causes the network to classify everything as the one class it has been shown. However, by training the network on examples of the 'healthy' class but also on random inputs for the 'alarm' class, any input which occurs after training which does not resemble one of the previously encountered 'healthy' inputs will automatically be classified as 'alarm'. The network effectively behaves as a novelty detector.

To illustrate this, a network was trained as follows. It had five inputs and one output. The 'healthy' (Class 1) input vectors consisted of elements a, b, c, d, e such that:

$a < b < c > d > e$ (Condition 1)

as illustrated in Table 17.1. 50 training examples satisfying Condition 1 were generated. A network with five inputs, three hidden neurons, and one output was trained to output Class 1 for this data. Additionally, random data with the same first-order statistics as the data for output Class 1 was synthesized; for this the network was trained to output Class 0. When tested on a new set of 100 inputs, half of which were produced by explicitly

Table 17.1: *Output Class 1 vectors are obtained using Condition 1. Output Class 0 vectors are synthesized from random numbers having the same mean as Class 1*

| | Input | | | | Output |
a	b	c	d	e	class
0.150160	0.241971	0.496722	0.338752	0.163327	1.0
0.752625	−0.258011	0.050505	−0.144331	0.085486	0.0
0.390102	0.582408	0.667979	0.252589	0.037113	1.0
−0.894841	0.933459	−0.331432	−0.835807	−0.459371	0.0
−0.406147	−0.263851	0.074262	−0.330817	−0.446870	1.0
0.024406	0.173021	0.477517	0.743378	0.155935	0.0
0.769972	0.797939	0.964704	0.768290	0.724058	1.0
0.705362	0.622344	0.909775	0.808566	−0.722170	0.0
0.574456	0.622694	0.686187	0.684142	0.684017	1.0
0.173560	−0.250082	−0.946428	−0.070469	0.570686	0.0

following Condition 1, and half of which were generated randomly, the performance was 93 per cent correct. For the randomly generated data there is a probability of 5 per cent of fulfilling Condition 1, and so the network is in fact performing to within 2 per cent of the inherent upper limit of performance.

A more rigorous justification for synthesizing the unavailable data with random numbers follows from the fact that training seeks to minimize the sum squared error over the training set. Consider a binary classification network with a single input v producing an output $f(v)$. The required outputs are 0 if the input is a member of Class A and 1 if the input is a member of Class B (not to be confused with Class 0 and Class 1 in the illustration given above). If the prior probability of any data being a member of Class A is P_A, and the prior probability of any data being a member of class B is P_B, and if the probability distribution functions of the two classes as functions of the input v are $p_A(v)$ and $p_B(v)$, then the sum squared error, E, over the whole training set is given by:

$$E = \int_{-\infty}^{\infty} P_A p_A(v)[f(v) - 0]^2 + P_B p_B(v)[f(v) - 1]^2 \, dv \qquad (2)$$

Differentiating this with respect to the function f:

$$\frac{\partial E}{\partial f} = 2p_A(v)P_A f(v) + 2p_B(v)P_B[f(v) - 1] \qquad (3)$$

and equating this to zero

$$f(v) = \frac{p_B(v)P_B}{p_B(v)P_B + p_A(v)P_A} \tag{4}$$

which is exactly the probability of the correct classification being B, given that the input was v.

So by training for the minimization of sum squared error, and using as targets 0 for Class A and 1 for Class B, the output from the network assumes a value equal to the probability of Class B.

Substituting the $f(v)$ corresponding to a trained network back into equation (1), we get:

$$E = \int_{-\infty}^{\infty} \frac{P_A p_A(v) P_B p_B(v)}{P_A p_A(v) + P_B p_B(v)} dv \tag{5}$$

So the minimum attainable error is when there is zero overlap between the distributions:

$$\int_{-\infty}^{\infty} P_A p_A(v) P_B p_B(v) \, dv = 0. \tag{6}$$

In this way it is possible to model the default class to produce an error less than the error to be expected from using uniformly distributed random variates.

It should be noted that the functional mapping, f, of a neural network can only assume the minimum error mapping as implied by equation (3) if the network has the necessary structure (number of neurons, suitable connectivity, etc.) and if the learning dynamics allow the solution, in the form of the final weight values, to be found iteratively.

17.4 IMPLEMENTATION

Good performance of a neural network is dependent on the following conditions:

(i)   The training vectors must be representative of the vectors which the network is later required to classify.
(ii)   The architecture of the network (i.e. its connectivity, weight sharing, activation functions, etc.) must be suited to the problem domain. In general, the kinds of neural network architectures catered for in off-the-shelf software packages are unsuitable for these specific alarm-detection applications.
(iii) For alarm-detection, where default training is used, the statistical distributions of the default class must be properly designed.

D620.86 SAF
Safety-critical System
Felix Redmill

D620.0045 HEN X

D620.86 COR

D005.133 PYL.

It is the responsibility of the end-user to ensure that the alarm-monitor is given representative examples during its training period. This may seem a strict requirement, but a valid analogue of the alarm-monitor is a willing but ignorant human helper. The helper cannot be of later value in signalling alarms if he or she is not shown representative examples of the normal functioning of the system during a training period.

Network architectures have evolved [Dodd 90] to a few specific types, all well-suited to the task of alarm detection. They vary from networks whose weights are well-defined at turn-on and which function quite well from the start, requiring training only to refine the weight values, to networks which are truly without knowledge of the application domain at turn-on and which require considerable training before they can distinguish alarms from normality.

Various statistical techniques are employed to refine the distributions used for the default class.

For the trials in progress, the algorithms were coded in C++ using Microsoft Windows 3.0. This graphics user interface (GUI) provides a flexible development tool and enables different user expertise levels to be incorporated easily. For instance, it is desirable that the development team has access to the fine adjustment of network architecture etc., so that all menu items are available to this level of expertise. Conversely, end-users will require an alarm monitor which is simple to operate and which requires no specialist skills beyond the ability to use a mouse, and so most menu items and other options are 'greyed out' for this level of expertise. A consequence of this design methodology is that the same developmental system can be used by its designers for assessing different architectures, default distributions, etc., and by the end-users for assessing the overall ergonomics of the system.

17.5 RELATIONSHIP WITH EXPERT SYSTEMS

The neural network alarm monitor, in its purest form, starts with no knowledge about the system it is monitoring. It learns everything by observing the environment and building an internal representation of 'normality'. This takes time and, for many potential application areas, there are well known 'rules' which the system should obey under normal conditions. It makes sense to use such prior knowledge in designing an alarm monitor.

Conversely, an expert system is pre-programmed with rules elicited from 'experts'. Learning, or modification, of these rules is not easily carried out on-line.

A real-world implementation of the neural network alarm monitor endeavours to make use of prior knowledge in the form of limit alarm data or other rule sets. It does this by using a network which, by virtue of its architecture and starting weights, performs initially, and without any training, as a rule-based system. Unlike the expert system, it then goes on to learn about the system it is monitoring and to update its internal model.

17.6 APPLICATION DOMAINS

The default-trained neural network is applicable in any domain where a number of sensors are monitoring a system of some kind and where an alarm is required to be set when the system strays out of a normal state. Examples include:

- **Manufacturing plant** where sensors monitor parameters of various safety-critical components to supply the alarm monitor with input.
- **Patient bedside units** which, with current technology, use limit alarms which must be set up by the medical staff. An adaptive monitor, such as the neural network alarm monitor, is able to adapt automatically to each new patient and track allowable changes in conditions such as the sleep/wake cycle.
- **Environmental monitoring** which can benefit from the neural network alarm monitor by adapting to an arbitrary set of sensor probes and signalling any change in the environment which may require further investigation.
- **Traffic monitoring** where a change from the normal distributions of density and speed of traffic may pre-empt an accident.

17.7 PERFORMANCE AND RESULTS

The major application domain so far investigated is the hospital intensive care unit (ICU). The neural network alarm monitor has been used to process data from several large hospital ICUs. It has been used on-line for a major trial at Southampton hospital where it has been shown to provide a useful degree of monitoring of critically ill patients and where, for comparative purposes, it has been used in conjunction with conventional limit alarms.

Figure 17.2 shows the output from the monitor when a network architecture is used which assumes no prior knowledge of the patient under observation. The output of the network is initially about 0.5, indicating that the network is uncertain about the state of the patient. After a period of learning, however, the network is better able to discriminate the state of the patient. Towards the end of the trace, the output rises, indicating a potential alarm condition.

Figure 17.3 demonstrates the input of prior knowledge concerning the acceptable excursions of the patient's vital functions. With these values input, the network behaves initially as a traditional limit alarm, learning a

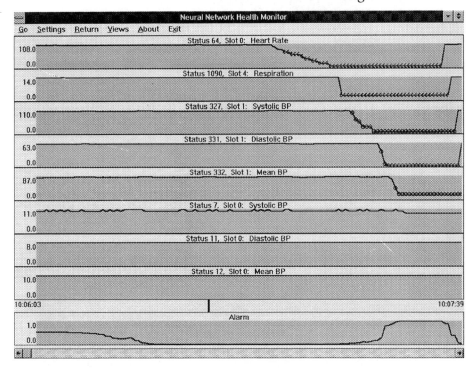

Figure 17.2: The neural network alarm monitor's output is shown at the bottom of the figure. The network used in this example starts with randomized weights and therefore gives an output of approximately 0.5. After a period of training, the output drops to a low value, indicating a stable patient, but rises when there is an abnormal response from the patient, indicating a potential alarm condition.

more refined model of the patient's behaviour through exposure to vital function data.

Overall, the comments of the ICU doctors and nurses have been favourable. The major problem with conventional limit alarms is that the limits cannot be set with sufficient insight resulting, often, in too frequent false alarms. This is made worse by the conventional systems' inability to recognize artefacts. The consequence of these shortcomings is that the conventional systems are frequently turned off, leaving the patient with no alarm monitoring at all. The neural network alarm monitor is largely immune from the major shortcomings of conventional limit alarms. We are working now to obtain objective performance measures using many days of patient data.

Another application area which is well suited to the neural network alarm monitor is environmental monitoring. Here a number of sensors are scattered widely across the environment. Monitoring these manually, or even deducing the rules of an expert system required to indicate alarm conditions, is impractical. An advantage of the neural network alarm

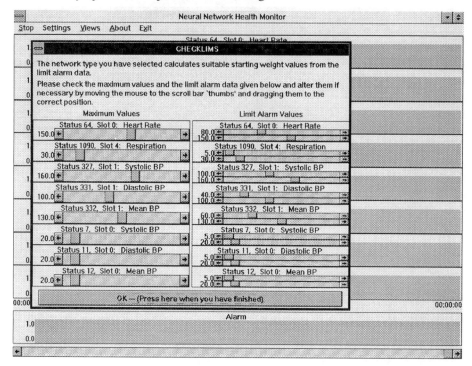

Figure 17.3: Here the user interface demonstrates the facility for inputting prior knowledge about the acceptable excursions of the various vital functions. The network, which starts to learn from these values, behaves initially like a conventional limit alarm, but is able to improve on this by exposure to data from the patient.

monitor lies in its ability to deal with a large number of sensory inputs, only a few of which might supply the information necessary to indicate an alarm. It is also tolerant of low quality sensor hardware, taking into account drift and fluctuation with other parameters, such as temperature. It does this by building an internal model of the inter-dependencies of the various inputs. If it is normal for an input to vary with temperature (assuming temperature is monitored by another sensor) then the monitor will become desensitized to this effect and will only give an alarm when the output of the sensor varies independently of temperature. Figure 17.4 shows the output of the neural network alarm monitor when the inputs are data from a set of sensors monitoring water quality. The monitor correctly shows an alarm towards the end of the trace where, in reality, there is a tidal event.

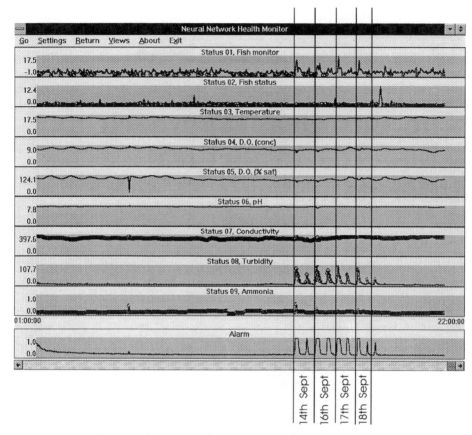

Figure 17.4: The neural network alarm monitor processing data from a river. The alarms towards the end of the trace are the result of a tidal event.

17.8 REFERENCES

[Dodd 90]   Dodd N: "Optimisation of Network Structure Using Genetic Techniques." In "Proceedings of the International Joint Conference on Neural Networks", IEE, San Diego, 1990.

[Gail 88]   Gail A, Carpenter and Grossberg S: "The Art of Adaptive Pattern Recognition by a Self-Organizing Neural Network." IEEE, 1988.

[Kohonen 88]   Kohonen T: "Self-organisation and Associative Memory." Springer-Verlag, 1988.

[McClelland 86]   McClelland J L and Rumelhart D E: "Parallel Distributed Processing: Volumes 1 & 2." Bradford Books, MIT Press, 1986.

18

The European approach to standards in medical informatics

Barry Barber

18.1 INTRODUCTION

There are a number of strands to the current development of European standards in Medical Informatics. The most significant of these are indicated below but the field is developing rapidly as the various activities mature. This chapter summarizes the work in progress and provides the contacts and references for further study and examination (the *Encyclopaedia of Data Protection* [Charlton 88] provides a comprehensive reference source on data protection).

18.2 ADVANCED INFORMATICS IN MEDICINE (AIM)

The Advanced Informatics in Medicine (AIM) programme developed out of an initiative called BICEPS. Funding for the exploratory phase was set at 20 MECU, and this was estimated to cover half the contracted costs of projects.

18.2.1   AIM Impact and Forecast

While the first phase of AIM was being developed, the AIM secretariat got together a group of specialists to explore the technical opportunities in the field of Medical Informatics - AIM Impact and Forecast [EC 91c]. This resulted in a report which set the scene for some of the more recent developments and outlined some of the key issues. I was involved in the examination of the legal, ethical and social issues, and this involvement led to the concept of the Six Safety First Principles for European Health Information Systems [Barber 90a, Barber 90b, Barber 90c, de Schouwer 90, EC 91c]. These principles required that European systems should:

(i)   Provide a safe environment;
(ii)   Provide a secure environment;
(iii)   Provide a convenient environment;
(iv)   Be legally satisfactory for users and suppliers;
(v)   Provide legal protection of software;
(vi)   Be multi-lingual systems.

18.2.2 Strategic Audit and Data Protection Working Conference

When the initial AIM contracts had been signed, the group were invited to review the work to be undertaken in the context of the requirements set out by the European Parliament when they endorsed the AIM exploratory programme. The greatest omission was found to be the lack of a programme of serious European work in the field of Data Protection and Information Systems Security in Health Information Systems.

As chairman of the Working Group (WG2) of the European Federation for Medical Informatics (EFMI) concerned with Data Protection and Information Systems Security, I was able to assist in the development of a European Commission (EC) AIM working conference to examine these issues in the light of the draft EC Directive on Data Protection [EC 90]. The conference was held in Brussels in the Spring of 1990, and the papers presented and the edited material from the working syndicates were published in 1991 [EC 91b]. It forms a worthy successor to the two monographs [Griesser 80, Griesser 83] of the International Medical Informatics Association (IMIA) working group in this area (WG4).

The conference was unusual in bringing together doctors, nurses, medical informaticians, lawyers, Data Protection Commissioners and computer security specialists.

18.2.3 AIM Phase 1

The first phase of AIM was extremely successful, and the results were exhibited at a special Euroforum in Seville in December 1990. An outline of the 42 funded projects and their participants is given in the references [EC 92b]. One issue that was raised by many participants was that of standards and what mechanisms existed to develop European standards. This groundswell of opinion provided the right basis for the subsequent initiatives undertaken by the AIM secretariat.

18.2.4 AIM Phase 2

The current three-year projects are now in progress and it is too early to know exactly how these activities will develop. However, one project, SEISMED (A Secure Environment for Information Systems in Medicine), is specifically aimed at the issues of Safety, Security and Privacy.

(a)   AIM SEISMED

The scope of SEISMED is closely related to the work of the Security and Data Protection Programme of the NHS Information Management Group of the Management Executive. It includes the following work packages:

- Survey;
- Risk analysis;
- High level policy;
- Legal framework;
- Code of ethics;
- Security in existing host systems;
- System design;
- Network security;
- Encryption;
- Reference centres.

(b)   AIM Liaison

All the AIM projects convene for two-day meetings at approximately two-monthly intervals to share their experiences. This process of integrating the work of the various projects provides a valuable perspective for all participants on the totality of the programme. Something that this has brought to light is security. Security issues have been found to arise in almost all projects, and it would be useful to explore these further. Unfortunately, however, the SEISMED resources have already been commited and cannot be diverted from their contracted purposes.

18.2.5   Council of Europe

The Council of Europe has been responsible for the development of several standards in Data Protection, the four most important being those listed below.

(a)   Convention 108

The Convention (No 108) for the Protection of Individuals with Regard to Automatic Processing of Personal Data [CEC 81] was issued in 1981 at about the same time as Recommendation R(81)1 on Automated Medical Data Banks. It sets the scene for considerations of Data Protection in a world-wide context. It is supported by a variety of supplementary recommendations on such matters as statistics [CER 83a], social security data [CER 83b], direct marketing [CER 86] and police data [CER 87].

(b)   Recommendation R(81)1: Automated Medical Data Banks

Recommendation R[81] on Automated Medical Data Banks [CER 81] was issued just before Convention 108, and it provides additional safeguards for Personal Health Information.

(c)   Working Party 12 Revising R(81)1

Working Party 12 is in the process of Revising Recommendation R(81)1 to take account of developments in technology and the experience of the last decade. During that time, health information systems have become very much more widely available, more clinical in use, more relied upon for support, and more ambitious in application.

(d)   Draft Recommendation on the Communication of Health Information in Hospitals: Ethical and Legal Issues

This draft recommendation [CER 92], which has only just become available, indicates the need for a 'Code of Good Practice' to regulate Medical Informatics Departments. It prescribes professional confidentiality clauses in contracts of employment; it makes recommendations on the handling of requests for information for purposes not originally specified, and for specific controls over micro-computers (including procedures for adequate back-up, for locking computers or rooms when they are unattended, for the storage of discs in locked cupboards, and for encrypting stored data where possible).

18.3 EUROPEAN COMMISSION ACTIVITIES

The European Commission has established a number of activities with an impact on the information systems standards area. The most important are the following.

18.3.1   European Directives

The Decision on Standardization in the Field of Information Technology and Telecommunications set the scene for the adoption of standards in Information Systems [ECD 86] and the Directive on The Minimum Safety and Health Requirements for Work with Display Screen Equipment [ECD 90], the UK equivalent of which was published by the Health and Safety Executive [HSE 92]. Undoubtedly, other EC standards will be adopted as they become available.

18.3.2   Draft Directive on Data Protection

The original draft of this Directive [EC 90] was issued in 1990, and the revised draft was expected to be available for discussion and comment during the summer of 1992. It is understood that substantial modifications will have been made to the original draft, and that it is likely to be influential in advocating significant changes to the UK Data Protection environment, either by direct changes in the law or by its interpretation of the existing Data Protection Act 1984.

18.3.3   Information Systems Security Initiatives

The European Commission has developed or supported a number of initiatives on security with a view to ensuring that its initiatives in the wider field of Telematics are not compromised by failures in this area [EC 82, EC 90, EC 92a, EC 92c]. The Information Technology Security Evaluation Criteria (ITSEC) [EC 91a] and the Information Technology Security Evaluation Manual (ITSEM) [EC 92d] are two of the more well publicised activities that have been given widespread support.

18.4 PRE-STANDARDS ACTIVITIES

The following specific initiatives set the European Standards activities in motion.

18.4.1   European Federation for Medical Informatics WG3

Jaap Nothoven van Gour, chairman of the EFMI Working Group on Standards (WG3), was particularly active in bringing the issues of Medical Informatics standards to the attention of the Medical Informatics community. Under his guidance, the working group forged a link with the AIM secretariat and set up a series of working meetings to discuss these issues.

18.4.2 Studley Castle Meeting

The Department of Health (DOH), the Information Management Centre (IMC), and the Computer Suppliers Association (CSA) set up an awareness meeting at Studley Castle to raise the understanding of Medical Informatics standards in the UK, and to bring UK participants up-to-date with developments within the EC and EFMI.

18.4.3 EC Study Mandate

The EC AIM secretariat established a requirement for an exploratory study into the requirements for Medical Informatics standards. The enabled project team (PT 007) of the European Workshop for Open Systems (EWOS) and Working Party 39 of the Comité de Normalisation (CEN) to be established to explore these issues. Both teams reported back with firm recommendations that there was a requirement for a standards committee to handle Medical Informatics standards, and they outlined the areas of work that were though to be needed. The EWOS team's report is listed as reference [EWOS].

18.5 CEN TC 251 MEDICAL INFORMATICS STANDARDS

Once these recommendations had been received, CEN set about exploring whether there was sufficient support from the member countries of the European Community to set up a standing Technical Committee. This led to the establishment of TC 251. This committee now meets approximately quarterly and, at the time of writing (Spring 1992), had held seven meetings. TC 251 has established a substantial programme of work in its Joint Directory of Work, the current version [CEN 91] being Version 1.4. In addition, it has set up seven working groups to handle the various elements of the work programme. These are listed below.

(i)   Health Care Information Modelling and Medical Records;
(ii)   Health Care Terminology, Semantics and Knowledge Bases;
(iii) Health Care Communications and Messages;
(iv)   Medical Imaging and Multi-media;
(v)   Medical Devices;
(vi)   Health Care Security and Privacy, Quality and Safety;
(vii) Intermittently Connected Devices.

18.6 EWOS EXPERT GROUPS ON HEALTH SYSTEMS

In addition, EWOS set up an Expert Group concerned with Open Systems Profiling for Health Information Systems, EG-MED, which handles the appropriate part of the CEN TC 251 work plan under the standing agreement between CEN and EWOS. It also has an Expert Group on Security (EG-SEC) to provide a security co-ordinating function within EWOS.

18.7 OTHER RELEVANT STANDARDS ACTIVITIES

There are many other initiatives which need to be linked into the activities of EWOS and CEN. These include the work of the International Electrotechnical Commission (IEC) which is in the process of developing standards for safety-critical computer systems. Indeed, Draft Standard 65 (Secretariat) 122 on 'Safety Related Software' [IEC 91] is currently being voted on internationally. When this has been adopted as an international standard, it could provide the basis for the development of guidance on dealing with the safety issues which are specific to health information systems.

The volume of work currently in hand is extensive. However, I should mention Working Group 6 of CEN TC251, currently chaired by Dr Kees Louwerse, which is concerned with Security and Privacy, Quality and Safety. Currently, this group meets every two months in Leiden.

18.8 UK BSI ACTIVITY

On receiving an invitation to participate in TC 251, the British Standards Institute was at first concerned about the problems of financing this work. They called a meeting at which it became clear to them that many UK individuals had already been working in Brussels with the AIM secretariat on standards issues. Those with experience of it were adamant that the UK should not sit on the sidelines but should be fully involved in this work.

At the preliminary meeting, the proposed work programme was discussed briefly while the administrative issues were debated at greater length. Eventually, the BSI agreed to the establishment of IST/35, the BSI equivalent of TC 251.

The meeting was initially convened in an ad hoc fashion, but it has since developed on a representative basis. It meets between the quarterly meetings of CEN TC 251 in order to consider the agenda and papers and to brief the UK delegation to TC 251. The secretariat is provided by the NHS Information Management Centre, and all the papers concerned with TC 251 and its working groups are available at the IMC so that UK specialists can be fully informed about all the various activities.

In addition, IST/35 has established a series of seven Mirror Panels to reflect the CEN working group structure. Mr Ray Rogers chairs IST/35 and I am the secretary of the committee; Mrs Pat Village administers the secretariat. The Mirror Panels support the work of the working groups by providing a forum for preliminary discussions as well as a reserve of experts on whom the working groups can call for technical support.

The UK is now well represented on all the European bodies. The Convener of WG3 is Tim Benson, and the Chairman of EWOS EG-MED is Adrian Stokes.

18.9 SECURITY AND RISK ANALYSIS

The current definition of information system security, adopted as the European standard, is that it comprises all the issues concerned with the confidentiality, integrity and availability of information systems. This includes the issues normally associated with data protection, but it goes further than the concerns of personal information.

In order to assess the security issues concerned with a system, it is necessary to carry out some form of risk analysis so that the severity of the counter-measures can be properly matched to the assessed risks. The Central Computing and Telecommunications Agency (CCTA) developed a method of handling risk analysis entitled the CCTA Risk Analysis and Management Methodology (CRAMM) [CCTA 91, Davey 90, Davey 91]. This method starts by defining the boundary of the systems to be examined and the data groups that need to be protected. Appropriate users are then interviewed in order to establish the implications to the organization of various types of security failure. These worst case scenarios then begin to indicate aspects of the security that must be considered in the package of appropriate security counter-measures. It is important to recognize that loss arising from system failure is multi-faceted and multi-dimensional.

While there are other risk-analysis techniques, the advantage of using CRAMM is that it is the approach to security used by the UK central government and, hence, its standards are well known and accepted in the UK security world. The key dimensions considered in CRAMM are described below.

18.9.1   Multi-Dimensional Loss

Loss may take one of numerous forms and is therefore multi-dimensional. Examples of the forms of loss are:

- Embarrassment;
- Personal safety;
- Infringement of privacy;
- Legal obligations;
- Commercial confidentiality;
- Financial loss;
- Disruption of activities;
- Loss of life attracts high counter-measures.

18.9.2   Threats and Vulnerabilities

After the initial data valuation, it is necessary to explore the specific threats to which the systems on site are subject and the vulnerabilities of the systems to these threats. Again, the results are reviewed and accepted by the management team. There is no flexibility in the scoring system utilized and the threats and vulnerabilities of the various data groups are explored so that an overall security requirement can be assigned to the data groups with respect to the risks facing them in terms of confidentiality, integrity and availability. From the measured security requirements, CRAMM selects appropriate security counter-measures for the systems under review from its knowledge base of over 1,000 counter-measures.

18.10 IMC SECURITY AND DATA PROTECTION PROGRAMME FOR NHS

Following its work in supporting the NHS through the process of registering for Data Protection purposes and handling the Subject Access procedures [NHS 88], the Information Management Centre (IMC) set up a programme to explore the security situation of the current generation of information systems and to prepare for the new generation of systems being planned by the Department of Health.

18.10.1   Changes in NHS Information Systems Usage

The key changes taking place with regard to the use of information systems within the NHS are as follows.

- More systems and terminals;
- More non-specialist system users;
- More reliance on systems;
- More clinical uses of systems;
- More sharing of information;
- More networked systems.

18.10.2   Consultation and Awareness Programme

The main drive of this work is in consultation and awareness seminars, but specific training sessions are also given on technical security issues and data protection. The various general security issues relevant to the NHS are being presented to small groups of 15 to 25 individuals for consideration and comment. This work started with the issue of the Top Level Security Policy [Barber 91a] and has developed as follows.

- Top-level security policy [NHS 92a];
- Risk analysis;
- Security of existing host systems;
- Small systems security;
- Baseline security [NHS 92b];
- Security in system development;
- Contingency planning;
- Security for users.

18.10.3   Supporting Security Reviews in NHS

The IMC programme supports a number of security reviews at key sites in order to apply CRAMM to the assessment of their security requirements. Some of the results of this work are outlined in references [Barber 91b, Barber 92].

18.10.4   Development of Guidance

Arising from the consultation and awareness seminars, practical guidance is being developed and published. The Top Level Information Systems Security Policy is in the process of being promulgated and Baseline Security is being published. Where guidance has been developed, the references are given in Section 18.10.2 above; other material will be published as soon as it has been adequately assessed.

18.10.5   Reviews Reveal Need for Serious Security

All the work undertaken so far reveals the need for much more serious security than the NHS has to date been accustomed to applying, and a significant effort is required to bring the current systems up to scratch and to ensure that new systems have adequate security designed into them. The following queries indicate the nature of some of the questions that are being explored [Barber 91b], and the lists show the topics being considered.

(a)   Where is That Record?

- Clinical implications;
- Loss of medical record;
- Loss of sub-records;
- Loss of data items;
- Modifications of data;
- Damage to health.

(b)   Erroneous Records

- Mis-identification;
- False positive test results;
- False negative test results;
- Wrong treatment;
- Will errors be discovered?;
- Malicious errors;
- Accurate and up-to-date.

18.10.6   Management Responsibility

The investigations by the IMC certainly suggest that there are important management issues to be addressed, and that they are squarely in the courts of all NHS managers, both clinical and non-clinical. These issues need to be addressed using the normal management approaches to other decisions on risks and dangers to both patients and organizations. The Department of Health is in the process of developing a Code of Confidentiality, but until this emerges the most coherent view of these issues is indicated by Henny [DGH 84].

The technicalities of handling information systems security may be different from other hazards, but the decisions on risk management and costs should be handled in the same way and at the same management levels. Risk has broad connotations; IT IS NOT SIMPLY AN INFORMATION TECHNOLOGY ISSUE.

18.10.7   Should Medical Systems Be Secure?

In considering the security of NHS systems of all sorts, we are concerned with how much Security we should install. CRAMM is a Government standard; we can certainly look for 'balanced security' but should we expect less security?

18.11 REFERENCES

[Barber 90a]   Barber B, Jensen O A, Lamberts H, Roger F, de Schouwer P and Zöllner H: "The Six Safety First Principles of Health Information Systems: A Programme of Implementation, Part 1: Safety and Security." Medical Informatics Europe 90, ed O'Moore R, Bengtsson S, Bryant J R and Bryden J S, Vol 40 Lecture Notes in Medical Informatics. Springer Verlag, 1990, pp 608-613, ISBN 3-540-52936-5.

[Barber 90b]   Barber B, Jensen, O A, Lamberts H, Roger F, de Schouwer P and Zöllner H: "The Six Safety First Principles of Health Information

Systems." In HC90: Current Perspectives in Health Computing, 1990, British Journal of Health Care Computing, 1990, ISBN 0948198 09 5.

[Barber 90c] Barber B et al: "The Six Safety First Principles of Health Information Systems." In: Data Protection and Confidentiality in Health Informatics: Handling Health Data in Europe in the Future, pp 296-314, ed CEC DG XIII/F AIM, proceedings of AIM working conference, Brussels, 19-21 March 1990, IOS Press, Amsterdam, ISBN 90 5199 052 9.

[Barber 91a] Barber B: "Towards an IT Security Policy for the NHS." In: HC91 Current Perspectives in Health Care Computing, pp 345-351, ed Richards B et al, British Journal of Healthcare Computing, Weybridge, UK, 1991, ISBN 0 948198 11 7.

[Barber 91b] Barber B, Vincent R and Scholes M: "Worst Case Scenarios: The Legal Consequences." In: HC92 Current Perspectives in Health Care Computing 1992, pp 282-288, ed Richards B et al, British Journal of Healthcare Computing, Weybridge, UK 1992, ISBN 0 948198 12 5.

[Barber 92] Barber B and Davey J, 1991, "The Use of the CCTA Risk Analysis and Management Methodology [CRAMM] in Health Information Systems." Paper submitted for MEDINFO 92.

[CCTA 91] Central Computing and Telecommunications Agency (CCTA): "CRAMM 1991 User Manual." CCTA, 1991, IT Security and Privacy Group, Riverwalk House, 157-161 Millbank, LONDON SW1P 4RT.

[CEC 81] Council of Europe: "Convention (No 108) for the Protection of Individuals with Regard to Automatic Processing of Personal Data." 28 January 1981, ISBN 92-871-0482-4.

[CEN 91] Comité Européen de Normalisation [CEN] TC 251: 1991 "Directory of the European Standardisation Requirements for Healthcare Informatics and Programme for the Development of Standards." CEN, Brussels, 1991 (also available from BSI Secretariat to IST/35 at NHS Information Management Centre, 15 Frederick Road, Edgbaston, BIRMINGHAM, B15 1JD, UK).

[CER 81] Council of Europe: "Recommendation on Automated Medical Data Banks R(81)1." Strasbourg, January 1981, ISBN 92-871-0495-6.

[CER 83a] Council of Europe: "Recommendation on the Protection of Personal Data Used for Scientific Research and Statistics R(83)10." Strasbourg, September 1983, ISBN 92-871-0317-8.

[CER 83b]   Council of Europe: "Recommendation on the Protection of Personal Data Used for Social Security Purposes R(86)1." Strasbourg, September 1983, ISBN 92-871-0924-9.

[CER 86]   Council of Europe: "Recommendation on the Protection of Personal Data Used for the Purposes of Direct Marketing R(85)20." Strasbourg, 1986, ISBN 92-871-0876-5.

[CER 87]   Council of Europe: "Recommendation Regulating the Use of Personal Data in the Police Sector R(87)15." Strasbourg, September 1987, ISBN 92-871-1587-7.

[CER 92]   Council of Europe: "Draft Recommendation on the Communication of Health Information in Hospitals: Ethical and Legal Issues." 29 April 1992, CDSP (92)8.

[Chalton 88]   Chalton S, Gaskill S and Sterling J A L: "Encyclopaedia of Data Protection, Vols 1 & 2." Sweet & Maxwell, London, 1988.

[Davey 90]   Davey J: "Risk Analysis and Management." In: Data Protection and Confidentiality in Health Informatics: Handling Health Data in Europe in the Future, pp 350-359, ed CEC DG XIII/F AIM, proceedings of AIM working conference, Brussels, 19-21 March 1990,   IOS Press, Amsterdam, ISBN 90 5199 052 9.

[Davey 91]   Davey J: "The CCTA Risk Analysis and Management Methodology [CRAMM]." In: HC91 Current Perspectives in Health Care Computing, pp 360-365, ed Richards B et al, British Journal of Healthcare Computing, Weybridge, UK, ISBN 0 948198 11 7.

[de Schouwer 90]   de Schouwer P, Barber B, Jensen, O A, Lamberts H, Roger-France F H and Zöllner H: "The Six Safety First Principles of Health Information Systems: A Programme of Implementation, Part 2 The Environment, Convenience and Legal Issues." In: Medical Informatics Europe 90, pp 614-619, ed O'Moore R, Bengtsson S, Bryant J R and Bryden J S, vol 40 Lecture Notes in Medical Informatics, Springer Verlag, 1990, ISBN 3-540-52936-5.

[DHG 84]   Department of Health Guidance, produced under the aegis of the Steering Group on Health Services Information (chaired by Edith Körner), A Report from the Confidentiality Working Group chaired by David Kenny, October 1984.

[EC 82}   European Commission: "Information Security Technologies - Rationale for Action." CEC/DGXIII/F/GEO182.

[EC 90]   European Commission: "Proposed Directive Concerning the Protection of Individuals in Relation to the Processing of Personal Data." COM(90) 314 final - including SYN 287, 288 and INFOSEC, Brussels, 13 September 1990.

[EC 91a]   European Commission: "Information Technology Security Evaluation Criteria [ITSEC], Provisional Harmonised Criteria." Version 1.2, June 1991, ISBN 92-826-3004-8.

[EC 91b]   European Commission: "Health Informatics 1991: Handling Health Data in Europe in the Future." ed CEC DG XIII/F AIM, proceedings of AIM working conference, Brussels, 19-21 March 1990, IOS Press, Amsterdam, ISBN 90 5199 052 9.

[EC 91c]   European Commission, AIM Requirements Board: "Impact Assessment and Forecasts of Information and Communications Technologies Applied to Health Care, Volumes I-IV." Pub. as "Perspectives of Information Processing in Medical Applications: Strategic Issues, Requirements and Options for the European Community" ed Roger-France F H and Santucci G, pp 213-256, Springer Verlag, 1991, ISBN 3-540-53856-9.

[EC 92a]   European Commission: "Information Security Technologies - Specification of Priority R and D Tasks." CEC/DGXIII/F/GE1190/GI Jan 1992.

[EC 92b]   European Commission: "Advances in Medical Informatics: The Results of the AIM Exploratory Action." ed Noothoven van Gour J and Christensen J P, CEC DG XIII/F AIM, IOS Press Amsterdam, 1992, ISBN 90 5199 058 8.

[EC 92c]   European Commission: "Information Security INFOSEC 92 - Security Investigations." January 1992, CEC/DGXIII/F/GEO182.

[EC 92d]   European Commission: "Information Technology Security Evaluation Manual [ITSEM]." To be published during 1992.

[ECD 86]   European Commission: "Decision 87/95/EEC On Standardisation in the Field of Information Technology and Telecommunications." December 1986.

[ECD 90]   European Commission: "Directive On The Minimum Safety and Health Requirements for Work with Display Screen Equipment." Directive 90/270/EEC, 29 May 1990.

[EWOS]   European Workshop for Open Systems: "Medical Data Interchange: Study and Investigation of Problems Related to Standardisation and the Relevance of Open Systems Standards in Medical Informatics - The Final Report of EWOS Project Team 007." Rue de Stassart 36, B-1050 Brussels.

[Griesser 80]   Griesser, G, Bakker, A, Danielsson, J, Hirel, J-C, Kenny, D J, Schneider, W and Wassermann, A I (Editors): "Data Protection in Health Information Systems: Considerations and Guidelines." IMIA Working Group 4, North Holland Publishing Co, 1980, ISBN 0 444 86052 5.

[Griesser 83]   Griesser, G, Jardel, J P., Kenny, D J and Sauter, K (Editors): "Data Protection in Health Information Systems: Where do we Stand?" IMIA Working Group 4, North Holland Publishing Co, 1983, ISBN 0 444 86713 9.

[HSE 92]   Health and Safety Executive: "Work with Display Screen Equipment: Proposals for regulations and Guidance." Health and Safety Commission, CD 42, 1992.

[IEC 91]   International Electrotechnical Commission: "Software for Computers in the Application of Industrial Safety-Related Systems." SC65A/WG9 Secretariat 122, Draft Document, November 1991.

[NHS 88]   NHS Management Executive Information Management Group: "The NHS Data Protection Handbook." Edited by the Information Management Centre, 15 Frederick Road, Edgbaston, Birmingham, B15 1JD, UK, July 1988.

[NHS 92a]   NHS Management Executive Information Management Group: "Information Systems Security: A Top Level Policy for the NHS." Developed by SCOLL for the Information Management Centre, 15 Frederick Road, Edgbaston, Birmingham, B15 1JD, UK, April 1992.

[NHS 92b]   NHS Management Executive Information Management Group: "Information Systems Security: Someone's Elses Problem - An Outline of 'Baseline Security'." Developed by SCOLL for the Information Management Centre, 15 Frederick Road, Edgbaston, Birmingham, B15 1JD, UK, 1992.

PART FIVE
CURRENT DEVELOPMENT OF STANDARDS

19

Deficiencies in existing software engineering standards as exposed by 'SMARTIE'

Colum Devine, Norman Fenton and Stella Page

19.1 BACKGROUND TO 'SMARTIE'

Despite the widespread introduction of new software engineering standards and methods, intended to help solve the so-called 'software crisis', there remains much scepticism as to their beneficial effect on software practice. Even where claims of 'improved quality' or 'greater productivity' seem plausible, these are not supported by hard scientific and engineering evidence. In fact, there has been almost no attempt to make an objective evaluation of standards and the methods which they specify. There is an urgent need for objective methods of independent assessment.

SMARTIE (Standards and Methods Assessment using Rigorous Techniques in Industrial Environments) is a collaborative research project within the U.K., funded by the Department of Trade and Industry (DTI) and the Science and Engineering Research Council (SERC) as part of their Information Engineering Research and Development programme. It is a measurement-based project whose major objective is to propose a widely applicable procedure for the objective assessment of standards and methods used in software development. We intend to provide a framework of measurement and evaluation in which hypotheses about the efficacy of standards and methods can be examined rigorously. We believe that such evaluation necessarily involves measuring those attributes of the software products which the standards and methods claim will result from their use. An important secondary objective is to influence positively the way that software engineering standards are written in the future.

The work to date on the SMARTIE project has produced a review [Fenton 91b] an analysis [Devine 91a] and a classification [Devine 91b] of software engineering standards. The analysis and classification have exposed several deficiencies in existing software engineering standards and those in draft form, notably:

(i)   Software engineering standards are written with a heavy bias towards process requirements. This is in stark contrast to traditional engineering standards where the emphasis is on product requirements.

(ii) It will prove impossible objectively to measure conformance to almost all of the requirements contained in software engineering standards.

(iii) While many of the standards claim that conformance to their requirements will result in a 'quality' product, few actually provide any definition of quality or guidance on how to measure it. The validity of such claims are highly questionable and should be treated with great caution.

It is our contention that these deficiencies must be overcome, and to this end we make some constructive proposals. Only then will we be in a position to provide a rigorous experimental approach to the evaluation of the efficacy of standards and methods. Without such rigour, the software developer is in the unacceptable situation of being forced to rely on unvalidated methods of development which may offer no real benefits.

19.2 INTRODUCTION

In recent years the software engineering world has witnessed the introduction of a wide range of tools, techniques, and methods which claim to improve the software development process or final software product in one or more ways. Much scepticism exists as to the beneficial effect of these technologies on software practice [Fenton 91a, Vessey 84, Card 87]. Few have ever been evaluated experimentally, and when the need arises to choose between competing technologies, any decisions taken are often made on the basis of unsubstantiated claims.

In short, the world of software engineering is severely lacking in the experimental rigour prevalent in many other disciplines, such as medicine, biological sciences, and even the social sciences [Mitchell 88]. Moreover some of the few published experimental investigations have subsequently been discredited or strongly criticized because of their poor theory and experimental design. For example, the experiment of Schneiderman et al [Shneiderman 77] led to a widely held view that flowcharts, as a means of program and design documentation, were no greater an aid to comprehension than pseudocode. As a result of this report flowcharts were shunned in the computing community. Yet, in one of the few truly rigorous software engineering experiments, Scanlan [Scanlan 89] comprehensively proved that flowcharts were a superior means of program documentation. Scanlan also exposed the experimental flaws in Shneiderman's and similar studies.

Even the most widely held beliefs in software engineering have little or no empirical evidence to support them. For example, Vessey and Weber [Vessey 84] examined in detail the empirical evidence to support the use of structured programming. They concluded that the evidence was 'equivocal' and argued that the problems surrounding experimentation on structured programming are '... a manifestation of poor theory, poor hypothesis, and poor methodology'.

If there is little evidence to support the efficacy of such universally accepted techniques as structured programming, what confidence can we justifiably place in novel, and at times competing, techniques such as object oriented design, formal methods, and software fault tolerance techniques?

Software engineering standards generally describe what are believed to be the current best practices for various aspects of the software development process. There is a widespread proliferation of such standards [Nash 87] and the number is rapidly increasing [Isaak 91]. Many of these standards prescribe, recommend, or mandate the use of various tools, techniques, or methods which have not, as we have already remarked, themselves been objectively validated. This immediately brings software engineering standards into conflict with the definition of a standard, as given in [BSI 81]: 'A technical specification or other document ... based on the consolidated results of science, technology and experience, aimed at the promotion of optimum community benefits ...'.

We might immediately conclude that the vast majority of software engineering standards are not in fact standards at all. This is a serious problem, but there is an even greater concern. The British Standards Institution guide just quoted [BSI 81] summarizes the aims of standardization:

> By providing technical criteria accepted by consensus, standards promote consistent quality and economic production ...

> The broad aims of standardization can be summarized as: ... protection of consumer interests through adequate and consistent quality of goods and services ...

The claims of 'improved quality' or 'greater reliability' [NIST 83, DoD 88, ANSI 86] which are made on behalf of software engineering standards are certainly consistent with these general aims of standardization. Unfortunately they are not supported by the hard scientific and engineering evidence expected for traditional standards. In fact, there has been even less work on objectively assessing the efficacy of software engineering standards than on the technologies prescribed within them [NCC 87]. In short, such assessment work, which would be considered mandatory for more traditional standards, is almost non-existent.

SMARTIE (Standards and Methods Assessment using Rigorous Techniques in Industrial Environments) is a measurement-based project whose major objective is to propose a widely applicable procedure for the objective assessment of standards and methods used in software development. An important secondary objective of the project is to influence positively the way that software standards are written in the future.

The work to date in the SMARTIE project has produced a review [Fenton 91b], an analysis [Devine 91a], and a classification [Devine 91b] of software engineering standards. The review included a comprehensive listing, by standards making body, of existing standards and those in draft form. The listing is not discussed in this chapter. In the analysis of standards, we investigated the contents of each standard according to specific criteria. The criteria and the results from the analysis are described in detail in Section 19.3.

We also present a detailed classification of the requirements contained in standards used in software development. In particular, we classify specific subsets of requirements. Any particular subset of requirements addresses a specific software process, product, or resource. The criterion on which the classification is based is the degree to which we can objectively measure conformance to these subsets of requirements. The results from the classification exercise are presented in Section 19.4.

Finally, in Section 19.5, we present our conclusions from the first phase of the SMARTIE project.

19.3 ANALYSIS OF SOFTWARE ENGINEERING STANDARDS

While the SMARTIE review [Fenton 91b] covers all existing software engineering standards, the more detailed analysis concentrates on a selection of standards concerned with verification, validation, and testing (VVT). These include complete standards, for example [NIST 83], [BSI 80], and the relevant sections of standards that cover all aspects of software development, for example, [MOD 91a] and [ESA 91]. The format for the analysis is described in Section 19.3.1 below. Following that, we present the results of the analysis of software engineering standards. We do not discuss the details of the analysis of each standard in this chapter; the reader is referred to [Devine 91a] for a complete description of this. Rather, we provide a summary of the main points discovered in the exercise and, in particular, we indicate the deficiencies in software engineering standards which make their objective assessment virtually impossible.

19.3.1 Format for Analysis

This section provides a list and brief description of the categories within which each standard was analysed.

(i) Standard identifier and title.   This identifies the standard being analysed.

(ii) Purpose of the Document. A brief statement indicating the objective of the standard.

(iii) Area of Application. A statement indicating, for example, whether the standard is, or claims to be, applicable to all software, applicable to data processing only, applicable to safety-critical software, for use in contractual situations. Any indication given of the market sector, for example military, is noted, as is regulatory use, if applicable.

(iv) Relationship to Other Documents.   An indication of what publications must or may be used in conjunction with the standard being analysed.

(v) History.   Information such as issue number, and whether it is a revision or a replacement of a previous document.

(vi) Structure and Content.   An overview of the area or topic covered, together with an indication of the overall structure of the standard.

(vii) Language. Whether the standard is easily comprehensible. Indications of terminology or jargon that are area-specific, for example, military terms.

(viii) Tools, Techniques and Methods.   Does the standard suggest or mandate the use of any specific tools, techniques, or methods?

(ix) Method of demonstrating compliance.   In this section, we take a broad look at the standard and ask of the requirements contained in it: Can we objectively measure conformance?

(x) Perceived effectiveness and validity. Are any objectives stated, or does the standard make any claims as to benefits accruing from its use? If so, are these objectively assessable or measurable in any way?

19.3.2   Structure, Content, & Language

In general, most of the standards analysed are well structured and easily read. All of the standards analysed, apart from [DoD 85], provide glossaries. Only [ESA 91, MOD 91a, MOD 91b, DoD 88] provide indexes. Some include tables [ANSI 86, NIST 83, DoD 88] and diagrams [ANSI 86, ANSI 87b, NIST 83, DoD 88] which add to the clarity of the text. A notable feature of two of the standards analysed [ANSI 83b, NIST 83], is the provision of example usage of the standard. This is a highly beneficial feature [Shanklin 91] and one which other standards would do well to follow. For some standards, however, none of these comments apply. [DoD 85] is particularly long and difficult to read. While [ANSI 87b] appears to be a well structured document, the subject of unit testing is handled in an overly complex manner. Interestingly, [IEE 88] warns that MIL-STD-2165 '... may be found difficult reading'.

19.3.3   Tools, Techniques, and Methods

The recommendations for the use of tools, techniques, and methods in standards vary greatly. At one end of the spectrum are standards which leave all responsibility in the decision to adopt and select appropriate tools, techniques, and methods with the user. For example, [ANSI 86] does not even provide a list of currently available technologies. At the other end of the spectrum are those standards which both mandate the use of specific tools, techniques, and methods and recommend others for specific tasks. An example is [MOD 91a] which also provides a list of currently available technologies, along with source references.

Of course, any requirement mandating the use of a specific tool, technique, or method is immediately subject to the criticism central to our argument: namely, that the tools, techniques, or methods are unlikely themselves to have been objectively assessed [Bassett 91]. This compounds the problem of assessing the standard.

19.3.4   Method of Demonstrating Compliance

In order to assess the efficacy of any technology we must, as a minimum, be able to measure the degree to which the technology is applied and the benefits obtained from application of the technology. In a traditional scientific discipline, such as medicine, we may measure the level of a drug administered to a patient and, at a later time, the reduction in that patient's blood pressure. These measurements are the minimum requirement in assessing the efficacy of the drug in lowering blood pressure. In order to assess the efficacy of a software engineering standard we must, at least, be able to measure the degree of conformance to the requirements of the standard, and measure the benefits gained from using that standard - for example, the reliability of the code produced. Only when we can satisfy both of these criteria are we in a position to consider any type of experimentation.

In this section and in Section 19.3.5 we present a broad indication of how feasible it is to satisfy both of these measurement criteria for existing standards. A more detailed investigation of the first criteria is presented in Section 19.4.

Firstly we consider some typical examples of requirements to which, we believe, we can objectively measure conformance.

In [NIST 83] the testing recommendations are as follows:

100% Statement coverage (Unit test);
100% Module Call (Integration test);
95% Module call (System test).

In [MOD 91a] the following requirements are specified as part of the dynamic testing phase:

Tests shall be monitored with a test coverage monitor. Tests shall continue until at least the following have been exercised:
(a) All statements
(b) All branches for both true and false conditions, and case statements for each possibility including, 'otherwise'.
(c) All loops for zero, one, and many iterations, covering initialisation, typical running and termination conditions.

The degree to which the user complies with all of these testing requirements may be measured manually or by the use of an appropriate automated tool such as [Pro].

Similarly, it would prove possible to measure compliance to the following requirements in [ANSI 83b].

Specify system and application software required to execute the test case.

and,

Specify names and titles of all persons who must approve this plan.

However, such requirements are greatly outweighed by a plethora of requirements to which it will never be possible to make an objective measure of conformance. For example, in [ESA 91] a requirement for unit testing is:

At a minimum the most probable paths through a module should be identified and tests designed to ensure that these paths are executed.

How do we determine the probability of paths? Are the probabilities subjectively assigned, or is there a method for assigning probability values to particular paths? No guidance is given on this requirement. Measuring conformance to such a requirement would be impossible.

Similar problems arise with the following test coverage requirement in [NIST 83].

100% of major logical paths.

Nowhere in the standard is the term 'major logical path' defined and measuring conformance to this requirement would also be impossible.

In fact, the majority of requirements tend to be even more vague than these particular testing requirements. For example, [ANSI 83b] requires that in the test plan document the user should:

> For each major group of features or feature combinations, specify the approach which will ensure that these feature groups are adequately tested.

No definition of 'adequate' is provided in the standard. Neither is any guidance provided on achieving an 'adequate' degree of testing. Measuring compliance to this requirement is impossible.

Similarly, in [BSI 80] the user must ensure that:

> ... the test specification is adequate to test the software to the required level of confidence.

and that

> ... input data and dummy software are ... suitable for the test.

How these should actually be achieved for the three levels of system complexity given in the standard code of practice is not stated. Measuring conformance to these requirements is impossible.

[ESA 91] provides the following requirement for the Software Verification and Validation Plan (SVVP).

> The SVVP shall ensure that the verification activities: are appropriate for the degree of criticality of the software ...

Measuring conformance to this particular VV&T requirement is thus impossible.

In [MOD 91a] the requirements for the review of the software specification are as follows.

> The software specification shall be reviewed by a review committee ... The review shall consider the correctness, completeness, consistency, absence of ambiguity, general style, and quality of document and its conformance to the code of design practice ...

Assessing the level to which the user has complied with such a requirement is impossible. No definitions are provided for the listed attributes, nor is any guidance provided on how to carry out such a task. Similar problems are encountered with the requirements for design descriptions, and source code.

These examples are only the 'tip of the iceberg'. Satisfying the first of our criteria for an experimental framework for assessing software engineering standards is, however, shown to be highly questionable.

19.3.5   Perceived Effectiveness and Validity

A feature of many software engineering standards are the claims they make relating to the benefits accruing from their use. For example, [ANSI 86] asserts that the application of the requirements of this standard will help ensure that:

> Software quality and reliability are enhanced.

The standard even requires the user to:

> Assess source code quality.

While [ANSI 83a] provides a measurable definition of software reliability, the same cannot be said for software quality. Similarly, [NIST 83] claims that it is:

> ... a basic guide for ensuring the production and maintenance of quality software.

And [DoD 88] claims that it:

> ... provides the means for establishing, evaluating, and maintaining quality in software and associated documentation.

Many more such claims exist. However, none of these standards actually define what they mean by 'software quality' or provide any guidance on its measurement. The claims made by such standards are untestable and should be treated with caution.

19.4 A CLASSIFICATION OF SOFTWARE ENGINEERING STANDARDS

We have chosen to classify standards (those investigated in the analysis exercise) according to properties of the requirements contained in them. In Section 19.4.1, we describe the framework for this classification. We classify those requirements which relate to a single process, product, or resource. In Section 19.4.2, we explain how the criterion on which the classification is based is the degree to which we can objectively measure conformance to the requirements. Such a classification enables us to identify those parts of standards for which an objective measure of conformance is possible.

A few classifications of software engineering standards and related topics have previously appeared in the literature [Nash 87, ANSI 87a, CEN 91], and a review of these and any relationships to the present classification is given in [Devine 91b].

19.4.1   A Classification Framework

In any manufacturing or development project, we identify *processes, products,* and *resources* as the three important classes of entities.

A **Process** is any specific activity or time period within the manufacturing or development project. Examples in software engineering include specific activities like requirements capture, designing, coding, and time periods like 'the first three months of the project'.

A **Product** is any artefact, deliverable, or document arising out of a process. Examples in software engineering include a design specification, a test plan, and a user manual.

A **Resource** is any item providing the input to a process. Examples in software engineering include a design team, a compiler, and a software test tool.

Anything that we are ever likely to want to measure or predict in software engineering is an attribute of some entity of one of the three classes. We make a distinction between attributes which are internal and those which are external.

Internal attributes are those properties of an entity which can be measured purely in terms of the entity itself. Examples include the time spent during system testing (an internal process attribute), or the algorithmic complexity of a software module (an internal product attribute).

External attributes are those properties of an entity which can only be measured with respect to how the entity relates to its environment. Examples include the experience of an individual (an external resource attribute), or the reliability of a software system (an external product attribute). This subject is discussed in detail in [Fenton 91a].

Any requirement in a standard can be described as primarily a process requirement, a product requirement, or a resource requirement. The emphasis in traditional engineering standards is on the 'measurable specification of quality requirements of products'. This is in complete agreement with the definition of 'standard' as given in the *Oxford Encyclopaedic English Dictionary*, 1991:

> **standard** ... an object or quality of measure derived as a basis or example or principle to which others conform or should conform or by which the accuracy or quality of others is judged (*by present-day standards*).

It would seem reasonable therefore that standards should concentrate primarily on product requirements. A good example in computer science is the compiler standards. These are based on product requirements since they specify a set of programs that must be compiled with specific results. However, for most software engineering standards the situation is very different. Very few requirements at all in software engineering standards are product requirements. The few product requirements are normally targeted at either the internal attributes of the final product or intermediate products, or the external attributes of the intermediate products. The potentially most important requirements, namely those specifying external attributes of the final product, are almost non-existent.

Even then, the requirements are vague, in sharp contrast to the rigorous manner in which the requirements of traditional engineering standards are specified. For example, the British Standards Institution's standard for pushchair safety [BSI 84] specifies, in measurable terms, the tests to be performed on the final product, as well as the safety levels of acid concentration in plastic components. Standards such as this reflect the vast amount of knowledge and experience embodied in the world of traditional engineering in contrast to software engineering. The impact of materials, structures, etc. on the quality aspects of the final product, namely safety in the case of [BSI 84], are all well understood and tested. This is certainly not the case for software engineering where many 'rule-of-thumb' ideas are embodied in the requirements of the standards. Thus, whereas the safety levels of acid concentrations in plastic components are well documented and understood, we do not have the same confidence in the relationship between the prohibiting of recursion [MOD 91a] and the resulting safety of software.

In software engineering standards, we find the emphasis almost entirely on process requirements. A shift from specifying product requirements to specifying process requirements is a shift away from an established link between conformance to the standard and end-product quality. The task of establishing the relationship between conformance to standard and product quality becomes even more difficult as we move from product to process to resource requirements, such as those specifying staff experience in [MOD 91a].

It is an interesting exercise to compare the distributions of requirements in [BSI 84] and [MOD 91a], while remembering that both standards are intended to improve the safety of particular systems. The requirements are broken down into four categories.

(i)   Process requirements;
(ii) Internal product attribute requirements;
(iii) External product attribute requirements;
(iv) Resource requirements.

The requirements in [BSI 84] are entirely product-based and are all specified in rigorous measurable terms. The statistics are these: of 29 requirements, all are product-based, 18 being external product requirements and 11 being internal product requirements. Thus, the proportion of requirements for external product attributes is almost twice that for internal product attributes. Moreover, the method of testing for conformance to the requirements is described in the appendices to the standard.

These observations are in sharp contrast to the distribution of requirements in [MOD 91a]. Here, there are 115 requirements, and these refer to a mixture of process, product, and resource. The majority of these, 88, or 77 per cent, are process-based. Only 13 of the requirements, or 12 per cent, are product requirements, 3 concerning people and 10 concerning tools and facilities. Of these, only a single one (Point 35.3, which asserts that systems must be checked for 'correct functionality') can be considered to be an external product attribute requirement (and this is highly debatable). 13, or 11 per cent, a relatively high percentage, of the requirements are resource based. Also, as our classification shows, the vast majority of the requirements in [MOD 91a] are written in such a way that we would not be able to provide an objective measure of conformance.

19.4.2   The classification of standards' requirements

The objective of the classification can be summarized as an attempt to provide an answer to the following question: 'To what degree can we measure conformance to the process, product, and resource requirements of software engineering standards?'

The classification scheme consists of a division into the three categories: process, product, and resource. The degree of detail present in the process, product, and resource requirements varies considerably from standard to standard. For example, where one standard provides requirements for general test plans only [NIST 83, ANSI 83b], another standard might provide requirements for unit test plans, integration test plans, system test plans, and acceptance test plans [ESA 91, DoD 88, ANSI 86]. To account for this, we take the following view of processes, products, and resources.

(i)   Processes

Our scheme groups processes in a particular way so as to obtain various 'levels'. For example, at the top level we have processes such as 'building' which is composed of the lower level processes 'coding' and 'testing'. In turn, the process of 'testing' is composed of the lower level processes 'unit testing', 'integration testing', 'system testing', and 'acceptance testing'.

Typical *internal* attributes of processes include the time and effort associated with each activity. Typical *external* attributes include the cost and effectiveness of each activity.

(ii)   Products

As with processes, we create groups to form various 'levels' of products. For example, at the top level we have products such as the user-delivered software which is made up of the source code and its associated documentation. This documentation is made up of the user manual and the support and maintenance manuals.

Typical *internal* attributes of products include size of specification documents and software product, and the number of known faults in the specification documents. Typical *external* attributes of products include the reliability of executable code; the completeness, accuracy, consistency, and correctness of specification documents; and the readability and quality of the user manual.

(iii) Resources

For our classification, we consider only one 'level' of resource. The resources adopted for the classification are Individuals, Physical Environment, and Tools.

Typical *internal* attributes of resources include the age and salary of an individual and the price of a software tool. Typical *external* attributes of the resources include the productivity of individuals and the reliability of any software tools used.

These 'levels' of process, product, and resource entities provide the necessary framework for the classification. Within this framework, for each software engineering standard requirement classified, we assess the degree to which we can measure the conformance to each process, product, and resource entity requirement.

Five degrees of increasing detail for each requirement are observed. For any requirement, a standard will be indicated as providing one of these degrees. These are indicated in Table 19.1.

In Table 19.2 we give examples of possible references for unit testing along with the appropriate code.

19.4.3   Results of Classification

The classification of software engineering standards has provided an interesting insight into their nature. Only one per cent of requirements

Table 19.1: Codes for the degree of detail given in any requirement

Code	Interpretation
	No reference
R	A reference only, with no indication of any particular attribute(s) which that entity should possess
S	A reference for which only a subjective measure of conformance is possible
P	A reference for which a partially subjective and partially objective measure of conformance is possible
O	A reference for which a totally objective measure of conformance is possible

Table 19.2: Example degree of detail for unit testing requirement

Reference	Code
No reference to unit testing	
Unit testing shall be carried out	R
Unit testing shall be carried out effectively	S
Unit testing shall be carried out so that all statements and the most probable paths are tested	P
Unit testing shall be carried out so that all statements are tested	O

relating to either a single process, product, or resource could be classified as providing an objective measure of conformance. Twenty-one per cent of requirements were classified as providing a partially objective and partially subjective measure of conformance. However, the majority of requirements in the standards were classified as providing either a subjective (51 per cent) measure of conformance or a reference only (27 per cent): a total of 78 per cent being judged altogether non-objective. Such a situation highlights the difficulty of objectively assessing the efficacy of software engineering standards.

Only 1 per cent of requirements actually addressed the final software product, and only a partially objective and partially subjective measure of conformance could be made for these.

Only 4 per cent of requirements addressed final product documentation. 10 per cent addressed resources. The majority of requirements (51 per cent) addressed intermediate products, while 34 per cent addressed process requirements. This is in sharp contrast with traditional engineering standards where the emphasis is almost exclusively on final product requirements.

19.5 CONCLUSIONS

The two measurement activities necessary for the objective assessment of software engineering standards, namely measuring conformance to the standard and measuring the benefits gained from application of the standard, are fraught with difficulty. The manner in which software engineering standards are currently written renders it impossible objectively to measure conformance to the majority of their requirements.

Further, many software engineering standards claim that their use will guarantee the production of a 'quality' software product. None of these standards, however, provides any definition of what they mean by 'quality', or guidance on how to measure it.

It is our contention that this situation must be improved if software engineering is ever to grow to the present level of maturity enjoyed by traditional scientific and engineering disciplines. Only then will we be in a position objectively to assess the efficacy of software engineering standards.

A first step towards achieving such a situation must be to change the manner in which software engineering standards are currently written. We believe that requirements must be written in such a way that:

(i)   Individual requirements in a standard should be restricted to a specific well-defined product, process, or resource. Ideally each such requirement should specify a measurable attribute of the process, product, or resource. This would ensure the possibility of establishing conformance to a standard objectively. Any requirement to which conformance can only be established by purely subjective means should be re-written or removed.

(ii) The specific benefits which the use of a standard is intended to bring should be stated clearly. Preferably, this should involve specifying desirable external attributes in measurable form. The intended benefit(s) which each requirement, or group of requirements, is supposed to influence should be clearly identified.

(iii) Standards should be restricted to cohesive collections of requirements. Ideally, they should be restricted to specific products or processes, for example, specific testing processes, or specific products like specification documents and design documents.

(iv) Until the use of a standard has been demonstrated to be effective for a range of products or processes to which it applies, it should only be called a 'proposed set of guidelines'. Such a set of guidelines should be supplemented by documentary evidence (preferably in the form of results from at least one case study) illustrating its successful application. If none exists, there can be no justification for its proposal as a standard.

19.6 REFERENCES

[ANSI 83a]   American National Standards Institute: "Standard Glossary of Software Engineering Terminology." ANSI/IEEE 729, 1983.

[ANSI 83b]   American National Standards Institute: "Standard for Software Test Documentation." ANSI/IEEE 829, 1983.

[ANSI 86] American National Standards Institute: "Standard for Software Verification and Validation Plans." ANSI/IEEE 1012, 1986.

[ANSI 87a]   American National Standards Institute: "Standard

Taxonomy for Software Engineering Standards." ANSI/IEEE 1002, 1987.

[ANSI 87b]   American National Standards Institute: "Standard for Software Unit Testing." ANSI/IEEE 1008, 1987.

[Bassett 91]   Bassett S, Cooper R, Fry J, Jones L, Kitchenham B, Law D, Linkman S, Mohammed W, Naeem T, Sadler C, and Shelley C: "State of the Art Report." DESMET Volume 1 - Main Report, November 1991.

[BSI 80]   British Standards Institution: "Code of Practice for Testing of Computer-Based Systems." BS 5887, 1980 (confirmed 1988).

[BSI 81]   British Standards Institution: "British Standard Guide - A Standard for Standards." BSO, 1981.

[BSI 84]   British Standards Institution: "Safety Requirements for Pushchairs." BS 4792, 1984.

[Card 87] Card D N, McGarry F E, and Page G T: "Evaluating Software Engineering Technologies." *IEEE Transactions on Software Engineering*, SE-13(7):845-851, July 1987.

[CEN 91] Comitée Européen de Normalisation: "Report on Study and Investigation Related to Information Systems Engineering." April 1991.

[Devine 91a]   Devine C, Fenton N, Littlewood B, Mellor P, and Page S: "Analysis of Standards." SMARTIE Project Technical Report 1.2 - Version 1.0, August 1991.

[Devine 91b]   Devine C, Fenton N, and Page S: "Classification of Standards." SMARTIE Project Technical Report 1.3 - Version 1.0, December 1991.

[DoD 85] Department of Defence: "Technical Reviews and Audits for Systems, Equipment and Computer Programs." MIL. STD 1521B, 1985.

[DoD 88] Department of Defence: "Defence System Software Development." DOD-STD-2167A, 1988.

[ESA 91] European Space Agency Board for Software Standardisation and Control: "ESA Software Engineering Standards." Issue 2, February 1991.

[Fenton 91a]   Fenton N E: "Software Metrics: A Rigorous Approach." Chapman and Hall, 1991.

[Fenton 91b]   Fenton N, Littlewood B, Mellor P, Devine C, Page S, Jacques D, Godliman R, McComish D, and Kelly M: "Quality Management and Software Engineering Standards - Review." Version 1.0, SMARTIE Project Technical Report 1.1, May 1991.

[IEE 88]   The Institution of Electrical Engineers: "Guidelines for Assuring Testability." IEE, 1988.

[Isaak 91] Isaak J: "Applications Environment Profiles." Computer, pp 69-70, February 1991.

[Mitchell 88]   Mitchell J and Welty C: "Experimentation in Software Engineering: An Empirical View." Int. J. Man-Machine Studies, 29, pp 613-624, 1988.

[MOD 91a]   Ministry of Defence Directorate of Standardization: "Interim Defence Standard 00-55: The Procurement of Safety Critical Software in Defence Equipment." Parts 1-2, 1991.

[MOD 91b]   Ministry of Defence Directorate of Standardization: "Interim Defence Standard 00-56: Hazard Analysis and Safety Classification of the Computer and Programmable Electronic System Elements of Defence Equipment." 1991.

[Nash 87] Nash S H and Redwin S T Jr.: "A Map of the World of Software-Related Standards, Guidelines, and Recommended Practices." Computer Standards and Interfaces, 6, pp 245-265, 1987.

[NCC 87] National Computing Centre: "The STARTS Guide." NCC, Oxford Road, Manchester, England, M1 7ED. 2nd Edition, 1987.

[NIST 83] National Institute of Standards and Technology: "Guidelines for Lifecycle Validation, Verification, and Testing of Computer Software." FIPS PUB 101, 1983.

[Pro] Program Analysers: "LDRA Testbed Static and Dynamic analyser." Program Analysers, 56 Northbrook Street, Newbury, Berkshire, RG13 1AN, United Kingdom.

[Scanlan 89]   Scanlan D A: "Structured Flowcharts Outperform Pseudocode: An Experimental Comparison." *IEEE Software*, pp 28-36, September 1989.

[Shanklin 91]   Shanklin R E Jr.: "Developing Standards With and For the

User." In *Fourth Software Engineering Standards Application Workshop*, pp 14-17. IEEE, 1991.

[Shneiderman 77]   Shneiderman B, Mayer R, McKay D, and Heller P. Experimental investigations of the utility of detailed flowcharts in programming. *Communications of the ACM*, 20(6): pp 373-381, June 1977.

[Vessey 84]   Vessey I and Weber R: "Research on Structured Programming: An Empiricist's Evaluation." TSE, 10: pp 397-407, July 1984.

20

Risk and system integrity concepts for safety-related control systems

Ron Bell and Dietmar Reinert

This chapter provides an overview of the concepts of 'risk' and 'safety integrity' in relation to safety-related electrical/electronic/programmable electronic systems. The chapter is an abridged version of Annex A of the emerging International Electrotechnical Commission (IEC) Standard: *Functional Safety of Electrical/ Electronic/Programmable Electronic Systems* [IEC 92]. Although based on Annex A, the authors have in a few instances deviated from the strict wording of the annex in order more properly to present their own views. Where this occurs, a note in the text has been added to alert the reader of the deviation. The concepts of risk, including 'tolerable risk', safety integrity, safety-related system, and system and software integrity levels, are discussed.

20.1 INTRODUCTION

Computer-based systems (generically referred to as programmable electronic systems (PES)) are increasingly being used to carry out safety functions. The design of certain equipment only becomes viable when it is to be controlled by a computer. The adoption of PESs for safety purposes has, potentially, many safety advantages, but these will only be realized if appropriate design and assessment methodologies are used. Many of the features of PESs do not enable the safety integrity to be predicted with the same degree of confidence that has traditionally been available for less complex hardware-based systems.

Several bodies have either published, or are developing, guidelines to enable the safe exploitation of PES technology. In 1987, in the UK, the Health and Safety Executive (HSE) developed guidelines for programmable electronic systems used for safety-related applications [HSE 87]. In Germany, a draft standard [DIN 90] has been published and, within the European Community, an important element in the work on harmonized European Standards, in connection with the requirements of the Machinery Directive, is concerned with safety-related control systems (including those employing PESs). In the USA, the Instrument Society of America (ISA) is well advanced in preparing a standard on programmable electronic systems for use in the process industries and, also in the USA, the Centre for Chemical Process Safety (CCPS), a Directorate of the American Institute of Chemical Engineers, is also preparing Guidelines for the Chemical Process Sector.

A major objective of all this work is the achievement of international standardization. In this context, the International Electrotechnical Commission (IEC) is developing two International Standards:

- *Functional Safety of Electrical/Electronic/Programmable Electronic Systems: Generic Aspects; Part 1, General Requirements* [IEC 92], a systems standard, the latest draft of which is currently being reviewed by all National Committees.
- *Software for Computers in the Application of Industrial Safety-Related Systems* [IEC 91], a software standard, the latest draft of which has already been the subject of a consultation exercise with all National Standards Committees.

The initial scope of the systems standard was limited to PESs, but this was increased to include all electrically-based safety-related systems (from simple electromechanical relay systems to complex PESs). Therefore, while the driving force to develop an international standard to provide a systematic risk-based approach came from the requirements relating to PESs, it has now been accepted that the fundamental principles relating to PESs should be applied to all electrical/electronic/programmable electronic systems.

A key feature of both of the above proposed international standards is their adoption of 'integrity levels'. That is, system integrity levels (for safety-related systems) and software integrity levels (for software within a safety-related system). In order to deal in a systematic manner with all the activities necessary to achieve the required system integrity level, for the safety-related systems, the systems standard adopts, as the key framework, an 'overall safety lifecycle' (see Figure 20.1). For all phases of this safety lifecycle, the systems standard specifies:

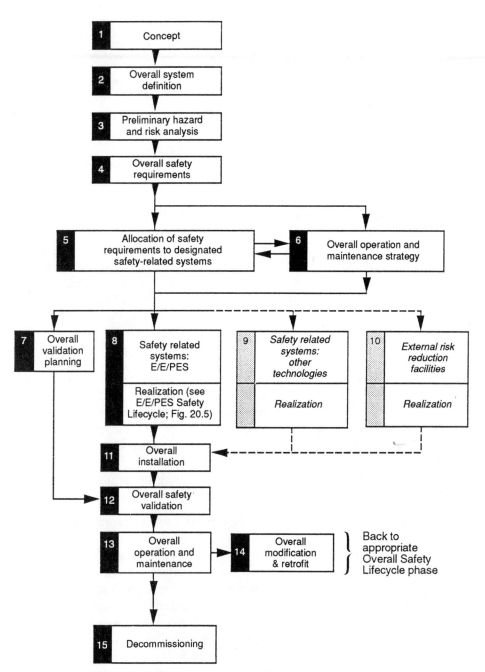

Figure 20.1: The overall safety lifecycle.
Note 1: Assessment and verification activities are not shown for reasons of clarity of the figure, but are relevant to all safety lifecycle phases.
Note 2: The activity phases in boxes 9 and 10 are shown in shaded format to indicate that the international standard does not deal with them in detail.

(i)   The Objectives to be achieved;
(ii)   The Requirements to meet the Objectives;
(iii)   The Scope of each phase;
(iv)   The required Inputs to each phase;
(v)   The deliverables required to comply with the Requirements.

The safety lifecycle could be applied to any safety-related system irrespective of the technology on which the system is based.

One of the major technical challenges, with respect to complex safety-related systems, is to develop measures and techniques which can be related to target safety integrity measures. Equally important is the need to relate the safety-integrity requirements for safety-related systems to the level of safety that the equipment under control (EUC) has to achieve. The purpose of this chapter is to outline the models that have been developed within the proposed IEC systems standard for linking the risk concepts for the EUC with the system integrity levels for the safety-related systems. One of the models is based on a quantitative approach (see Section 20.9) while the other is based on qualitative parameters (see Section 20.10).

20.2   RISK

20.2.1   General Concepts

An abbreviated form of the definition of risk given in the IEC systems standard [IEC 92] is: 'The combination of the frequency and the consequence of a specified hazardous event'. The concept of risk always has two elements: the frequency with which a hazard occurs and the consequences of the hazardous event.

The main tests that are applied in regulating industrial risks are very similar to those we apply to daily life. They involve determining whether:

(i)   The frequency is so high, or the outcome so unacceptable that it must be refused altogether; or
(ii)   The risk is, or has been made, so small as to be insignificant; or
(iii)   The risk falls between the two states specified in (a) and (b) above and that it has been reduced to the lowest level practicable, bearing in mind the benefits flowing from its acceptance and taking into account the costs of any further reduction. Any risk must be reduced so far as reasonably practicable, or to a level which is 'as low as reasonably practicable' (ALARP principle). If a risk falls between the two extremes (i.e. 'intolerable' and 'negligible') and the ALARP principle has been applied, then the resulting risk is the tolerable risk for that specific application.

This 'three zone' approach is shown in Figure 20.2.

In some cases the ALARP principle is applied in quite a rough-and-ready way, by making a rapid judgement. But in the case of major risks, it is often necessary to apply a much more formal process of assessment. The tolerable risk level for a specific application may be stated in a qualitative manner (by determining the risk parameters for a specific application sector (see Section 20.10)) or in a quantitative manner (for example, by deducing that the hazardous event leading to a specific consequence shall not occur with a frequently greater than 1 in 104 years (see Section 20.9)).

The purpose of determining the tolerable risk level is to state what is deemed reasonable with respect to both the frequency of the hazardous event and its specific consequences. Safety-related systems are designed to reduce the frequency of the hazardous event and/or its consequences.

20.2.2   Tolerable risk levels

The 'tolerable' zone may be thought of as a 'justifiable' zone in that it is possible to justify the risk by showing that it is ALARP. In general, ALARP

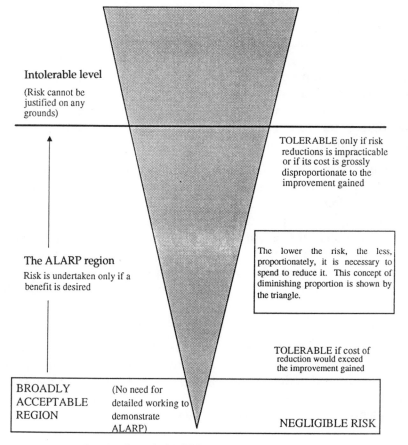

Intolerable level

(Risk cannot be justified on any grounds)

TOLERABLE only if risk reductions is impracticable or if its cost is grossly disproportionate to the improvement gained

The lower the risk, the less, proportionately, it is necessary to spend to reduce it. This concept of diminishing proportion is shown by the triangle.

The ALARP region

Risk is undertaken only if a benefit is desired

TOLERABLE if cost of reduction would exceed the improvement gained

BROADLY ACCEPTABLE REGION

(No need for detailed working to demonstrate ALARP)

NEGLIGIBLE RISK

Figure 20.2: Levels of risk and ALARP.

will be applied in such a way that the higher or more unacceptable a risk is, the more, proportionately, those responsible for the risk would be expected to spend to reduce it.   Where the risks are less significant, the less, proportionately, it is worth spending to reduce them. Below the 'tolerable zone' the levels of risk are so insignificant that they need not claim attention, and those responsible for the risk need seek no further improvement provided that these low levels of risk will be attained in practice. Nevertheless, those responsible for the risks might decide to reduce them even further. The concept of diminishing proportion is shown in the triangle in Figure 20.2.

Tolerable risk levels are an expression of society's preferences and involve consideration of many factors. They are usually set, implicitly or explicitly, by interested parties within the application sector dealing with the particular risks. Determination of the tolerable risk level takes into account the specific hazardous consequences for the application under consideration. In many instances, the tolerable risk levels are not defined as such, but are implicit in the consensus about what constitutes current good practice.   However, where there is a lack of consensus, or insufficient experience to judge the value of current practice, more explicit analysis of the costs and benefits may need to be undertaken.

Tolerable risk levels depend on many factors, for example, severity of injury, number of people exposed to danger, frequency at which a person or people are exposed to danger, and the duration of the exposure. Important factors are the perceptions and views of those exposed to the hazardous event. In arriving at what constitutes the tolerable risk level for a specific application, a number of inputs are considered. These include:

(i)   Guidelines from the appropriate Safety Regulatory Authority;
(ii)   Discussions and agreements with the different parties involved in the application;
(iii) Industry standards;
(iv)   International discussions and agreements: the role of national and international standards is becoming increasingly important in arriving at the tolerable risk levels for specific applications;
(v)   The best independent industrial, expert, and scientific advice from advisory bodies;
(vi)   Legal requirements relevant to the specific application.

The purpose of the risk level is to state what is deemed tolerable with respect to both the frequency of the hazardous event and its consequences. It is the equipment under control which poses the hazard; the safety-related electronic systems are designed to reduce the frequency and/or the consequences of the possible hazardous events.

20.2.3   Quantified Tolerable Risk Target

One way in which a tolerable risk target can be obtained is for a number of consequences to be identified and tolerable frequencies allocated to them. This matching of the consequences to the tolerable frequencies would take place by discussion and agreement between the interested parties (e.g. safety regulatory authorities, those producing the risks, and those exposed to the risks).

To take into account ALARP concepts, the matching of a consequence with a tolerable frequency can be done through 'risk classes'. Table 20.1 shows four risk classes (I, II, III, IV) for a number of consequences and frequencies. Table 20.2 defines each of the risk classes, and this introduces the concept of ALARP. The descriptions of the four risk classes are based on the zones in Figure 20.2. Classes II and III are at the extreme ends of the ALARP regions.

For a given application sector, Table 20.1 would be developed and would be used to specify the tolerable risk. In the tolerable zone, the aim would be to achieve Risk Class III (see definitions in Table 20.2). The risks within these risk class definitions are those risks that are present when risk reduction measures have been put in place.

Table 20.1 would be developed taking into account a wide range of social, political and economic factors. Each consequence would be matched against a frequency and the table populated by the risk classes.   For

Table 20.1: Risk classification of accidents

| | Consequence | | | |
Frequency	Catastrophic	Critical	Marginal	Negligible
Frequent	I	I	I	II
Probable	I	I	II	III
Occasional	I	II	III	III
Remote	II	III	III	IV
Improbable	III	III	IV	IV
Incredible	IV	IV	IV	IV

Table 20.2: Interpretation of risk classes

Risk class	Interpretation
Class I	Intolerable risk
Class II	Undesirable risk, and tolerable only if risk reduction is impracticable or if the costs are grossly disproportionate to the improvement gained
Class III	Tolerable risk if the cost of risk reduction would exceed the improvement gained
Class IV	Negligible risk

example, 'Frequent' in Table 20.1 could be an event that is 'likely to be continually experienced' which might be specified as a frequency greater than 10 per year.

The 'risk class' approach is one mechanism that can be used to determine the tolerable risk for a specific application or to enable a tolerable risk to be specified in an application-specific standard.

20.2.4   Qualitative Risk Targets

The approach adopted in Section 20.2.2 led to a numerical risk target. An alternative approach is to specify risk targets according to a qualitative scale. Such a scheme is outlined in Section 20.10.

20.3 ROLE OF SAFETY-RELATED SYSTEMS

Safety-related systems contribute towards the tolerable risk level being met. A safety-related system:

(i)   Implements the required safety functions necessary to achieve a safe state for the equipment under control, or maintains a safe state for the equipment under control; and

(ii)   Achieves, on its own or with other safety-related systems, the necessary level of safety-integrity for the implementation of the required safety functions.

Note that part (i) of the definition specifies that the safety-related system must perform the safety functions which would be specified in the functional requirements specification. For example, the functional requirements specification may state that when the temperature reaches 'x', valve 'y' should open to allow water to enter the vessel.

Part (ii) of the definition specifies that the safety functions must be performed by the safety-related system with the degree of confidence appropriate to the application, in order that the overall safety level is achieved.

Safety-related systems can broadly be divided into two types.

(i)   Safety-related protection systems which, if activated, put the EUC into a safe state. In the context of the process industries, safety-related protection systems are normally not actively controlling the EUC but, in the event of failures of the main control system, come into action and put the EUC into a safe state (e.g. an emergency shutdown system in a chemical plant, activated when the main process control system fails).

(ii)   Safety-related continuous control systems, which maintain a safe state by continuing to perform the necessary safety functions in the event of failures of the EUC control system, for a specified period of time (because a safe state is not reached by shutting down the EUC, for example, in a flight control system on an aeroplane).

Note that the above descriptions have been modified from the descriptions given in the systems standard [IEC 92]. This has been done to aid clarity of the concepts. The variation is one of emphasis rather than of conflict.

It should be noted that a person could be an integral part of a safety-related system. For example, a person could receive information from a display screen associated with a control system and perform a safety task based on this information.

20.4 SAFETY INTEGRITY

Safety Integrity is defined as 'The likelihood of a safety-related system satisfactorily performing the required safety functions under all the stated conditions within a stated period of time'. Safety integrity is considered to be composed of two elements:

(i) Hardware integrity (Ih): that part of the safety integrity of safety-related systems which relates to random hardware failures in a dangerous mode of failure.

(ii) Systematic integrity (Is): That part of the safety integrity of safety-related systems which relates to systematic failures in a dangerous mode of failure. Systematic failures may result from errors in specification or design, and would include common cause failures arising, for example, from environmental influences. It should be noted that measures to reduce random hardware failures will not necessarily have a corresponding effect on systematic integrity.

The required safety integrity of the total combination of safety-related systems involved in a given application must be of such a level as to ensure that:

- The failure frequency of the safety-related systems does not allow the hazard frequency to exceed that required to meet the tolerable risk level; and/or
- The safety-related systems modify the consequences to the extent required to meet the tolerable risk level.

Figure 20.3 illustrates the general concepts of risk reduction when safety-related protection systems are part of the risk reduction mechanism. The general model for this diagram assumes that:

(i) There is an EUC with a control system;
(ii) There are associated human factor issues;

(iii) The safety protective features comprise:

- E/E/PES safety-related systems,
- 'Other technology' safety-related systems,
- External risk-reduction facilities.

The various risks specified in Figure 20.3 are described below.

EUC Risk: The risk existing for the specified hazardous events for the EUC, its control system, and associated human factor issues. No designated safety protective features are considered in the determination of this risk.

Intermediate Risk: The risk existing for the specified hazardous events for the EUC, its control system, and human factors issues, but with the addition of the risk existing for the E/E/PES safety-related systems.

Actual remaining risk: The risk existing for the specified hazardous events for the EUC, its control system, and human factor issues, but with the addition of the risk existing for the E/E/PES safety-related systems, 'other technology' safety-related systems, and external risk reduction facilities.

The EUC risk is a function of the risk associated with the EUC itself, taking into account the risk reduction brought about by the EUC control system. To ensure that unreasonable claims are not made for the safety integrity of the EUC control system, the systems standard [IEC 92] places constraints on the claims that can be made.

A risk reduction to the tolerable risk level is achieved by a combination of all the safety protective features and is determined using the concepts outlined in Sections 20.2.1 and 20.2.2. It should be noted that in some situations the tolerable risk level may be achieved solely by E/E/PES safety-related systems (i.e. the intermediate risk may actually be less than the tolerable risk). The minimum risk reduction (ΔR), to achieve the tolerable risk, from a starting point of the EUC risk, is shown in Figure 20.3. The risk model outlined above, and shown in Figure 20.3, is particularly applicable to safety-related protection systems as distinct from safety-related continuous control systems.

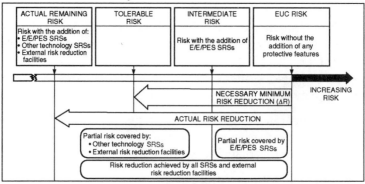

Figure 20.3: Risk reduction - general concepts.

20.5 RISK AND SAFETY-INTEGRITY

It is important that the distinction between risk and safety-integrity is fully appreciated. Risk is a measure of the likelihood of a specified hazardous event occurring. This can be determined for different situations, for example, EUC risk, intermediate risk, tolerable risk, actual risk - see Figure 20.3. Tolerable risk levels are determined on a societal basis and involve consideration of societal and political factors.

Safety Integrity applies solely to safety-related systems and is the likelihood of a safety-related system satisfactorily performing the required safety functions. Once the tolerable risk level has been set, and the necessary risk reduction estimated, the safety integrity requirements for the safety-related systems can be apportioned.

The role that safety-related systems play in achieving the necessary risk reduction is illustrated in Figures 20.3 and 20.4.

20.6 SYSTEM AND SOFTWARE INTEGRITY LEVELS

To cater for the wide range of risk reductions that safety-related systems have to achieve, it is useful to define a number of system integrity levels for both safety-related systems and safety-related software.The systems standard [IEC 92] has adopted 4 system integrity levels, level 4 being the highest and level 1 the lowest (see Table 20.3).

Then, in the requirements specifications for the safety-related systems, it should be clearly stated which system integrity level should be achieved by each system.

The software in a safety-related system is an integral part of that system,

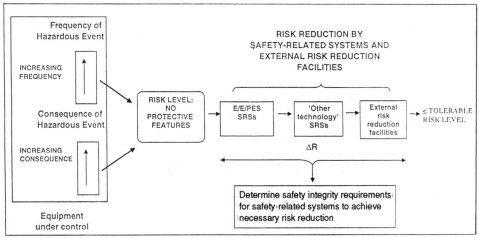

E/E/PES = Electrical/electronic/programmable electronic systems
SRSs = Safety-related systems

Figure 20.4: Risk and safety integrity concepts - safety-related protection systems.

Table 20.3: System integrity levels - target failure measures for safety integrity

System integrity level	Target safety integrity	
	Safety-related continuous control sytems (dangerous failures per hour)	*Safety-related protection systems (probability of failure to perform its design function on demand)*
4	$\geq 10^{-9}$ to $< 10^{-8}$	$\geq 10^{-5}$ to $< 10^{-4}$
3	$\geq 10^{-8}$ to $< 10^{-7}$	$\geq 10^{-4}$ to $< 10^{-3}$
2	$\geq 10^{-7}$ to $< 10^{-6}$	$\geq 10^{-3}$ to $< 10^{-2}$
1	$\geq 10^{-6}$ to $< 10^{-5}$	$\geq 10^{-2}$ to $< 10^{-1}$

is a contributor to how that system functions, and is a determinant of whether the system achieves its required safety integrity level. Thus, the safety-related software in an individual safety-related system of required system integrity level N is itself required to be at least of software integrity level N. For example, if an individual safety-related system has a system integrity level 2 designation, then the safety-related software in that system shall be of software integrity level 2, or greater, in order to ensure that the software does not reduce the system integrity of the system of which it forms a part.

20.7 SAFETY INTEGRITY TARGETS

The target safety integrity failure measures for the four system integrity levels are specified in Table 20.3. Two failure measure parameters are specified, one for continuous control safety-related systems and one for safety-related protection systems.

Note that for continuous control safety-related systems, the safety or integrity measure of interest is the 'rate of occurrence of dangerous failures' (x per unit time). For safety-related protection systems, the safety integrity parameter of interest is the probability of failure on demand (y per demand).

The target safety integrity is sub-divided into target values for hardware integrity and systematic integrity. These are required to be greater than or equal to the safety integrity target. The hardware integrity requirements are specified in Tables 20.4 and 20.5.

20.8 ALLOCATION OF SYSTEM INTEGRITY LEVELS

The safety-related systems and external risk reduction facilities have to be specified such that, as a minimum, the tolerable risk level is achieved. The standard [IEC 92] does not state the tolerable risk levels for specific applications and, consequently, cannot define the required system integrity levels for safety-related systems for any given applications. These should be

Table 20.4: Hardware integrity: safety-related protection systems

System integrity level	System fault requirements	Type 1 safety check (check of all safety functions)	Type 2 safety check check to detect all faults (including unrevealed)	EUIC put in safe state when fault detected	Quantitative hardware integrity analysis	Other requirements
1	• When a failure occurs the safety function may not be performed and the fault may lead to a dangerous mode of failures of the SRS between TYPE 1 SAFETY CHECKS	A or M	A or M	A or M	R	—
2	• When a single fault occurs the safety function shall always be performed; • Accumulation of unrevealed faults between TYPE 1 SAFETY CHECKS may lead to a dangerous mode of failure of the SRS	A or M	A or M	A or M	R	—
3 OPTION 1	• When a single fault occurs the safety function shall always be performed; • The single fault shall be detected automatically or the ability of the safety functions to be performed shall not be affected by the accumulation of three faults between TYPE 2 SAFETY CHECKS; • All faults shall be detected by the TYPE 2 SAFETY CHECK	A	A or M	A	R	—
3 OPTION 2	• When a single fault occurs the safety function shall always be performed; • The single fault shall be detected automatically or the ability of the safety functions to be performed shall not be affected by the accumulation of two faults between TYPE 2 SAFETY CHECKS; • All faults shall be detected by the TYPE 2 SAFETY CHECK	A	A or M	A	HR	—
4	• When a single fault occurs the safety function shall always be performed; • The single fault shall be detected automatically or the ability of the safety functions to be performed shall not be affected by the accumulation of three faults between TYPE 2 SAFETY CHECKS; • All faults shall be detected by the TYPE 2 SAFETY CHECK	A	A or M	A	HR (based on 'worst case' assumptions)	Components restricted to 'well tried'

See Notes to Tables 20.4 and 20.5 at the foot of Table 20.5.

Table 20.5: Requirements for hardware integrity: safety-related continuous control systems

System integrity level	System fault requirements	Type 1 safety check (check of all safety functions)	Type 2 safety check check to detect all faults (including unrevealed)	Quantitative hardware integrity analysis	Other requirements
1	• When a failure occurs the safety function shall always be performed; • Accumulation of unrevealed faults between TYPE 1 SAFETY CHECKS may lead to a dangerous mode of failure of the SRS	A or M	A or M	R	—
2	• When a single fault occurs the safety function shall always be performed; • If a second fault occurs during the detection and repair of the first fault, the probability that this shall lead to a dangerous mode of failure of the SRS shall be 'remote'	A	A or M	R	—
3	• When two faults occur the safety function shall always be performed; • All faults shall be detected by the TYPE 2 SAFETY CHECK	A (carried out prior to the start-up of the EUC)	A or M	HR	—
4	• When two faults occur the safety function shall always be performed; • All faults shall be detected by the TYPE 2 SAFETY CHECK	A (carried out prior to the start-up of the EUC)	A or M	HR (based on 'worst case' assumptions)	Components restricted to 'well tried'

Notes to Tables 20.4 and 20.5: Hardware integrity requirements
1. A = Automatic.
2. M = Manual.
3. HR = Highly Recommended; this means that the measure or technique is Highly Recommended for this System Integrity Level. If the measure or technique is not used then the rationale behind not using it should be detailed and justified.
4. R = Recommended; this means that the measure or technique is Recommended for this System Integrity Level as a lower recommendation to HR recommendation and can be combined with other measures or techniques as part of the package of the measures/techniques.
5. Type 1 safety check' shall ensure that all the safety functions are being performed by the E/E/PES safety-related systems.
NOTE: This is solely a check that the safety functions are being performed. A 'Type 1 safety check' will not necessarily identify that there is a fault in the SRS (e.g. a fault in one channel of a redundant channel architecture may be detected).
6. Type 2 safety check' shall ensure that all the faults (including those that remain unrevealed in the system) are detected.

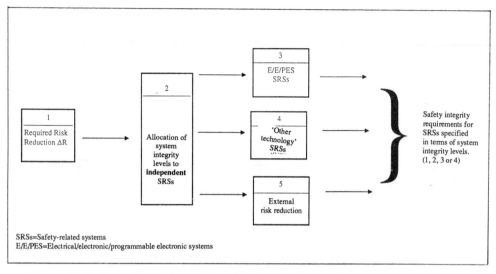

Figure 20.5: Overall model - safety-related protection systems.

specified in application-specific standards.

The overall model for safety-related protection systems is shown in Figure 20.5. This figure illustrates the key steps in moving from the required risk reduction to assigning the system integrity levels to the safety-related systems. At the apportionment stage, reached at Boxes 3, 4 and 5 (see Figure 20.5), the   system integrity level requirements are specified for individual safety-related systems. Each system at this stage will be specified by System Integrity Level 1, 2, 3 or 4.

An example to illustrate this is given in Figure 20.6. In this case the risk reduction is achieved by four safety-related systems (SRS # 1, 2, 3, 4). The allocation is as follows:

(i)   SRS # 1 (Hardwired) = System Integrity Level 2;
(ii)   SRS # 2 (PES) = System Integrity Level 2 (also, the safety-related software of SRS # 2 is allocated an Integrity Level of 2 to match the System Integrity Level 2);
(iii)   SRS # 3 (Other Technology, e.g. hydraulic) = System Integrity Level 2;
(iv)   SRS # 4 (External Risk Reduction, e.g. fire-fighting measures) = System Integrity Level 1.

The methods used to allocate the system integrity levels to the safety-related systems and external risk reduction facilities depend, primarily, upon whether the tolerable risk target is specified explicitly in a numerical manner or in a qualitative manner.   These approaches are termed 'quantitative' and 'qualitative' methods respectively.

Overviews of the quantitative and qualitative methods are given below.

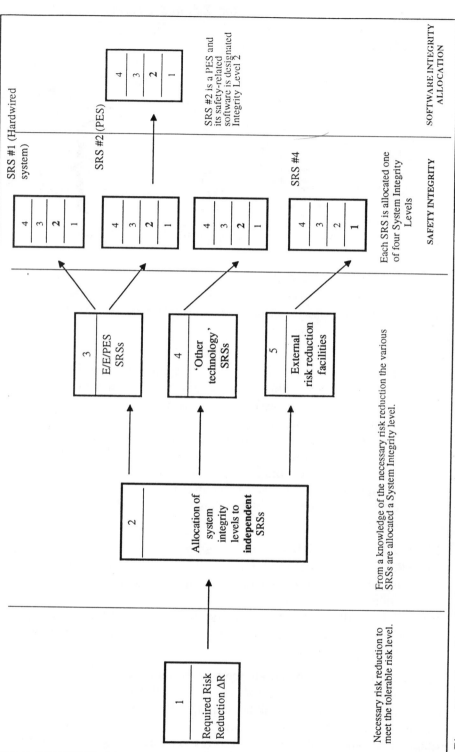

Figure 20.6: *Overall model showing system integrity level allocation to SRSs #1, 2, 3 and 4: example for safety-related protection systems*

20.9 QUANTITATIVE METHODS

A quantitative method can be used when:

(i) The tolerable risk has been specified in a numerical manner (e.g. that a specified consequence should not occur with a greater frequency than once in 104 years); or

(ii) Numerical targets have been specified for the system integrity levels for the safety-related systems. Such targets have been specified in the international standard (see Table 20.1).

Population of Table 20.1 with tolerable risk frequencies (F_t) allows a quantitative safety target for the EUC to be specified. The EUC risk is made up of two components: the consequence of the hazardous event and the frequency with which that event could occur without any protective features being present. The frequency associated with the EUC risk, without any protective features (F_{np}), is a function of the various components making up the EUC (including the EUC control system and human factor issues) and may be determined by:

(i) Analysis of failure rates from comparable situations;

(ii) Data from relevant databases;

(iii) Calculation using appropriate predictive methods.

The importance of the EUC risk in the determination of the system integrity levels of the safety-related systems can be seen by reference to Figure 20.7 which provides an example of a single safety-related protection system. For such a situation:

$$PFD_{ps} = F_t/F_{np}$$

For this case:

- F_{np} is the 'demand rate' on the safety-related protection system;
- PFD_{ps} is the probability of failure 'on demand' of the safety-related protection system, which is the safety integrity failure measure for safety-related protection systems (see Table 20.1).

It can be seen that determination of F_{np} is important because of its relationship to PFD_{ps} and, hence, the system integrity level.

The necessary steps in obtaining the system integrity level (when the consequence C remains constant) are illustrated below, and in Figure 20.7, for the situation where the whole risk reduction is achieved by a single safety-related protection system which must reduce the hazard rate of F_{np} to, as a minimum, F_t.

(i) Determine the hazardous frequency without the addition of any protective features;

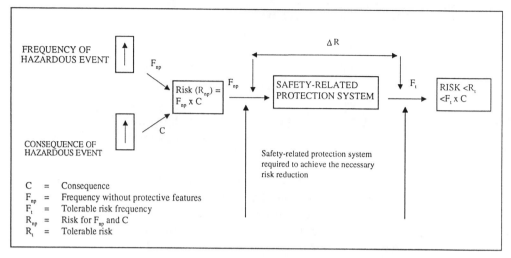

Figure 20.7: Safety integrity level determination for single safety-related protection system.

(ii) Determine the consequence without the addition of any protective features;

(iii) Determine, by using Table 20.1, whether for frequency (F_{np}) and consequence a tolerable risk level is achieved. If interpolation of C and F_{np} leads to a Risk Class I, then further risk reduction is required. Risk Class IV or III would be tolerable risks. Risk Class II would require further investigation.

On the basis that protective features are required to achieve a tolerable risk, the following steps are necessary:

(i) Determine the tolerable frequency (F_t) for specified consequence (C) from Table 20.1 - that is, starting with the known consequence, the tolerable frequency can be determined from the row in which Risk Class III is shown;

(ii) Determine the probability of failure on demand for the safety-related protection system (PFD_{ps}) to meet the risk reduction (ΔR) required. For a constant consequence this gives:

$$PFD_{ps} = F_t/F_{np}$$

(iii) With PFD_{ps} determined, the system integrity level can be obtained from Table 20.3 (e.g. for PFD_{ps} lying between 10^{-3} and 10^{-2}, the system integrity level = 2).

20.10 QUALITATIVE METHODS

20.10.1   Risk Graph: General

The numeric method described above is not applicable when the risk (or the frequency component of it) cannot be quantified. However, several qualitative methods have been developed to allow the system integrity levels of safety-related systems to be determined from a knowledge of the risk factors associated with the EUC. This section describes the 'risk graph' method [DIN 89].

In order to simplify the procedure when a qualitative approach is adopted, a number of parameters are introduced which make it possible to describe the nature of the hazardous situation when safety-related systems fail or are not available. From a number of possible parameters, which affect the system integrity level allocated to the safety-related systems, four are chosen which:

- Allow a meaningful graduation of the risks to be made;
- Contain the key risk assessment factors.

20.10.2   Risk Graph Synthesis

The following simplified procedure is based on the following equation:

$$R = F \times C$$

Where:

R = Risk with no safety-related systems in place;

F = Frequency of the hazardous event with no safety-related systems in place;

C = Consequence of the hazardous event.

The frequency of the hazardous event (F) is made up of three influencing factors:

(i)   Exposure to the hazardous zone;
(ii)   The possibility of avoiding the danger;
(iii) The probability of the hazardous event taking place without the addition of any safety-related systems (but having in place external risk reduction facilities).   This is termed the 'probability of the unwanted occurrence'.

This produces the following four risk parameters, descriptions of which are given in Table 20.6.

(i)   Consequence of the hazardous event (C);
(ii)   Frequency and exposure time to the hazard (F);
(iii) The possibility of avoiding the hazardous event (P);
(iv)   The probability of the unwanted occurrence (W).

Table 20.6: Classification of risk parameters

Risk parameter	Classification	Comments
CONSEQUENCE (C)	C_1 Minor injury. C_2 Serious permanent injury to one or more persons; death to one person. C_3 Death to several people. C_4 Very many people killed.	1. The Classification system has been developed to deal with injury and death to people. Other Classification schemes would need to be developed for environmental or material damage. 2. The interpretation of C_1, C_2, C_3 and C_4 the consequences of the accident and normal healing processes shall be taken into account.
FREQUENCY AND EXPOSURE TIME (F)	F_1 Rare to more often exposure in the hazardous zone. F_2 More frequent to permanent exposure in the hazardous zone.	3. See Note 1 above. 4. This parameter takes into account: • Operation of a process (supervised (operated by skilled/unskilled persons) or unsupervised) • Rate of development of the hazardous event (suddenly/quickly/slowly) • Ease of recognition of danger (seen immediately/detected by technical measures/detected without technical measures) • Avoidance of hazardous event (escape routes possible/not possible/possible under certain conditions) • Actual safety experience; (such experience, may exist with identical EUC/similar EUC or may not exist).
POSSIBILITY OF AVOIDING THE HAZARDOUS EVENT (P)	P_1 Possible under certain conditions. P_2 Almost impossible.	
PROBABILITY OF THE UNWANTED OCCURRENCE (W)	W_1 A very slight probability that the unwanted occurrence will come to pass and only a few unwanted occurrences are likely. W_2 A slight probability that the unwanted occurrences will come to pass and few unwanted occurrences are likely. W_3 A relatively high probability that the unwanted occurrences will come to pass and frequent unwanted occurrences are likely.	5. The purpose of the 'W' factor is to estimate the frequency of the unwanted occurrence taking place without the addition of any safety-related systems (E/E/PES or 'other technology') but including any 'external risk reduction facilities'. 6. If little or no experience exists of the EUC under consideration, or a similar EUC, the estimation of the 'W' factor may be made by calculation. In such an event a 'worst case' prediction shall be made.

20.10.3   Other Possible Risk Parameters

The above risk parameters are considered to be sufficiently generic to deal with a wide range of applications. There may, however, be applications which have aspects requiring the introduction of additional risk parameters (for example, the use of new technologies in the EUC). The purpose of the additional parameters would be to estimate the necessary risk reduction more accurately (see Figure 20.3).

20.10.4   Risk Graph Implementation

On the basis of the risk parameter classification scheme adopted (and the graduations within that scheme), it is theoretically possible to arrive at a great many combinations of the risk parameters used. These give rise to a 'risk assessment package'. However, practical implementation of a risk graph (see below) reveals that significantly fewer than the maximum number of combinations have any practical significance (because of the dominance of certain risk parameters), and this simplifies the risk graph.

For example, in the risk graph of Figure 20.8 in which risk parameters C, F and P are dominant, there are only eight practicable combinations. An explanation of this risk graph is as follows.

Use of risk parameters C, F and P lead to one of eight outputs, these being mapped on to one of three scales (W1, W2 and W3). Each point on these scales (a,b,c,d,e,f,g or h) is an indication of the necessary minimum risk reduction that has to be met by the safety-related systems.

The mapping on to W1, W2 or W3 allows the necessary contribution of the external risk reduction facilities to be applied. The offset feature of the scales for W1, W2 and W3 is necessary to take into account the contribution made to risk reduction by the external risk reduction facilities. This gives, at this point on the risk graph, an indication of the necessary risk reduction that has to be met by E/E/PES and 'other technology' safety-related systems.

The risk scales for W1, W2 and W3 are then mapped on to the system integrity levels. This mapping is carried out in a pragmatic way to take into account the current good engineering practice in the specific application sector. On the basis on which the risk graph has been constructed, these System Integrity Levels represent the safety integrity requirement allocated to the E/E/PES and 'other technology' safety-related systems.

It should be noted that the exact definition of the parameters (S1, S2, F1, F2, P1, P2) would need to be clearly specified for the application sector International Standard.

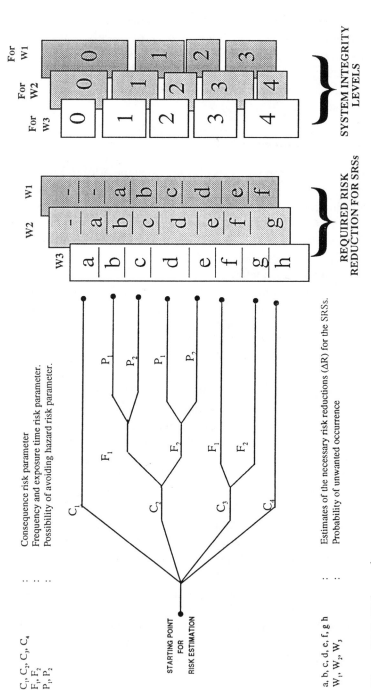

C₁, C₂, C₃, C₄ : Consequence risk parameter
F₁, F₂ : Frequency and exposure time risk parameter.
P₁, P₂ : Possibility of avoiding hazard risk parameter.

a, b, c, d, e, f, g h : Estimates of the necessary risk reductions (ΔR) for the SRSs.
W₁, W₂, W₃ : Probability of unwanted occurrence

Figure 20.8: Risk graph.

20.11 SUMMARY

This chapter has reviewed the current position with respect to the emerging IEC International Standard *Functional Safety of Electrical/Electronic/ Programmable Electronic Systems: Generic Aspects* [IEC 92] with respect to the model employed linking the risk of the equipment under control to the system integrity levels of the safety-related systems. The key elements of this proposed standard and the proposed model are:

- A 'risk-based approach' is adopted in the determination of the safety integrity requirements for the safety-related systems;
- A major objective of this proposed international standard is to enable the development of application-specific and sector-specific international standards; this will enable tolerable risk targets to be set for specific applications;
- Four system integrity levels have been adopted, and these are directly related and complimentary to the four software integrity levels that have been defined for the international standard dealing with safety-related software [IEC 91];
- The model linking the risk of the equipment under control to the safety integrity of the safety-related systems allows for both qualitative and quantitative approaches.

It is hoped that the proposed model, together with the proposals for system integrity levels, including the quantitative target failure measures, will be accepted by National Committees. The 'risk system integrity level' model should provide a useful basis for the development of future application-specific standards.

20.12 REFERENCES

[DIN 89] DIN: "Grundlegende Sicherheitbetrachtungen für MSR - Schutzeinrichtungen." DIN V 19250, Beuth Verlag, Berlin, January 1989.

[DIN 90] DIN: "Principles for Computers in Safety-Related Systems" (Grundsatze für Rechner in System mit Sicherheitsaufgaben). DIN V VDE 0801, January 1990. Available from Beuth Verlag, Berlin, FRG.

[HSE 87] Health and Safety Executive: "Programmable Electronic Systems in Safety-Related Applications." Two documents: 1, *An Introductory Guide* ISBN 011 8839062; 2, *General Technical Guidelines* ISBN 011 8839063. HSE 1987. Both documents are available from HMSO, PO Box 276, London SW8 5DT (Telephone orders: 071-873-9090: Fax 071-873-8463).

[IEC 91] International Electrotechnical Commission: "Software for

Computers in the Application of Industrial Safety-Related Systems." SC65A/ WG9 Draft Document, (IEC reference 65A Secretariat 122) November 1991.

[IEC 92]   International Electrotechnical Commission: "Functional Safety of Electrical/Electronic/Programmable Electronic Systems; Generic Aspects: Part 1, General Requirements." SC65A/WG10 Draft Document, Version 5, (IEC reference: 65A Secretariat 123) January 1992.

21

Towards safe road transport informatic systems

Peter Jesty and Tom Buckley

21.1 INTRODUCTION

There is now a marked increase in the use of computers and programmable electronic systems (PES) in the road transport industry. The principal reason for this is the increased possibilities which software can bring to enable systems either to perform functions which would be impractical with traditional techniques, or to increase efficiency.

In such situations, the overall safety of the operator or of the final product often depends on the correct functioning of the computer or PES, which therefore comes under the category of safety-critical computing. Safety-critical software can be developed for all aspects of road transport, both in-vehicle and at the road side. The most obvious examples are in the use of computers to control sub-systems such as brakes, steering, engine, etc. Less obvious examples are when computers are used to control variable message traffic signs, or in navigation systems that give detailed instructions as to which route should be taken.

A CEC-funded research programme for 'Dedicated Road Infrastructure for Vehicle Safety in Europe' (DRIVE) [DG XIII 91] was commenced in 1989. This was instigated to investigate the use of Road Transport Informatic (RTI) systems to solve some of the major problems associated with road transport, including congestion, pollution, injuries and fatalities. Applications being investigated include intelligent cruise control, collision warning, platooning of vehicles, automatic navigation (in some cases with centralized control), traveller information, and automatic toll collection. Some of these applications require communication between vehicles, while others require communication between a vehicle and the roadside. Some require programmable systems or computers inside the vehicle, while others need a network of large computers spread over a wide area. Whatever their objective, it is essential that the addition of one or more of such new systems does not create a less safe road transport environment than exists at present, and preferably should create a safer one.

This chapter is concerned with the work done in the DRIVE I project 'DRIVE Safely' (V1051) by a consortium consisting of TUV Rheinland in Germany, TNO Delft in The Netherlands, Program Validation Ltd, and the Safety Critical Computing Group at the University of Leeds, the last two being in the United Kingdom. The task of DRIVE Safely was to produce a proposal for a European Standard for the development of safe RTI systems [DRIVE 92].

21.2 APPROACH

We wished to take an approach which would lead to a document that would:

- Be based on current accepted good practice;
- Conform to the (draft) standards that were then available;
- Be acceptable to the road transport industry;
- Permit future development.

The first year of the three-year project was spent reviewing the available documents that might give us some guidance as to how to proceed. While, at that time, three principal sets of documents giving guidance on currently accepted good practice had been published [Redmill 88, STARTS 86, HSE 87], the situation with respect to standards was less clear-cut. Soon after we started our project, the two draft Defence Standards [MOD 91a, MOD 91b] were published, closely followed by the early drafts of the IEC Standards [IEC 91, IEC 92].

These two proposals were very different indeed. The Defence Standards, which have 'Interim' status, state that all software is either safety-critical or not, and prescribe a development route for safety-critical programs that is based upon the application of mathematical methods for specification, design and verification. The IEC documents use five integrity levels and require that the higher the integrity level, the greater the care that must be given to its design. Various development techniques are then identified as being suitable for each integrity level. There is no specified limit as to what can be attempted.

Unfortunately, neither of these two sets of interim or draft standards fully solves the current problems faced by industry. There are already many safety-critical systems in existence which could not be developed according to the interim defence standards, and their removal is not a viable option. In addition, the apparently sensible attitude taken by the IEC/SC65A/WG9 Standard is flawed. The requirement that different design techniques should be used for different integrity levels implies that some methods are demonstrably better than others. There is no scientific or quantitative basis for this assumption [Jesty 90a].

The situation is therefore one in which control over safety-critical software is being called for, but in which there is no agreement as to how, in detail, it should be done. In other words, this is not the time to write a standard, but many people are saying that they want one! Furthermore, we discovered during a presentation which we gave, as a part of our project, to representatives of European motor manufacturers that a document worded in the dictatorial manner of the interim defence standards would be considered unacceptable. It was therefore clear that for this, and other, reasons, we would have to base our document on the IEC draft standards, though we had to solve the problem of how to give a meaningful idea to software integrity levels.

21.2.1   Type Approval

Like in some other industries, any equipment intended for use either on the road or at the road side must be subject to 'Type Approval'. This is 'a way of making sure that cars and goods vehicles are safe for use on the road, without having to inspect and test every single one' [DoT].

These regulations are, however, about 20 years old and do not cover the special problems of programmable sub-systems. We had already reviewed the method currently used by the aviation industry to certify software [RTCA 85], but while this was useful we were very much aware that it was in need of being updated - and, indeed, was in the process of being updated.

Reviewing our progress, then, we had come to the conclusion that we should propose that there should be two integrity levels for software (c.f. the interim defence standards), but that the guidelines on how safety-critical software should be developed would follow (part of) the IEC draft standards. All this changed, however, when we came across the ITSEC documents for the certification of secure software [DTI 91], which showed us how to put meaning on to a number of integrity levels for software. This is described below.

21.3 THE PROPOSAL

The proposal is divided into five main Parts. Part A covers the generic system aspects of risk assessment and overall development philosophy.

Part B covers the specification and architecture of (programmable) electronic systems. The safe design of the software is covered in Part C, while the hardware aspects are covered in Part D. Throughout the design and

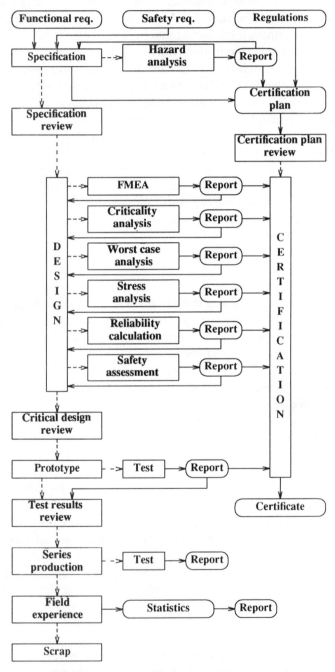

Figure 21.1: The safety system development lifecycle.

implementation of any programmable electronic system or sub-system, there should be a process of assessment, and the mechanism by which a Certification Authority should carry this out is described in Part E. A further part, Part F, contains a glossary of terms used throughout the document.

The document is based around the system safety development life cycle shown in Figure 21.1. While this basically follows the standard waterfall model, it should be noticed that certification is seen as a concurrent process that follows the development. This is in marked contrast to current Type Approval, which only occurs at the 'prototype' stage.

21.3.1   Estimation of Integrity Levels

Before the design of new equipment is started, the risks that will be associated with it have to be identified and classified. A hazard analysis must therefore be performed to attempt to identify a 'preliminary hazard list'. In road transport, one is dealing with equipment that can be either in a vehicle or at the road side. In addition, the failure of any part may not necessarily always lead to a serious incident since a skilful driver can sometimes bring the situation back under control. Contrariwise, a 'simple' failure can sometimes lead to a serious accident. In order to classify the hazards into one of five levels of risk, we therefore decided to use the likely controllability of the situation should a hazard occur; the results are shown in Figure 21.2. The controllability category for each hazard defines an

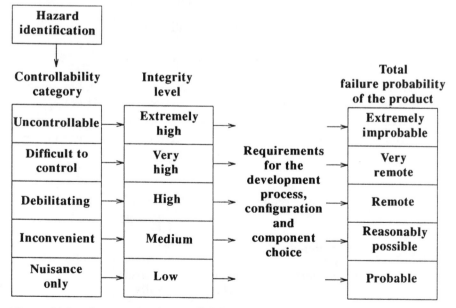

Figure 21.2: The concept of controllability.

integrity level required for the design of the new (sub-)system, which in turn defines the requirements for the process of development. The aim is to produce, and to be able to demonstrate that one has produced, a system whose total probability of failure is also shown in Figure 21.2.

21.3.2   Specification

The requirements specification for each safety-critical sub-system is drawn up in terms of its functional safety requirements and its safety integrity requirements (see Figure 21.3). The safety functional requirements specify those functions which must be carried out by the safety-critical control system should a hazardous failure occur, either in the technical process or in the safety-critical system itself.

The safety integrity requirements specify those measures necessary to ensure that all safety functions are performed in order to meet the estimated integrity level. They are divided into measures to avoid systematic and random failures and those to control them [DIN 89].

21.3.3   Safety by Design

Failures may be of two main types, random or systematic. Random failures can occur at any time and are due to a degradation in the hardware. Systematic failures are the result of a fault in some stage of the life-cycle of a system, and can occur in either hardware or software. There are three principal measures that can be taken against such failures.

(i)   Quality - mainly effective against systematic failures;
(ii)   Reliability - against random failures;
(iii)   Configuration - mainly against random failures.

Quality is achieved through the application of a suitable quality management system that should conform, at least, to ISO 9000 [ISO 87].

The reliability of hardware components can be increased by using good quality components, and, possibly, by derating them. The environment, both inside a vehicle and at the roadside, can be very hostile, so tests must

Safety requirement specification		
Functional safety requirements	**Safety integrity requirements**	
	Measures to avoid faults	**Measures to control faults**

Figure 21.3: Safety specification.

be carried out to ensure that the hardware will perform correctly under all conditions, and in all the required geographical locations. These include tests for temperature, humidity, vibration, shock, salt mist, dust, sand and the action of fluids [Trier 87]. Tests must also be carried out to ensure electro-magnetic compatibility such that no electronic component causes excessive interference to others, or is affected by any of them. If safety cannot be sufficiently obtained with quality control (measures for fault avoidance) during the development and production phases, as well as by improving the reliability of the system, then measures must be taken to control failures during the operational phase.

A system's architecture (configuration) should ensure that any faults occurring do not lead to an unsafe situation. One particular problem of random hardware faults and systematic faults in hardware or software is that they may produce a common mode failure in all channels simultaneously, unless they have each been designed diversely. It must also be remembered that the safety requirements specification itself is a potential cause of common mode failures.

The first basic safety requirement of RTI for all levels of integrity is that a single fault should never lead to a dangerous situation [Asmuch 91]. To obtain this goal, errors in the state of the system must be detected and an appropriate protection measure must be carried out.

The second requirement is that, if an error is undetected, it should never lead to a dangerous situation, even in combination with one or more other faults.

These safety requirements can mainly be fulfilled with the aid of two methods. The first uses the comparison of the results of redundant systems, while the second uses test procedures to detect faults in systems.

We need to distinguish between processes with a safe state and those without a safe state. In the former, the process can be switched into the safe state after the detection of dangerous failures, for example, by switching off the power supply (fail safe design). In the latter case, fault tolerant structures are required to perform the operation continuously after failure detection (fail operational design). Fault tolerance is achieved by redundancy, which is the provision of additional elements or systems so that any one can perform the required function, regardless of the state of operation or failure of any other. A further possibility is to continue operation by degrading functional capabilities or performance in case of failures (fail soft design).

A safety-critical system may take the form of a protection system or it may be part of a control system. Protection systems receive several inputs from the monitored process, and their sole purpose is to transfer the process into a safe state if they recognize a transition of the process to a potentially dangerous state. Control systems use information from the process to influence the process operation; in this case we have to distinguish between processes with a safe state and those without a safe state. If the safety-critical system is part of the control system it is often more economical, particularly in complex systems, to separate the safety tasks from the main tasks.

21.4 TOWARDS THE DEVELOPMENT OF SAFE PROGRAMMABLE ELECTRONIC SYSTEMS

21.4.1 The Nature of the Problem

Traditional engineering products can be considered to be developed in two stages, design and production, as shown in Figure 21.4a. An idea is first developed into a design until one or more prototypes are created. Once it has been confirmed that these prototypes do represent what is required, the production stage is entered. Essentially, this produces multiple copies of the same system. It is assumed that, once the prototype is type approved, the design is 'correct' and so, providing quality control is maintained during production, any failures will be due to wear and/or random faults in a component. The conformity of produced items to their specification is often checked at regular intervals. This is the basis of type approval.

Unfortunately, the development of software does not follow these same stages in the same way (see Figure 21.4b). The production phase (producing multiple copies) is trivial and software is one hundred per cent reliable - it can never change, and so always causes the same thing to be done. Thus, any faults in software appear during the requirements or design stages, and if they are not discovered they remain as systematic design faults in the production model.

The development of fault-free software is notoriously difficult for two principal reasons.

(i)   Software is a digital system, and any state can follow any other state - the feature that provides flexibility;

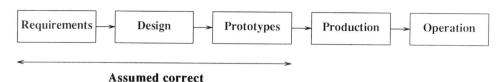

Assumed correct

Figure 21.4a: Development of traditional engineering product.

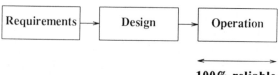

100% reliable

Figure 21.4b: Development of software engineering product.

(ii)   Its potential for complexity - the feature that provides the increased functionality.

These, of course, are the reasons for which it was being used in the first place!

Since software cannot, in general, be fully black-box tested, it can be seen from the above argument that its evaluation must be done by certifying the development process rather than the final product. This is achieved in the civil aviation industry by the methods laid down in *Software Considerations in Airborne Systems and Equipment Certification: DO-178A* [RTCA 85]. The basic message of DO-178A is that, if they are to obtain certification of their products, 'designers must take a disciplined approach to software requirements definition, design, development, testing, configuration management and documentation'.

21.4.2   The Proposals for Software

Our document addresses a number of problems simultaneously.

(i)   It gives guidance on how safety-critical software should be designed and implemented, at a time when there is no absolute consensus as to how this should be done;
(ii)   It introduces the certification of software into the existing Type Approval systems;
(iii) It provides a meaningful mechanism for handling the safety integrity of a software sub-system.

These three topics will now be discussed individually, and we will show that by allocating certain tasks to the Certification Authority, a practical solution to these problems can be achieved without holding back any advances that may be made in the area of safety-critical computing, or handicapping the European motor industry. The proposal currently only deals with the design, implementation and certification of new systems.

(a)   Design and Implementation Methodologies

Section 21.2 concentrated on pointing out the difficiencies in the two sets of draft standards. There is, however, much in common between them and the various guidelines that preceded them [Redmill 88, STARTS 86, HSE 87]. The draft standards are only flawed in that their authors have tried to impose rules as to which development methodologies may, or may not, be used before a general consensus has been reached.

Our approach to this problem is to recognize the lack of consensus and to acknowledge it, rather than ignore it [Jesty 90b]. Engineering knowledge usually advances in one of two principal ways; either by research or by experience (learning by one's mistakes). We therefore require a standard or guideline which fosters 'best practice', but which at the same time permits the subject to develop in the light of experience. A standard on its own cannot achieve this properly as it is purely a document, and the change mechanism can be extremely slow.

There is a consensus shared by workers in the area of safety-critical computing that, since it is so easy for software to be developed in a haphazard manner, all safety-critical software should be formally and independently assessed before being permitted to become operational. Our approach is therefore to combine the job of independent assessor or Certification Authority with that of information disseminator in the following manner, though we do acknowledge that there will be political and economical problems in setting up such a body.

The proposal is therefore definitive in those areas where there is an undisputed consensus, and is based on the proposals in IEC/SC65A/WG9 [IEC 91]. However it gives more open guidance when it covers the methodologies that should be used.

The result of each phase of the software life-cycle is one or more documents (and sometimes code) which can be classified as being either a plan, a specification or a report. The proposal specifies the contents of the documents and their interrelationship. Those documents that must be made available to the Certification Authority will depend on the integrity level being designed for, as explained below.

It is during the creation of the Software Design Plan that the developer must consult with the Certification Authority as to which method(s) may be used for the development. The advantage of this system is that the Certification Authority will, over the years, gain in experience as to which techniques are the most suitable and will therefore be able to influence the techniques used by the industry and to guide it in the 'best' direction.

(b)   Software Certification

Certification implies some form of official approval of a software product which in turn implies that the software performs in accordance with the claims of the software producer. It is, to a certain degree, an implied 'second' guarantee. (Whereas hardware guarantees are actually useful, a typical software supplier's guarantee is often virtually worthless [Bryan 88]). This second guarantee is given by an independent authority to which the software suppliers submit their products for testing and assessment. The certifying body puts its reputation and prestige at risk in endorsing the software and while there may be no financial penalty should the software fail, the resulting loss of credibility to the certifying body can be of serious consequence. Because of this risk, the wording used by the certifying authority can be expected to be very precise; and, in turn, the customer for safety-critical software has to be aware of the certification process so as to avoid falling into the trap of assuming that certification means that the software is perfect.

Software certification can have at least three meanings or levels of guarantee.

(i)   The software is correct;
(ii) The software is correct in that it provides the service as described in its top-level requirements specification.
(iii) The software has been tested and appears to be correct, and it appears to have been produced in accordance with good software engineering practices and in accordance with a recognized relevant standard.

These interpretations of what is meant by certification become progressively weaker. The first says that the software will provide its intended service and that there will be no unexpected side effects. That is to say, that it does the job it is meant to do and it does nothing else besides. It is virtually impossible to give such a guarantee for any but the simplest software product.

The second level is saying that if the specification is correct then the software is correct, but in any case the software does what its designers thought it should do.   This level of certification is possible for small systems. If it can also be shown that the specification is complete, then the software can be certified as having no unwanted side effects and we have in effect moved up to the first level.

The third level is the most commonly used in practice; it is the method by which the civil aviation authorities certify the software components of airborne computer equipment.

There are two basic problems that force certification down from the top level to the bottom level. The first is the difficulty of knowing that one has derived a complete, unambiguous and correct specification from the initial requirements - a universal problem. The second is the problem of testing and/or proving the implemented system against the specification; this is an area being addressed by the use of formal methods.

(c)   Integrity Levels

As shown in Figure 21.2, the objective of designing a (sub-)system to a particular integrity level is to achieve a specified probability of failure. In some forms of engineering this can be achieved by designing in a certain way, or by using certain components. It is then possible to demonstrate that, when a product has been designed to, say, a very high integrity level, it indeed has a lower probability of failure than one designed to, say, a medium integrity level. This is because all failures are assumed to be due to random faults.

Software, however, cannot have random faults; any faults that exist will be systematic faults in the design. The 'probability of failure' does not therefore have the same type of meaning: in fact, it is very difficult to find any criteria by which two software programmes may be compared in a manner analogous to that of Figure 21.2, especially since it is possible for even a 'very badly' designed program to be correct, or, contrariwise, a 'very well' designed program still to have faults. Thus, since it is not possible to assure that one design methodology will produce a demonstrably better product than another, using the criterion of the probability of failure, we have rejected this interpretation of integrity levels.

The probabilities of failure in Figure 21.2 ultimately give the road user confidence in the equipment. We have therefore extended this notion into the idea of levels of confidence, which we map on to the integrity levels. This is an idea also being proposed for secure software [DTI 91]. The principle is that the more one knows about the design and implementation processes of a piece of software, the greater the confidence that one can place in it. This knowledge is gained through the documentation produced, and so the requirements for certification at a particular integrity level are specified in terms of the documents required for inspection. Thus, for example, while a software developer may use a formal specification language for a system of any integrity level, a formal architectural specification would only be required for inspection by the Certification Body for the higher integrity levels. The conformance quality of any software tools to be used in the development - in particular, compilers - is also specified.

We have then extended this idea into the certification of the overall system design by giving tables of measures required for each level of confidence required.

Thus, we believe that a methodology of specifying the requirements for the development process, AND the gaining of a corresponding level of confidence by means of evaluation, gives a meaning for software products that corresponds to the use of integrity levels in traditional engineering products.

21.4.3   Evaluation Mechanism

We have shown that the certification of a programmable RTI system is a long term process that proceeds in parallel with the development of the product. We propose that this should be done by Licensed Evaluation Centres, which would be companies that specialize in this work. These companies would be licensed by a central organization, such as the European Organization for Testing and Evaluation, so that their decisions would be valid throughout the European Community. Thus, a producer of a new RTI product would contact a Licensed Evaluation Centre early in its development and maintain a close liaison with it until the product was certified.

21.5 FUTURE WORK

The work that we begun in DRIVE Safely is now being enhanced in the DRIVE II programme within a project called PASSPORT. This project will take many of the philosophies developed in DRIVE Safely and produce guidelines for their implementation, based on the experience gained in performing case studies on some of the RTI systems being developed for field trials during DRIVE II.

Further, with the advent of the Single European Market, it is, of course, essential that a certification process is repeatable by any authorized body. The problem of achieving this will also be addressed by PASSPORT.

DRIVE Safely was only able to concentrate on basic programmable electronic systems, and in DRIVE II we would like to extend our studies to the safe development of more complex systems, such as networks and databases, as well as to the related areas of the safe development of application-specific integrated circuits and custom designed, very-large-scale integrated circuits.

As part of the United Kingdom Safety-Critical Systems Research Programme, we are associated with a project called MISRA, the partners of which are either vehicle or vehicle component manufacturers. The goal of this project is to produce guidelines for the development of in-vehicle software.

21.6 CONCLUSION

We belive that we have been successful in proposing the basis for a set of standards for the development of safe RTI systems that is both meaningful and workable. The solution that we propose is pragmatic and uses the Certification Authority as the mechanism by which best practice is disseminated throughout the industry. The integrity level required of a (sub-)system is mapped on to a confidence level for the final product. This is to be achieved through varying the levels of knowledge gained by the Certification Authority by means of the documentation supplied by the developer.

21.7 ACKNOWLEDGEMENT

The work described in this chapter was funded under the European Community's DRIVE I Programme.

Dr Tom Buckley died during the latter stages of the work described in this chapter.

21.8 REFERENCES

[Asmuch 91]   Asmuch W, Heuser G, Trier H, and Sonntag J: "Proposal for a Guideline for Safety Related Electronics in Road Transport Systems". 13th International Technical Conference on Experimental Safety Vehicles, November 1991.

[Bryan 88]   Bryan W L and Siegel S G: "Software Product Assurance". Elsevier Science Publishers, 1988.

[DG-XIII 91]   DG-XIII, "Advanced Telematics in Road Transport", Proceedings of the DRIVE Conference (Vols 1 & 2), Elsevier, February 1991.

[DIN 89]   DIN VDE V 0801: "Principles for Computers in Safety Related Systems". Germany, 1989.

[DoT]   Department of Transport: "How to Get Type Approval for Cars and Goods Vehicles". Vehicle and Component Approvals Division, Department of Transport, Bristol, UK.

[DRIVE 92]   DRIVE Safely: "Towards a European Standard: The Development of Safe Road Transport Informatic Systems (Draft 2)", DRIVE Project Number V1051, July 1992.

[DTI 91]   Department of Trade and Industry: "UK IT Security Evaluation and Certification Scheme, Description of the Scheme". UKSP01, March 1991.

[HSE 87]   Health and Safety Executive, "Guide to Programmable Electronics Systems in Safety Related Applications: Introduction", Her Majesty's Stationary Office, UK, 1987.

[IEC 91]   International Electrotechnical Commission: "Software for Computers in the Application of Industrial Safety-Related Systems." SC65A/WG9 Draft Document, November 1991.

[IEC 92]   International Electrotechnical Commission: "Functional Safety of Electrical/Electronic/Programmable Electronic Systems." SC65A/WG10 Draft Document, Version 5, January 1992.

[ISO 87]   ISO 9000, "Quality Management and Quality Assurance Standards - Guidelines for Selection and Use", International Standards Organisation, 1987. (Equivalent to BS 5750)

[Jesty 90a]   P H Jesty, T F Buckley, K M Hobley, and M West, "DRIVE Project V1051 - Procedure for Safety Submissions for Road Transport Informatics", Colloquium on Safety Critical Software in Vehicle and Traffic Control, IEE, February 1990.

[Jesty 90b]   Jesty P H, Buckley T F, and West M: "Critical Software - A Pre-standard and its Certification". Proceedings of SafetyNet 90 Conference, Viper Technologies, Worcester, October 1990.

[MOD 91a]   UK Ministry of Defence: "Interim Defence Standard 00-55, The Procurement of Safety-Critical Software in Defence Equipment". Issue 1, 5 April 1991.

[MOD 91b]   UK MINISTRY OF DEFENCE: "Interim Defence Standard 00-56, Hazard Analysis and Safety Classification of the Computer and Programmable Electronic System Elements of Defence Equipment". Issue 1, 1991.

[Redmill 88]   Redmill F J (Ed.): "Dependability of Critical Computer Systems 1". Elsevier Applied Science Publishers, 1988.

[RTCA 85]   Radio Technical Commission for Aeronautics: "DO-178A: Software Considerations in Airborne Systems and Equipment Certification", RTCA, US, 1985.

[STARTS 86]   STARTS Public Purchaser Group, "The STARTS Purchasers' Handbook: Software Tools for Application to Large Real Time Systems", NCC publications, 1986.

[Trier 87]   Trier H and Stall E: "Development of Methods for Assessment of the Safety of Electronic Systems in Motor Vehicles". VdTUV Research Project Number 232, 1987.

22

Defence standard 00-56: background and revision

Kevin Geary

This chapter explains the background to Interim Defence Standard 00-56 and its forthcoming revision. The coincidence of the standard's emergence with an increasing sociological awareness of safety issues is discussed in relation to safety management. Practical and project factors are considered, and proposed improvements in the widely promulgated Interim DEF STAN 00-56 (1991) are outlined.

22.1 INTRODUCTION

Development of Interim Defence Standard (IDS) 00-56, *Hazard Analysis and Safety Classification of Computer and Programmable Electronic System Elements of Defence Equipment* [MOD 91a], began early in 1989, based on the existing procedures of a large defence contractor. The impetus was due to the need to place Interim Defence Standard 00-55 [MOD 91b] in context. The first draft was promulgated for public comment in mid-1989 and was also applied to live projects. Lessons learned then contributed to the specification which led to the publication of the current Interim Standard.

22.2 BACKGROUND

In the past, hazard analysis of relatively simple mechanical systems could be performed subjectively by examination. There was adequate confidence in this process because the detail of functional mechanisms was visible.

Such analyses were often based on lessons learned from experience.

Like many design rules, safety considerations have evolved reactively and, as reports of recent civil disaster inquiries have taught us, they are still doing so. Where established design practices are relatively stable, design safety rules have matured to an acceptable level. However, with systems becoming ever more complex due to the increasing pace of technological evolution and the ever increasing demands for sophisticated functionality, often implemented through software, the hazard analysis exercise is no longer straightforward. In these circumstances, it is unwise to rely on developing safety rules reactively. Technology in general is no longer sufficiently stable to be able to consolidate experience before newer technological advances are implemented with even greater degrees of sophistication and sensitivity, thereby increasing the scope for root causes of accidents. Further, safety has become 'fashionable' and the sociological climate is nowhere near as forgiving as it used to be. Accidents are becoming more unacceptable and there is widespread recognition that they are usually preventable.

This new awareness has placed the safety assessment and certification process much more in the limelight and, as a result, the need for evidence of design safety has received wider recognition. Safety assessment requires demonstration that safety management has been properly applied. This is accomplished by knowledgeable oversight and documentary evidence. In Interim Defence Standard 00-56 there is a requirement to record safety criticality status and, where relevant, the safety management activities carried out throughout the lifecycle of the system. Such evidence, recorded in a *Hazard Log*, is central to the documentary evidence that would be required by a safety assessor.

22.3 ACCEPTABLE RISK

Deliberations on safety criticality inevitably lead to the question 'What is an acceptable risk?'. Deciding on the acceptability of risk is unfortunately not always a quantitative judgement; it may be biased by emotions. Public opinion, albeit strongly influenced by what constitutes a good news story, and the resulting political opinion, has a significant influence on what is an acceptable risk. For example, we accept a probability of death by road accident of *1 in 10,000*, but a risk of death of *1 in 1,000,000* for an uncontrolled nuclear release from a power station [HSE 87a] can cause reactions resulting in expensive public enquiries, mass demonstrations, and Parliamentary questions.

As an example of public sensitivity, reporting of Tornado losses in the early phase of the Gulf War illustrated how relatively few losses for such military action still raised public concern and political comment. More recently, there has been much press coverage of the call for the questioning in person of the A10 pilots involved in the accidental death of nine British servicemen in the 1991 Gulf War.

The issue of human fallibility does not seem to be of great concern [Tuler 89] to the public at large. Although many notable disasters are directly attributable to human failure, society still seems to be prepared, under many circumstances, to rely on the familiar human operator and show a lack of trust in automated systems, especially those in which there is little general understanding and no visibility of the operating mechanism. However, reversion to manual control is not possible for many modern defence systems because humans are not sufficiently quick or accurate in their reactions to substitute for computerized real-time control. There are similar problems in civil systems where automation of safety-critical tasks is less prevalent due to the unwillingness to trust automation.

What constitutes an unacceptable hazard is judged differently by different people. The term 'accident', used in the general sense, has a wide meaning which can refer to any unintended event that may or may not cause damage or harm. Prime factors in determining acceptability are severity of consequence and frequency of occurrence. An unintended event that causes damage could range from a minor scratch on some paintwork to large-scale destruction of property and lives. When it comes to the grey area of deciding whether a system is in one category or another, arguments occur between those who have economy and schedules as their prime objective and those concerned with prevention of what the safety assessors consider to be unacceptable accidents.

The problem of deciding what is an acceptable risk is complicated by the need to attribute a measurement of risk, in the form of a probability of accident per some unit of measure. But what is the unit of measure to be? It could be constituted by units of time, such as mission hours, units of activity, such as number of projectiles fired, units of distance, such as passenger miles, or units of demand, such as the likelihood of accident per single missile. Random failure distributions, which constitute a measure of physical degradation, are not readily transferable to systematic failures that may or may not manifest themselves in an unsafe way. The severity of consequent system failures is predetermined with respect to specific operational circumstances at the time of incidents [Harbison 91]. Moreover, the general lack of a universal metric hinders direct comparisons being made between industry sectors. Therefore, problem-specific metrics are likely to remain in use for some time unless there is a breakthrough in the perception of accident measurement criteria.

The issue is not just a Ministry of Defence (MOD) problem; it needs to be tackled on a national basis. The difference between civil considerations and military ones is that the military makes use of systems that are designed to be hazardous, but only to an enemy and only where and when intended. Nevertheless, current civil and military activities associated with safety-critical software are complementary in that current MOD priorities [MOD 87] equate to the class of civil safety considerations for systems that are potentially lethal.

22.4 RATIONALE

There are several NATO, Defence or Naval (and civil) Engineering standards which lay down design rules for safety for various categories of military equipment. Many of these standards call for a hazard analysis to be conducted. Often, there may be a chicken-and-egg situation wherein the system, or some aspect of the system, has to be recognized as potentially hazardous before a safety-related design standard is invoked.

Recognition of hazards may result from experience. For example, in systems incorporating explosives, policy makers automatically perform a high-level mental hazard analysis because experience over many years has taught us that explosives can be dangerous. Mature safety policies thus evolve, an example being AOP-15 [NATO 85] which is a NATO standard that applies to explosives and calls for a hazard analysis to be performed.

The need to assess the safety of systems with sophisticated control mechanisms has been focused by the increasing use of software-based control and the concurrent concern over the integrity of safety-critical software and its interaction with computing hardware. This raised the issue of deciding when software should or should not be classified as safety-critical. In searching for a suitable model standard, it became apparent that there was little available which offered guidance on safety-critical software-based systems. All the existing standards, guidance, or *de facto* procedures for hazard analysis of systems or components [Stoddard 90] were those applied to plant in the traditional heavy construction, nuclear and chemical industries.

Another observed general problem was that hazard analysis was sometimes applied in the latter stages of development, close to acceptance. With no definitive policy or obligatory or advisory standard, hazard analysis may be progressed by subjective judgement exercised by a committee. Although this practice may traditionally have been applied successfully to relatively simple technology, it is not sufficiently effective when applied to modern complex systems of high functionality. Further, there is a school of thought which has it that group decision making, such as by committee, is not as sound as many would believe [Hammond 92]. Two significant contributory documents containing some guidance on hazard analysis of systems are MIL STD 882B [US 84], which is a high-level document, and the HSE Guide [HSE 87b] which includes a description of Fault Tree Analysis.

Requirements for consistency, clarity, and methodical argument in hazard analysis inevitably lead to the need for a standard. Good engineering management regarding safety demands that safety-critical systems and components are identified at an early stage. Furthermore, in order to avoid an unnecessary increase in budget and time in non-critical system projects, such systems should be exempted from safety policy requirements as early as possible in their lifecycle.

22.5 PROJECT FACTORS

The lack of methodical or timely hazard analysis, or deficiencies in the auditable documentary safety evidence, will introduce a high risk of incurring significant delays and extra costs through a need to carry out expensive re-work at a late stage in a project. In the Channel Tunnel project, it was discovered that a simple safety aspect, such as the width of shuttle doors (apparently overlooked during design), can be very costly to correct after production [BBC 91].

If safety assessment is left until final safety certification is required, say for embarkation, certification processes may reveal unacceptable safety risks which had not been previously realized. This results in a delay to, or refusal of, certification and, consequently, deferred introduction into service and project costs and timescales which are significantly extended while safety features are dealt with retrospectively.

Project risk assessment (not to be confused with *safety* risk assessment, which may use similar methodologies such as Fault Tree Analysis) is therefore accorded a high profile as an essential management aid. This being so, early implementation of hazard analysis and *safety risk* classification will form a significant contribution to the reduction of *project risk* whenever safety is a factor. Indeed, there are already cases of preliminary hazard analysis, using Interim Defence Standard 00-56, being employed during bid assessment to optimize cost trade-offs [Taylor 91].

The usual means of addressing safety is to set up a project safety committee, although this is not always the case for smaller projects. Yet, design is normally perceived to be the critical path to project success, with the work of the project safety committee often being seen as an ancillary procedure and occasionally as a necessary evil. It is not unusual for early design decisions to be made before the project safety committee has established itself and, in those circumstances, the hazard analyses may not be finalized until the design is almost complete. The work of the project safety committee may therefore follow the design, rather than making a contribution to the design process. This approach tends to assume that the design is tolerably safe, and it results in the safety committee's role becoming one of producing safety papers and gathering approval from the various safety advisers.

If the safety committee operates in a reactive fashion, a great deal of the work of its members will inevitably be taken up in negotiating compromise, sometimes accompanied by protracted and detailed technical discussion. This contrasts with the more effective, efficient, creative, and safe alternative of the committee contributing to design safety, with approval following almost by implication.

The initiative for Interim Defence Standard (IDS) 00-55 [MOD 91b] was a proactive measure aimed at reducing the risk to safety from software specification and design flaws. Interim Defence Standard 00-56 is also proactive in its approach to design safety. Its objective is to identify component safety-criticality in the context of the system so as to enable the optimum use of resources by focusing on the safety-critical elements and apportioning a safety classification to each. Resources can then be optimized by applying the appropriate safety design rules to the critical components, for example by applying IDS 00-55 to safety-critical software. (As yet there is no equivalent of IDS 00-55 for computing hardware, although the IEC-SC65/WG10 document [IEC 91] will address this area.)

Because it takes a proactive approach to safety management, IDS 00-56 can be used as a tool for controlling costs by identifying and targeting the critical areas of the system. In contrast, the more blunt approach of a reactive safety policy may lead to unnecessary expenditure by making some parts of systems not only safer but also much more expensive than they need to be - and even then, usually only after learning the hard way.

On a more general level, the IDS 00-56 approach offers a way towards greater efficiency of safety management tasks. Uniformity of the requirements for a safety case, and of the manner and format in which the evidence for the safety case is presented, would enable a single definitive interface to be derived between projects and an infrastructure incorporating the various safety assessment and certification bodies. This would greatly ease current project burdens of interfacing individually to several different safety advisers, and would facilitate improved efficiency in assessment and certification by providing a single central facility for the co-ordination of safety advice.

22.6 CAUSAL LINKS

Increased complexity of system design creates increased scope for root causes of accidents. Systems are becoming more sensitive to apparently insignificant or unexpected events and the causal links are no longer readily apparent. The old tale about the lack of a horseshoe nail resulting in the loss of the kingdom is an illustration of a causal link which was not perceived before the event. Under a reactive approach to safety rules, the response would be to analyse such a scenario after the event. The likely resultant policy would be that all farriers would be instructed by law to carry a minimum of 500 horseshoe nails at all times - in the days of the story, no doubt on pain of death - which adds a new dimension to the safety-criticality of nails.

Such retrospective action would reduce the risk of a recurrence of the event but, as with all accidents, would not reverse the first occurrence - which we would wish to avoid. However the IDS 00-56 philosophy facilitates a proactive approach to safety management so that an assessment can be carried out and an early informed judgement made about the critical components of a system, including the project's logistics and the system's maintenance. With such a policy in place, the accident may be avoided in the first place.

The criticality of correct functioning of the system has special significance for the safety assessment of defence equipment. Civil systems are designed to be 'fail safe', which normally involves the system ceasing to function or having its control switched from automatic to manual. Most safety standards take this approach, with the obvious exception of fly-by-wire aircraft. Many defence systems, however, may have a role such that the *success* of their mission can be regarded as safety-critical. For example, the mission of a defensive weapon may be to protect a vessel from deliberate hostile acts by shooting down enemy missiles. If it fails, human lives and the vessel are likely to be lost. Under such circumstances, it must be recognized that, although an individual life could be put at risk from the system, a far greater risk would be incurred if the system failed to perform its mission to defend.

22.7 SENSITIVITY

Although not safety-critical, the problems with the Hubble space telescope illustrate the sensitivity of refined technology to a minor physical event compounded by human deviations [Joyce 90]. An investigation found that a tiny fragment of non-reflective coating had flaked off a metering rod cap, resulting in an erroneous reading based on reflected light. During testing, results showing misalignment of instrumentation were incorrectly blamed on the test device, and an aberration detected by an older instrument was dismissed. At the time, the contractor's quality assurance department was understaffed, and so the relevant quality control procedure was not enforced. It is well known that the telescope, costing $1.6bn, suffers degraded performance. In this example, as with many accidents, it is a combination of erroneous events and actions that come together within the same time frame to open a path between the triggering event and the consequence.

It might be possible to establish causal links to show that almost everything is safety-critical. However, common sense must prevail in determining the depth and detail of analysis and the importance of causal links. IDS 00-56 hazard analysis progresses in a hierarchical top-down fashion, enabling each level to be examined and decisions to be made as to which of the lower-level elements (i,e. the most critical elements) should be targeted for analysis in greater depth. It should be recognized that nothing is 100 per cent safe; even living eventually results in death. A reasonable and acceptable degree of risk must therefore be assumed, otherwise the costs of analysis may become disproportionate to the benefits, and we could end up establishing a causal link between project management and shortened life expectancy.

22.8 SOFTWARE

Examples of causal sensitivity may be seen in software-based systems. The software industry has long been used to the software 'bugs' that dog computing systems. Software is discrete, complex, and ultra-sensitive to apparently minor deviations in program or data. Until recently, we have been able to tolerate software errors as long as they did not cause too much inconvenience or loss of system availability. However, the ACARD report [ACARD 86], published in 1986, publicly expressed concern over software being used for safety-critical applications. Attention was then turned to the significance of software in safety-critical systems. Action was started, with the objective of reducing the safety risks, resulting from software flaws, in defence equipment. Following much deliberation and consultation, Interim Defence Standard 00-55 has been produced for application on MOD projects.

22.9 EXPERIENCE

Trial application of the first (1989) draft IDS 00-56 on live projects was enlightening. It was interesting to note that experience of live application generated observations which contradicted some of the comments received concerning the style of the Standard. It was therefore possible to form an evaluation based on experience of use as well as on theoretical judgement. Other projects have subsequently applied the published (1991) Interim Standard and have confirmed observations from the initial trials.

One observation on the use of the Standard under current procurement policy is that it may be difficult at present for assessment contractors to quote a fixed price for the whole job. There are two main reasons for this. Firstly, there is a lack of experience in price estimation against the tasks involved. Secondly, the amount of assessment work is dependent on the design contractor's procedures and documentation and on the nature of the system being assessed and its operational environment. Typical contractual strategies so far have been either to predefine the top level hazards to be investigated or to let a running contract and then, progressively, to define the various work packages and negotiate a series of smaller fixed-price contracts for them. The latter approach seems to be preferred by both clients and contractors.

22.10 EVOLUTION

The current version of the IDS 00-56 carries a title which reflects its initial role in relation to IDS 00-55. The first (1989) draft of IDS 00-56 attempted to simplify safety classification too much, but both comment and experience of use indicated that safety classification is not simplifiable to an elementary level. Initial impressions of complexity often fade when implementors learn to apply IDS 00-56. With a change of the current title, the Standard should be capable of having its scope expanded to system-wide safety risks associated with systematic and random failures, where software is only one aspect of system design. When analysing the system it is important to include consideration of the contribution to safety by the human operator as part of the 'system' [Lucas 90] and consideration of the possible need to balance system-initiated hazards with defence against greater hazards from hostile acts.

Significant proposed changes to the current Interim Standard include:

(i)   The standard is to have two parts, a requirements part (the current Interim Standard updated) and a new guidance part;

(ii) The two parts of the standard are to be written by different teams;

(iii) The standard will be at system level and its scope system-wide;

(iv) A formal mathematical specification of the safety classification criteria will be created and published in the guidance part.

This final feature is a quality enhancement measure, and publication of the formal specification is an important pragmatic concept for prospective tool development. It will provide a formal mathematical specification for tools and should thereby promote consistency between them.

Although safety policies usually only address peacetime, detailed press reporting of war activities and losses, and the resultant social and political concern, may mean that such policies will need to be reviewed. Despite the Allies' success, the 1990 Gulf War provided abundant material for media analysis, albeit mostly speculative, on the availability, reliability, and performance of complex weapon systems. Whatever the military perspective, it is the kind of coverage that attracts attention and discussion.

22.11 CONCLUSION

Software is only a component of a system, and it is the system that may be dangerous, not the software on its own. Any viable hazard analysis must therefore consider the system in its operational environment in order to arrive at a classification for the system and its components, including software criticality. It is inefficient to carry out individual component-oriented hazard analyses, so the scope of IDS 00-56 should be broadened to system level. The principles of the current IDS 00-56 are generic and capable of accommodating the wider system scope.

When carrying out a hazard analysis of a system or component, it is necessary to include the operational scenario in which the system will be used. Hazard analysis for the identification of safety-critical components cannot be performed by analysing the components in isolation; it must include relationships with the real world.

Experience has shown that hazard analyses can be variable in the depth, completeness and timeliness of their application and, when problems related to safety and assessment are discovered at a late project stage, resolution of deficiencies can pose considerable risk to project criteria. Interim Defence Standard 00-56 represents a significant step forward in procedures to introduce definitive engineering disciplines to the area of safety management.

It is widely recognized that discovery of design flaws late in development means delays and added expense, with post-production changes typically costing 100 times more to correct than if found during the specification and design phases. The value of the standard to projects is in providing a safety management framework, which includes milestones in the risk analysis process and which enables safety contributions to be made at the most safety-critical and cost-effective stages of a project - specification and design. To view the Standard as merely a documentary procedure, adding to costs, is to overlook its greater strategic advantage as a tool for project risk reduction by significantly reducing the probability of unexpected objections at the safety certification and acceptance stages.

When the principles of the standard are adopted to a wider scope, project management efficiency should be improved. The standard's documentation and consultation scheme could provide a single project interface to the many system safety advisory and certification bodies that inevitably become involved with certification of a defence system.

Predictive methods will never replace experience but, if used in conjunction with experience, they should enhance the designers' ability to exploit advancing technology, while maintaining safety at acceptable levels and achieving it at optimum cost.

This new standard does not in itself provide all the answers, but it has already served to focus minds on the issues of acceptable risk and on the infrastructure necessary for the application of engineering thoroughness to safety management.

Disclaimer
Views expressed are those of the author and do not necessarily represent those of the Department.

22.12 REFERENCES

[ACARD 86]   Cabinet Office: "Software - A Vital Key to UK Competitiveness." An Advisory Council for Applied Research and Development Report, HMSO, London, 1986.

[BBC 91]   BBC News: "News report on Channel Tunnel delay of 6 months and £100M lost revenue for safety modifications to shuttle exit doors." BBC1 6 o'clock News, 8 April 1991.

[Hammond 92] Hammond J: "A Risky Shifty Business." *Project Management Today*, March 1992, p. 8.

[Harbison 91]   Harbison S A: "Safety Objectives in Nuclear Power Technology." *Reliability Engineering and System Safety*, Vol. 31, No. 3, Elsevier Applied Science, London, 1991, pp 297-307.

[HSE 87a]   Health and Safety Executive: "The Tolerability of Risk from Nuclear Power Stations." HMSO, London, 1987.

[HSE 87b]   Health and Safety Executive: "Programmable Electronic Systems in Safety Related Applications." HMSO, London, 1987.

[IEC 92]   International Electrotechnical Commission: "Functional Safety of Electrical/Electronic/Programmable Electronic Systems." SC65A/WG10 Draft Document, Version 5, January 1992.

[Joyce 90]   Joyce C: "A Flake of Film Foiled Hubble." *New Scientist*, 1 Dec 90, p. 21.

[Lucas 90]   Lucas D: "Looking Facts in the Face." *Professional Engineering*, July/Aug 1990, pp 28-29.

[MOD 87]   Ministry of Defence: "Draft MOD Policy Statement for the Procurement and Use of Software for Safety Critical Applications." *D/CSSE/4/22*, 14 Dec 1987.

[MOD 91a]   Ministry of Defence: "Hazard Analysis and Safety Classification of Computer and Programmable Electronic System Elements of Defence Equipment." *Interim Defence Standard 00-56*; Directorate of Standardization, Glasgow, 1991.

[MOD 91b]   Ministry of Defence: "The Procurement of Safety Critical Software in Defence Equipment." *Interim Defence Standard 00-55*; Directorate of Standardization, Glasgow, 1991.

[NATO 85]   NATO: "Guidance on the Assessment of the Safety and Suitability for Service of Munitions for NATO Armed Forces." *Allied Ordnance Publication 15 (Stanag 4297)*; NATO Military Agency for Standardization, March 1985.

[Stoddard 90]   Stoddard R: "Are There Bugs In The Program?" *Defence Computing*, February 1990, p. 10.

[Taylor 91]   Taylor M: "Hazard Analysis of an Active Dipping Sonar System." *Proceedings of the ASSC Seminar on the Use of Hazard Analysis in Avionics Systems Development*, IEE 29 Nov 1991, ERA ASSC Agency Doc. No. 330/2/61; ERA Technology Ltd., 1991.

[Tuler 89]   Tuler S, Kasperson R E and Ratick S: "Human Reliability and Risk Management in the Transportation of Spent Nuclear Fuel." In *Reliability on the Move: Safety and Reliability in Transportation*; ed. Guy G B, Elsevier Applied Science, London, 1989, pp 169-194.

[US 84]   US Department of Defense: "System Safety Program Requirements." *Military Standard 882B*; DOD, Washington DC, 1984.

Index